The Privatization of Police in America

An Analysis and Case Study

JAMES F. PASTOR

McFarland & Company, Inc., Publishers
Jefferson, North Carolina, and London

363.289
P293p

LIBRARY OF CONGRESS CATALOGUING-IN-PUBLICATION DATA

Pastor, James F., 1957–
    The privatization of police in America : an analysis and
case study / James F. Pastor.
        p.   cm.
    Includes bibliographical references and index.

    ISBN 0-7864-1574-6 (softcover : 50# alkaline paper)

    1. Police, Private — United States.   2. Police — United States.
I. Title.
HV8291.U6P37   2003
363.28'9'0973 — dc22   2003019130

British Library cataloguing data are available

©2003 James F. Pastor. All rights reserved

*No part of this book may be reproduced or transmitted in any form
or by any means, electronic or mechanical, including photocopying
or recording, or by any information storage and retrieval system,
without permission in writing from the publisher.*

Cover photograph ©2002 Corbis Images

Manufactured in the United States of America

McFarland & Company, Inc., Publishers
  Box 611, Jefferson, North Carolina 28640
    www.mcfarlandpub.com

11/03

To my wife, RoseAnn, and my mother,
family, and friends, and to
the memory of my late father.

Table of Contents

Preface

This book addresses the impact and implications of private policing on public streets. It is the result of over twenty years of experience and study, which culminated in my doctoral dissertation at the University of Illinois at Chicago. The dissertation was defended on September 10, 2001, the day before the terrorist attacks on Washington, D.C., and New York City. At that time, private policing was not a mainstream issue. It was a subject only academics would debate and worry about. In fact, the nuances of private policing, such as its functions and constitutional implications, were issues even most intellectuals had not given much thought to.

In light of the terrorist attacks of September 11, 2001, the emphasis on security has intensified, which will likely continue for years to come. While security is often viewed as a governmental function, the private sector has always played a significant role in public safety. Private policing will no doubt increase as a response to heightened security concerns. As we go forward, one significant fact will become increasingly obvious: "security" is larger and more substantive than the simple presence of guards or perception of safety. With this in mind, this book discusses a number of substantive legal and public policy issues that relate to the provision of security services.

The issues are many and diverse. While people generally express the need for safety and security, what people consider the "proper" amount varies widely. Since security is subjective by its nature, it is difficult to determine what and how much is appropriate. Unfortunately, these are not the only questions raised by security. Legal and public policy issues, such as constitutional concerns and the potential to create a dual system of policing — one for the rich and another for the poor — are even more difficult to resolve. Many worry about the impact of security efforts on the protections provided by the constitution. Such concerns have been subject of some debate within intellectual circles. However, these are not esoteric issues anymore. They now resonate within the security industry and throughout society. This book will address these questions.

We must assess the issues surrounding security from a larger perspective — to do this we must take a step back. Prior to the advent of municipal police departments, private citizens regularly acted as the protectors of the law and public order. When the first modern police force was formed in England in 1829, it was the first time government appointed and authorized officers performed law enforcement and public order functions. Subsequently, government-based policing became the dominant mode, with private policing taking a subservient role. This monopoly by the public police lasted almost 150 years.

Private policing reemerged in the 1970s. At that time, the ratio of public to private policing shifted from 1.4:1 in favor of public police to the current ratio where private security personnel outnumber public police by a multiple of three (Cunningham, et al., 1991; and Walsh, et al., 1992). In some states, such as California, the current ratio is 4:1 in favor of private security (Cunningham, et al., 1991). Accordingly, the security industry outspends public police by 73 percent. It also employs 2½ times the workforce (Cunningham, et al., 1991). Private policing has annual revenues over $52 billion, with the industry employing approximately 1.5 million people. In contrast, public police spend $30 billion, with a workforce of approximately 600,000 (Cunningham, et al., 1991). These statistics illustrate the deep roots of private police in the public safety of this country. Indeed, some authors argue that private security is the primary protective resource in contemporary America (Connors, et al., 2000; and Benson, 1996).

Going beyond the broad statistical significance of private security, the scope and import of such services raise many provocative questions. For example, do private police officers perform the traditional "observe and report" function, or do they act more like public police officers, emphasizing legal authority, particularly law enforcement? Are order maintenance techniques, widely utilized in community policing, among the functions of private police? Under what conditions are security guards deemed "public actors"? How have courts viewed the application of constitutional protections relative to actions of security providers? What important public policy questions are raised by the use of private police patrols?

These questions are addressed here through an inclusive examination of private policing. Privatization of police services includes diverse considerations from conceptual, historical, economic, legal, and functional approaches. These approaches provide the backdrop for a case study on a private policing patrol arrangement in a community on the south side of Chicago. I examined this rather unusual provision of private police service in a variety of ways, including interviews, document research, and ride-alongs with the officers during their patrols. All of these methods provided insight into the phenomenon of private policing on public streets.

From my observations, I draw several conclusions. First, the importance and impact of security will continue to be heightened in the years to come. As the above statistics illustrate, the impact of private security is already significant, with three to four times the personnel and budgets of public police. This book demonstrates that these ratios are likely to increase in favor of private security. Consequently, the influence and significance of private security will also increase.

Second, the magnitude of security services issues is sufficient reason to examine them. Anyone who doubts the importance of these issues should consider the recent terrorist incidents, the media and public reaction to those incidents, and the implications of a sustained terrorist campaign. This book makes the case that private security will be an instrumental component of any public safety initiative — whether in response to terrorism or to more common crimes. Many people are coming to realize that private policing is much too complex as an industry and too important as a crime reduction technique to overlook.

Finally, while there has been a national trend toward the use of private security personnel in public areas, there has been little study of its implications. Typically, modern institutions of public justice have required legislative action and public debate to confer police power to governmental officials and authorities (Shearing and Stenning, 1983). In contrast, the development of private security has been largely invisible, with little legislative and public debate (Shearing and Stenning, 1983). The lack of research on this topic is glaring and the remedy long overdue.

Privatization arrangements raise important constitutional and public policy considerations. As observed by McKenzie in his study of home-owner associations, the trend toward placing more and more power into the hands of such associations resulted from governmental inaction. As a consequence of this governmental inaction, typical functions of government gradually shifted to private associations and corporations (McKenzie, 1994). This is a key premise of this book: if government fails to provide adequate protection from crime (or from terrorism), then people will seek protection through private security. However, since most of the development of private security has been conducted in the context of contracts and client accounts, there has been little analysis of the larger issues related to the use of private patrols. This book will address these issues.

Chapter I discusses the concepts of personal security and constitutional rights, especially the tension between security and liberty. This tension may become unbearable in a sustained terrorist campaign. The competing interests and principles underlying these opposing concepts exist in an extremely delicate balance, as Chapter I shows.

Chapter II presents the concept of privatization. Included in the discussion are the major tenets advanced by proponents and opponents of privatization. These two sides debate whether *any* current governmental service should be privatized. As with the tension between security and liberty, there are compelling arguments on both sides. An examination of these arguments provides an overview of the general characteristics of privatization and a framework for discussing the use and implications of private policing.

Chapter II also looks at the particular characteristics and respective functions of private and public policing. These groups—one publicly funded and governmentally controlled, and the other privately funded and controlled by corporations—have increasingly become interrelated to the extent that it is difficult to discern any differences in their functions or roles. Upon presenting the respective roles, the focus of this study narrows to the privatization of policing, with a detailed discussion of the particular issues and theories raised by various authors.

In the third chapter, I present a brief historical overview of the nature of policing, along with a discussion of the advent of public policing. This discussion illustrates how policing once operated. Before the formation of public police, the role of the citizen was paramount in providing order and enforcing the law. Over time, certain societal conditions paved the way for publicly funded police officers. Chapter III traces public policing from those early days to contemporary times. Following this overview, the chapter presents some statistics on the extent and involvement of private policing.

Interestingly many factors converged to set the stage for the emergence of public policing, including crime, economic considerations, order maintenance techniques, and the notion that government was the proper authority for the provision of public safety services. Ironically, these same issues dominate the discussion of today's emergence of private policing. This discussion, covered in Chapter IV, will help the reader understand why private policing has reached its current state of prominence in the public safety industry.

The fifth chapter analyzes court decisions relating to the use of police powers by private security personnel. Historically, courts viewed constitutional protection as inapplicable to private security. Over time, courts gradually recognized that private security was providing a significant law enforcement function. As a consequence, courts have crafted certain tests to make constitutional protections relevant to private policing.

Following this analysis, certain examples of private security patrols from various areas of the country are presented in Chapter VI. Some of these examples involve private security officers performing a public safety function exclusively, without any involvement of public police. Others involve a combination of efforts, with private police acting as a supplement to the public police. Together these examples represent the spectrum of possible arrangements for contemporary public and private safety services, showing how and why private policing is used.

How private policing is used — the specific functions a private force performs — is key to how the courts interpret the applicability of constitutional protections. For this reason, the case study in Chapter VII devotes much attention to what the private police officers actually do in the course of their patrols. Important to this chapter is the concept of "police powers." This term describes various functions used in policing to demonstrate the assertion of legal authority. The assertion of legal authority may stem from one of three broad functions. The most assertive function is law enforcement, which focuses on the most serious crimes. The second function is order maintenance, which involves less serious crimes or incidents which tend to disrupt public order. Finally, the least intrusive function is observation and reporting. In their traditional role, private police simply observe the crime and report it to public police. Each of these functions is examined in the case study.

The case study entailed three different research components. The key component was direct observation in a series of ride-alongs with the private police officers as they performed their patrols. In this way, by watching and listening as situations unfolded, I was able to directly assess the specific functions of the officers. I had a front row seat for what police officers sometimes call the "greatest show on earth." The show is often humorous. It is also melodramatic. It is often dangerous and even deadly.

The second component was interviews with the private police officers. Hoping to more fully appreciate and understand their actions, I probed their recollections and feelings about particular incidents. I also asked broader questions regarding their functions and roles, their backgrounds (including experience and training), and their understanding of legal authority and constitutional provisions. I also conducted a series of interviews with other key participants to develop a better understanding of the overall patrol program. In each case, the interviews were designed to assess the stated and actual functions of the privatized police patrols, as well as to provide a better understanding of the political, administrative, and situational factors surrounding the arrangement.

Finally, I analyzed documents related to the patrol program. This analysis also sought to assess the particular functions conducted by the private security personnel, and to shed light on other aspects of the arrangement. Such documents included daily reports, contracts, referendums, legal pleadings, and any other document pertaining to the patrol program, especially policies and procedures.

In summary, this book examines issues that up until now have been largely ignored by the police, the security industry, academics, and policy makers. While the subject of privatized policing has been previously addressed, prior studies were limited in their scope. Some previous works have focused on legal issues, but lack a data analysis component. There are a number of studies by practitioners within the security industry; these typically hail the use of private police by pointing out environmental improvements or the reduction of crime rates. Such studies, however, predictably fail to address the larger legal or public policy issues inherent in the use of private policing. This book examines largely unexplored territory in private policing, including unintended or unanticipated consequences, such as constitutional violations and the development of a dual system of policing.

There are numerous individuals who have contributed to this document, often in ways that they may not be aware. Certainly, a special thank you is warranted for my dissertation chairman, Richard Johnson. Professor, your patience and good nature was absolutely fundamental. Your patience and insight to direct the seemingly disparate aspects of this document into a much more cogent work was essential — and most appreciated.

I would like to directly thank each member of my doctoral dissertation committee, Wayne Kerstetter, Jess Maghan, Melissa Marschall, and Evan McKenzie, all of whom contributed their time and efforts toward this work. Each member contributed in different ways. I was very fortunate to have such quality, caring people who took time away from their respective projects to help me complete this document. The academic standards exhibited by each member was both inspiring and exacting. Your suggestions and critiques have enabled me to present this document in a manner substantially strengthened from my earlier versions. Thank you for the considerable help afforded to me. In addition, of special note is Joseph N. DuCanto, who helped me see the value and significance of private policing. Your insight into this subject was significant.

To my late father, and to my mother, I thank you for the selfless efforts designed to help your children be the best that they could be. I thank you for helping impart a desire to learn, and your focus on education. Over the many years of my educational and experiential growth, I have kept the lessons derived from your teachings. My hope is that someday my mission will resonate to help you understand the gravity and import of this document.

To my wife, Rose Ann, I thank you for your considerable love, patience, support, and encouragement. Without such I could not have struggled through this process. It has been a long, often difficult, process which you made possible. I greatly appreciate all that you have done to help make this happen. There have been so many examples of how you have made a difference, I cannot even fathom to count them. All I can say is thank you.

Finally, thanks to all my friends and collogues at Calumet College of St. Joseph for your support and interest in this work. Of special note are President Dennis Rittenmeyer, Ph.D., Dean Michele Dvorak, Ed. D., Graduate Director David Plebanski, Ph.D., Law Enforcement Management Director Michael J. McCafferty, J.D., and Assistant Director James McCaleb, Ph.D.

I

Personal Security and Constitutional Rights: Post–9/11 America

In the aftermath of the terrorist incidents of 2001, this country has been faced with many fundamental questions related to security. Since the framework of this country is built upon and around a constitution, it is important to assess security in light of constitutional protections. Questions are being posed as to how we should appropriately — and legally — respond to the threat of terrorism. Questions like, just how far is the Bush Administration prepared to push the constitutional envelope? Or in pursuit of national security, are we sacrificing the very rights we say we are fighting for? These questions, and others, were posed in a recent magazine article on the conflict between security and constitutional rights (see Klein, 2002: 4). This article is similar to many others by well-intended journalists and authors. This debate is the heart of this book.

The debate between security and constitutional rights is, at its core, a conflict of the principles of human life versus the principles of liberty. This can be illustrated by two statements from people who have spent their professional lives involved with security and the constitution. Laurence Tribe, a renowned constitutional attorney and professor at Harvard, stated that "if we get accustomed to a system of detention and surveillance, we may wake up and find to our dismay that we live in a state that has sold far more of its liberty in exchange for its security than it would be willing to do." On the other hand, U.S. Attorney General John Ashcroft stated that "the security we are fighting for is not security for nothing. We're not destroying rights. We're protecting rights" (Klein, 2002: 4–6).

What Is Security?

These statements focus on two separate principles—liberty versus personal safety. Security is, in its essence, the pushing and pulling between the desire for safety and the constraints of the constitution. The positions articulated by Tribe and Ashcroft are both intellectually correct. They accurately represent the debate between two ideological extremes. There are numerous complex, substantive issues related to these viewpoints. Before we delve into these ideological positions, it would be useful to step back and analyze the issue of "security" from a more personal perspective.

Ask any adult what they think "security" means. You will always get an answer. Everyone has their own understanding of what "security" means. We all have had experiences in which our personal safety seemed at risk. Many of these fears have been unfounded. Many have not. Each year thousands, even millions, of people become victims of crime. They are living proof that security is not just some "concept," it is real and the consequences can be deadly. Indeed, many of the victims are no longer living—they have been the victims of the ultimate breach of security—they have been murdered. As clinical as this statement sounds, the cold, hard reality is that security can mean the difference between life and death. It is not an esoteric concept. It is an everyday issue in some people's lives. To others, it is a brief moment of sheer terror.

Security is an ideal which most people desire. Some characterize it as peace, others view it as tranquility or serenity. Still others view it as the absence of fear or terror. At both linguistic extremes is the notion of safety, and freedom from harm or injury. These concepts, however, do not adequately describe the personal, psychological or even societal implications of security. This is partly because security is an issue for which everyone has a frame of reference. For some, the question of security is raised when a stranger appears on their doorstep. For others, concerns are produced when confronted on a dark street corner by a strange or suspicious person. Still others perceive the notion of security when they lie awake at night hearing strange sounds in the house. Others worry about their security when they hear all too familiar sounds—of gunfire from gang members fighting over control of the neighborhood drug market. These examples—and countless others—are our own personal "war stories" relating to security, or the perceived lack of security, in contemporary America.

These personal examples are part of the broad notion of security. At this level, we all contribute to the debate or the societal discourse. Everyone has an opinion of security, some grounded in real experiences, others based more on fears, often driven by movies or television news reports. Nonetheless, each person has a concept of security. Undeniably, this is not simply an adult phenomenon. Children are often irrationally afraid of monsters in the closet. Children are also reasonably afraid of gang members and drug dealers who terrorize their neighborhood. In Israel or even in this country, many are afraid to go to the corner café for fear that terrorism will wreak havoc.

When you strip away the irrational fears from the reasonable concerns, the concept of security begins to take some shape. While acknowledging that everyone has a personal concept of security, it is just as important to accept the fact that most people do not understand the larger, substantive issues related to security. It can be argued that most people have never had occasion to intellectually analyze the concept. This is not said to slight any reader, or any person who worries about their own safety, or the safety of their family and community. Most people are just busy making a living, raising their children, babysitting their grandchildren, and pursuing passions and hobbies. Most people do so in a way that is devoid of the intellectual issues surrounding security. Indeed, this can be viewed as a positive reflection of American society. We have been quite blessed, and are even downright unique, in our ability to function as a free and relatively secure country. While it is true that not all people in this country are equally safe or secure, most Americans have a level of safety and security which people in many foreign countries can only envy. Unfortunately, this may not be sustainable. There are disconcerting trends and potentialities that may adversely — and substantially — impact the notion of security in contemporary America.

Now consider the concept of liberty. What does liberty mean to the average person? If asked, most people would probably respond with words like freedom, personal rights, and privacy. Clearly, these words engender concepts of living in a free society, being free to live without governmental interference, or simply being "left alone to do as one pleases." Each of these concepts invoke the notion of freedom. Hence, liberty and freedom are inherently interlinked. At the personal level, freedom, or being able to do as you desire, has always been limited in some reasonable capacity. The classic example is falsely yelling "fire" in a crowded theater. We all understand that there are limits to our freedom. Such limits typically revolve around reasonable times, places and circumstances.

From a societal perspective, the issue of freedom is even more complicated. The complication is, in essence, the result of an aggregate of millions of individual liberties potentially competing — or actually competing — with other individuals. It is quite amazing that the framers of the constitution were able to yield the delicate balance that allows individual liberties to exist in a societal structure.

Much can be said on this issue. There have been treatises and other comprehensive and authoritative documents which probe the core of this delicate balance. The depth and breadth of these works stand apart from the focus of this book. Nonetheless, it is important that the reader view the larger context of the constitutional protections afforded to citizens of this country.

Most people are aware that the U.S. Constitution (and the Bill of Rights) limits the power of government, or governmental actors. While the constitution and the Bill of Rights are two separate documents, written at different times for different reasons, most people think of the constitution as encompassing both documents. As such, we will speak of the constitution to include the Bill of Rights.

The more important issue is the constitution's intent to limit the powers of government. It was and is designed to take power away from government, and give rights to the people. Hence, the Bill of Rights— incorporated into the constitution — enumerates certain rights afforded to citizens that limit the ability of the state (government generally) to perform certain actions against its citizens.

The key question, in our context, is whether constitutional protections apply to private police. The answer is not simple or straightforward. Nuances and implications permeate the question. At this point, it is sufficient to state that the answer provides a backdrop to the larger issue of security versus liberty. Underlying the tension between security and liberty is the implementation of private policing patrols within a public environment. This changes the dynamics of constitutional applicability, thereby potentially undermining citizen rights in our quest for security.

With this framework established, think again of the statements made by Tribe and Ashcroft. As stated earlier, their respective statements are both intellectually correct, and they represent the debate between two ideological extremes. Certainly, both would argue compellingly and convincingly as to the merits of their particular point of view. Tribe would view constitutional rights as supreme, or at least, superseding in importance to other forces facing this country. Ashcroft would view human life or the safety of citizens as superseding certain constitutional prohibitions. Indeed, each point of view is correct.

Obviously, both ideological positions respect the notions or concerns of the other. Those who worry about constitutional rights would not advocate loss of lives in the quest to maintain liberty. These individuals would certainly care about the safety of citizens. Conversely, those individuals who advocate greater safety and security would not throw away over two hundred years of constitutional safeguards in order to save a few lives. They also understand the value of liberty. Undeniably, many lives have been sacrificed in both civil and foreign wars to maintain the freedoms afforded to citizens of this country.

When considering the two extremes, the issue is not as simple as constitutional rights versus personal security. Instead, the issue is the tendency, or the side in which one is allowed "room for error." In this way, the issue is the protection of freedom, knowing that some people are likely to die because terrorists or even common criminals are given certain freedoms inherent in this society. The injuries or even deaths caused by violent attacks are analogous to brave soldiers who fought in wars to protect the freedoms and liberties derived from the constitution. Hence, some must die to protect the values and principles of the larger society.

On the other hand, proponents of greater security would see the issue as being defenders of the sanctity of life, inherent in the human right to be free from fear and violence. Here the emphasis is on safety and security, with constitutional safeguards a secondary issue. Proponents of this viewpoint would raise questions like, why worry about constitutional rights when our lives and the lives of our children are at stake? This point of view may consider diminishing constitutional protections as worth the price of safety and security. In any case, advocates of security would likely argue that it is not "our" rights or liberties which are at stake, it is those of the "bad guys," the terrorists and the criminals—who may not even deserve rights.

These are generalized arguments, but the gist of their positions is accurate. They are presented to demonstrate the well-founded positions of both ideological views. At this level the debate is not merely opinion versus opinion. Instead, the debate rests on compelling values and principles versus equally compelling values and principles. At the core of this debate, it is not simply security versus liberty. More accurately, it is questions like these which reveal the inherent conflict:

- How much security is appropriate?
- What level of protection is necessary?
- When does security become overbearing or even destructive to liberty?
- Which principle is more important, security or liberty?

These questions, or questions with a similar refrain, were posed at the advent of public policing in the early-to mid–1800s. Most people in contemporary America view the presence of large municipal police departments as "normal." This was not always the case. Private citizens performed the job of the "police" for centuries prior to the advent of public police departments. Undeniably, this country was founded on the premise that private citizens were the protectors of law and order.

When municipal police departments were being formed, there was a great controversy over "government" enforcing laws, which would inevitably impact the rights of citizens. At that time, the debate sounded as it does now. On one side, those who were deeply concerned with freedom and such things as constitutional rights viewed the use of government-employed police officers as troubling. Many believed that the police would become a repressive arm of the government, and the rights of citizens would be violated and even trampled. On the other hand, those people who were deeply concerned about law and order rightly desired and clamored for safety and security. At that time, major cities were overcrowded with immigrants, who often were involved in crimes or other forms of public disorder.

These circumstances weighed heavily on the debate. How would the criminals be controlled? How can the police (government) be controlled? These refrains were of great concern to civil liberty advocates and security proponents of the 19th century. As a result of this tension between rights and security, the American system attempted to accommodate both opposing ideologies. After literally thousands of court cases and innumerable legislative and executive initiatives, the American system is again at a crossroad.

In contemporary America, the tension between security and constitutional rights is again evident. Now the dynamic has changed. While many still worry about the power of the government to usurp the rights of its citizens, another player has entered the stage. This player is more subtle, almost invisible within the debate. Indeed, the focus of the debate still rests heavily on the government, through officials like Attorney General Ashcroft, advocating more power to suppress crime (and now terrorists), while civil libertarians, like Professor Tribe, caution against too much power (government) to undermine the constitution. Meanwhile, an entity commonly known as "security" silently expands its influence and scope throughout American society.

While this debate will likely sustain itself for years, its nuances need to be expanded to include a larger audience, and another player — private security. The debate is not just intellectual. This is so even though most people have never considered the constitutional, psychological, operational, and economic issues surrounding the use of privatized police services. The issues relating to the tension between security and constitutional rights need to be communicated to the larger society.

This tension is made more dynamic by an intriguing and creative evolution in our quest for a more secure environment. That is, private security patrols on public streets. This arrangement is part of a larger trend of privatization. It is intended to provide a secure and stable environment. In this sense, this is a study of security — more pointedly private security patrols on public streets—and its implications upon society. Before we delve into the details, it would be helpful to first consider a couple of premises.

Security Premises

There are two basic premises related to security in contemporary America. One may seem to be common sense, while the other may raise questions or even controversy:

1. The notion of public safety is changing to include private police actively working in conjunction with and separately from traditional police departments and law enforcement agencies. This demonstrates a sort of "back to the future" situation because in early America, private citizens historically performed law enforcement and order maintenance functions.

2. As a result of this new policing model, citizens and communities will desire increased use of private security personnel and methodologies, including the widespread utilization of private police patrols on public streets and in public areas.

The first premise should not seem unusual to those who have paid attention to the security industry. The genesis of this premise can be traced to a clear, discernable trend. This trend is often referred to, in the generic sense, as partnerships between public and private policing. In these arrangements, the roles and functions of the two groups intersect. Most arrangements are little more than informal communication networks between public and private police officers. However, there are other more comprehensive arrangements, where private police perform order maintenance and law enforcement roles, similar to what has traditionally been the domain of public police departments. Thus, we may be witnessing a resurgence of private policing as it once operated prior to the advent of large municipal police departments.

Prior to the establishment of police departments, private citizens regularly acted as the protectors of the law and public order. When the first modern police force was formed in 1829, Britain's Robert Peel did away with the assorted groups of parish constables, soldiers, and roughnecks who previously did the job. Shortly thereafter, the first American municipal police departments were formed. Government appointees rather than private citizens filled these roles. When this occurred, private policing took a subservient role to government initiated policing. Of course, government based policing grew to be the dominant mode.

As illustrated by the statistics presented earlier, private police are now deeply rooted in the public safety industry of this country. Beyond the raw numbers, current circumstances illustrate a rather dramatic change in the role of private police in contemporary America. In fact, private security is expanding back into public streets where they once operated. In several locations around the country, private security personnel are acting in a patrol function, either to supplement or sometimes even to replace public police departments. There are dramatic examples, such as the towns of Sussex, New Jersey, and Reminderville, Ohio, which fired their police officers and replaced them with private security guards.

To illustrate the nuances of a privatization arrangement, this book is based on a case study of a specific site in a Chicago neighborhood where private security personnel patrol public streets. In this somewhat unusual arrangement, the private patrols are independent of and act as a supplement to the Chicago Police Department. They are independent in the sense that they do not operate under the purview of the public police. They are supplemental in the sense that the private patrols act in concert with the Chicago Police Department. These patrols are accomplished within the same environment, performed in a similar manner, and even resemble the public police both in appearance and weaponry. (See Chapter VII for more on this arrangement.)

Of course, municipal police departments conduct much of their work on public streets, alleys and parks. The security firms also operate within the same environment. As such, they are illustrative of the growing use of private security personnel into areas traditionally within the domain of municipal police departments. How they do their job, and the environment in which they perform, are important considerations regarding the viability of security patrols, including the applicability of constitutional prohibitions. These are particularly important considerations since private police officers are armed with handguns and appear almost exactly as do tactical police officers—who typically perform their jobs in a much more aggressive fashion than the average police beat officer. Thus, we see how the nature of law enforcement is changing as the first premise states.

The second premise relates to the debate between security and liberty. When considering the possible responses between security and liberty, one dominant goal will surface. That is, people will desire more security and personal safety (Azano, 2001: 174). Despite the well-founded constitutional arguments raised by Laurence Tribe, people will tend to err on the side of safety and security. The intensity and duration of this emphasis will likely depend on the frequency of subsequent terrorist attacks. While it is impossible to accurately predict future events, it is reasonable to presume that terrorism, at some level, will be a factor in American society for some time to come.

Given this reality — or at least this assertion, the natural question is, what can society do to counter or contend with terroristic violence? Even more common crimes create fear and terror. Think of the impact of armed robberies, drive-by shootings, and child abductions. Clearly, these are traumatic events, both for the family of the victim(s) and the entire community. Hence, the question of violence is not confined to terrorism. It is relevant at many levels, and for many types of crimes. It relates to the perception of individuals, to communities, to corporations, and of society as a whole. The questions raised in this research are particularly relevant in a society struggling with balancing security and constitutional protections. For example,

- Do such private police officers perform the traditional "observe and report"[1] function, or do they act more like public police officers, thereby emphasizing legal authority, particularly law enforcement?
- Are the order maintenance[2] techniques widely utilized in "community policing" among the functions of private police?
- If order maintenance techniques are utilized by private police officers, does the use of such require legal authority?
- Do the functional aspects of private police patrols conform to the constraints of constitutional protections?
- Are private police forces accountable for their actions, and if so, how and to whom?
- What implications does private policing have on larger public policy, including the incidence of terrorism, and the development of a dual or two-tiered system of public safety?

This research addresses these questions, through an analysis of the functions of private policing — as they operate on public streets in a Chicago neighborhood known as "Marquette Park."[3] The focus is to investigate whether private police are inclined to use police powers in the performance of their patrol function. If so, considering the relevant facts related to their functions, does their use of police powers conform to applicable constitutional prohibitions?

There are a number of factors which may contribute to the increased use of private police on public streets. In general, such factors are appropriate and pragmatic responses to current socioeconomic and political conditions. These factors include crime (or fear of crime), certain economic and operational issues, and order maintenance techniques (commonly utilized in community policing). These factors require further explanation.

A number of criminological studies have assessed fear of crime and its effects on people, especially urban dwellers. Criminal acts, and their accompanying fears, are related to: urban flight (Sampson, 1983; and McLennan, 1970); feelings of insecurity, paranoia and other psychological problems (Smith and Hill, 1991; and Liska, et al., 1982); the tendency toward violence (Hsieh and Pugh, 1993); and a host of other responses. These studies, and others, reveal that crime (or the fear of crime) has many problematic effects. Certainly, one of the principle tenets of terrorism is the spreading of fear or "terror" within society (Wardlaw, 1982: 36; Davis, 1982: 116; Ezeldin, 1987: 33). One of the many responses to crime, or its related fears, is to provide a more secure environment. Private security patrols could be viewed as a means to provide public safety services which the public police will not or cannot provide.

A number of other economic and operational issues could also be related to the trend toward private policing on public streets. Financial constraints may facilitate the use of private security firms for certain policing functions (see Cox, 1990; and Connors, et al., 2000). For example, there are a number of operational aspects of public policing—such as staffing and the tendency to be reactive—which may burden already stretched municipal budgets. Economic constraints never cease, and the economic impact of terrorism will likely be problematic for both public and private coffers.

Finally, the emphasis placed on "community policing" may result in certain unintended consequences. Community policing is commonly used by public police departments throughout the country. In essence, this approach seeks a closer, more intimate contact between the police and citizens in a given area or community. This is accomplished by allowing community involvement in the decision making of the police command structure. It also emphasizes patrol officers getting out of their squad cars and interacting more closely with people in residences, businesses, schools, parks, and community centers (Moore and Trojanowicz, 1988; and Trojanowicz and Carter, 1990).

One result of this approach is that the police are taking on a broader mission that moves away from the legalistic and reactive roles that have traditionally dominated policing. Instead, community policing techniques seek to reduce or negate the conditions which are deemed to create crime. Stated another way, community policing techniques seek to address the root causes of crime (Roth, 1994). The focus is not just on arrests, but on other factors which affect their responsiveness to citizens and the quality of life within the community. Consequently, the nature of this work requires police officers to spend significant time on matters that are not traditionally associated with law enforcement.

Considering the economic constraints associated with community policing, police departments may not be able to sustain the substantial financial commitment of police resources and personnel. This may result in police departments being forced to contract out certain services to private security. An example of outsourcing, at least partially attributable to community policing, can be found in statistics from police departments in Canada. In 1991, the shift toward this model of policing began to take place. That year there were 61,500 police officers and 104,800 private security guards in Canada. By 1998, the number of police officers declined to 54,311, while the number of private security guards doubled to more than 200,000 (Palango, 1998). As illustrated by these statistics, private security could be used to fill public safety functions previously performed by municipal police departments.

While this policing model has achieved some success, it remains to be seen whether these programs are sustainable. Will the funding for this broader mission continue? If not, will the public settle for a reduction in police services? Can the services provided by public police be contracted to private providers, and if so, by whom and at what cost?

The costs are not just financial. There are also functional, legal, constitutional, and public policy implications. Regardless of how these questions are ultimately answered, it is undisputed that the police are taking on a broader mission, without any guarantee that the money and the personnel needed to sustain these programs will continue into the foreseeable future. Should the public continue to demand a broader role from public police departments, then private security is in a unique position to perform certain functions, such as order maintenance on public streets, which is a critical aspect of the community policing model (Moore and Trojanowicz, 1988; Kelling, 1995; Palango, 1998; Robinson, 1997; Seamon, 1995; Kolpacki, 1994; Johnston, 1992; and Connors, et al., 2000).

It appears that the relationship between public police and private security will become increasingly important in the future. Many authors say the growth of the private security industry is a response to the inability of the "outmodeled" public police to cope with crime and disorder (Cunningham and Taylor, 1984; Benson, 1990; and Johnston, 1992). The term "outmodeled" essentially means that the current policing model, as exhibited by community policing techniques, may become less viable, even unsupportable. If this is true, private security could fill the demand for public safety left unfulfilled by government. This is even more likely in a terroristic environment, where random or symbolic violence is accomplished despite the best efforts of government.

The above factors have converged to create a new model of policing. The key to this new model is the growing use of private police to perform certain police functions. The increased use of private police has, in turn, fostered an increased use of surveillance, with less emphasis on strict law enforcement. In practical terms, the concept of "surveillance" could range from the use of sophisticated technology to physical order maintenance techniques, including conducting searches and seizures of suspects on public streets and facilities.

What impact occurs when private security fills or at least shares the role traditionally maintained by public police departments? My assertion is that the impact is unclear, and relatively unstudied. This is especially true of the larger constitutional and public policy issues surrounding the widespread utilization of private policing. The task of order maintenance requires certain police powers, which will inevitably be utilized by private police. This brings up other questions. Will the utilization of police powers by private police officers result in a more secure environment? Will it increase the incidence of constitutional violations?

Some authors also ask whether we are witnessing the growth of a dual provider of public safety services, which may compete with — or even replace — governmental sponsored policing. There are many provocative concerns related to this question, including the possibility that private police will serve the rich, while the public police will focus on the poor (see Johnston, 1992; and Zielinski, 1999; and Kaplan, 1994). One result of a dual public and private provision of policing, according to Shearing and Stenning, would be an "unobtrusive but significant restructuring of our institutions for the maintenance of order, and a substantial erosion by the private sector of the state's assumed monopoly over policing and, by implication, justice" (1983: 496).

This statement illustrates the core of the current state of policing. While security firms have become increasingly involved in policing, the nature of the role played by government has also changed, thereby resulting in a two-tiered or dual system of policing. While these dual systems have co-existed for generations, until recently a critical component has been lacking. That is, private security patrols on public streets. This has occurred with little discussion or research. While courts have provided some oversight, there still is a level of scrutiny maintained by private security which is not even available to public police (Shearing and Stenning, 1983). This involves the constitutionally guaranteed rights afforded to citizens of this country. Such constitutional concerns can adversely impact important public policy issues.

Court decisions relative to private policing have varied substantially over time and among jurisdictions. In the early part of the 20th century, courts largely maintained the principle that constitutional protections were not applicable to actions of private security personnel (see *Burdeau v. McDowell*, 256 U.S. 465, Supreme Court, 1921). Currently, however, courts may deem private security personnel as "state actors" depending upon certain factual findings related to the extent of governmental involvement, and the nature of the property being policed. The term "state actor" is a legal determination in which courts deem an individual who otherwise is not a sworn police officer or governmental official as being a representative of the government due to a factual connection or "nexus" with government. If an individual is deemed a "state actor" then constitutional prohibitions become applicable even though the individual is otherwise a private citizen.

The decision-making process is relatively straightforward. The court would examine the facts of the case to determine whether the private police officer is a state actor. This critical consideration is to assess whether constitutional protections apply. If the private police officer (or officers) is deemed a state actor, then this decision triggers applicable constitutional prohibitions. Conversely, if the private police officer is not deemed a state actor, then constitutional protections do not apply. If constitutional protections do not apply, then evidence obtained in violation of constitutional protections, such as the 4th Amendment prohibition against unreasonable searches and seizures, could be used against the accused. The accused could be convicted with the use of evidence that would have been excluded had the individual been arrested by the public police.

Generally speaking, if private police officers function similar to public police, then they will be deemed state actors. Conversely, if they function in the traditional mannerisms of private security personnel — such as limiting themselves to the "observe and report" function — then the private police officers are likely to be deemed private citizens.

The fact that private security personnel may or may not be deemed state actors presents substantial public policy implications especially considering the ever increasing role of private security in areas traditionally considered public — such as streets and businesses frequented by the general public. This use of private security personnel demonstrates a compelling potential for increased public safety, since another layer of protective services would be provided to the public. However, as discussed above, such arrangements may adversely impact constitutional protections, thereby being potentially destructive.

Without a doubt, this struggle impacts one of the most cherished principles of this democracy. That is, whether individual rights may be breached by those who are not officially acting in a public capacity. Stated another way, what implication does privatization of police services have on public safety, and on the constitutional framework of this country? These questions are provocative, thereby requiring consideration. Hopefully this book can help frame and shape the future relationship between security versus liberty.

II

Privatization and Public Safety

To fully understand privatization in its relationship to public safety, it would be helpful to first examine the concepts of public and private. Much of the privatization literature, whether from advocates or from opponents, views the concepts of "public" and "private" as two distinctive entities (see Tolchin, 1985; Clemow, 1992; and Hebdon, 1995). Unfortunately, the distinction is not that clean. In fact, Shearing and Stenning (1983) argue strongly against using this dichotomy. They state these distinctions do little more than confuse the issue, since they assume the existence of definable boundaries (Johnston, 1992: 25). Because this basic premise is not as clear-cut as most people assume, it would be helpful to discuss how this has come about.

The distinction between public and private has deep historical roots. It relates to the gradual expansion of government. One key role of government was to keep the concept of "king's peace" within land deemed to be "public" (Reynolds, 1994: 2; and Benson, 1990: 29). King's peace was a term used to describe law and order. As royal power grew, kingships began to extend king's peace to places where the king traveled; then to churches, highways and bridges (Reynolds, 1994: 2; and Benson, 1990: 29). Implicit in this movement to extend king's peace into wider and more defined areas was the notion of property ownership. Since the king had, in effect, ownership of all public property, he could declare king's peace in any area viewed as public property (Johnston, 1992: 205). In this way, the more the king expanded his territory, the larger the influence and power derived from his domain.

However, the distinction between public and private was never truly clear. For example, Johnston (1992) questions whether a privately owned tavern should be considered within the public domain. He explained that while a tavern may be privately owned, it is frequented by the general public. This involvement of the public provided the theoretical basis for the king to assert that any disturbances within the establishment violated the king's peace (Johnston, 1992). In this way, the influence of government into events or actions which occurred on private property was justified by the need to maintain law and order. While this does not seem unusual by contemporary standards, the assertion of king's peace on private property was an important development in the gradual expansion of government.

The nature of the "public" and "private" distinction is effectively addressed by Donahue. He argues that the apparent distinction between the two is a "good deal messier than it appears" (Donahue, 1989: 8). He explains that every government agency consists of private citizens who perform "governmental" functions. These citizens are motivated by the same hopes and fears as any other person. Similarly, every private firm is deeply political both within its internal structure, and in its dealings with the larger society (Donahue, 1989: 8). This statement recognizes that even in private corporations, there are both internal and external power struggles. From this point of view, the issue is not simply government (i.e., public sector) versus business (i.e., private sector). Instead, Donahue's larger point was that the public and private sectors are not two distinctively separate entities. Accordingly, it is instructive to think in terms of government and business as being owned by individuals.

Individuals staff both government and business. They are motivated by certain incentives and sanctions. These incentives and sanctions range from money, power, honor, and prestige; to the avoidance of pain, punishment, and other organizational and interpersonal sanctions (Donahue, 1989: 37; and Benson, 1990: 133). Individuals usually assess these incentives and sanctions, and then often act in accordance with the structural policies and constraints placed upon them. Hence, the concept of privatization is also about individuals, not simply what is public and what is private. Kolderie agrees with this notion when he states, "We cannot talk simply about a public sector and a private sector" (1986: 17).

The focus on the significance of individuals, not the institutions which employ them, acts as the baseline of the public-private distinction. It effectively turns the attention away from the terms "government" and "business." The importance of this re-directed view is manifest in the language of the federal government's policy on privatization. The policy states that "government should not compete with its citizens" (Donahue, 1989: 37). The response by Donahue is "Unless government is staffed exclusively by aliens, this ringing declaration has no real meaning" (Donahue, 1989).

While this was stated somewhat in jest, Donahue made his point very clear. Implicit in his statement is the assertion that even policy makers in the government seem to buy into the notion that citizens are those who work for businesses, and government workers are merely employees, not citizens. Of course, this inference does not withstand sound logic. What is clear is this: the concepts of public and private domains relate to each other in complex, dynamic, contradictory, and sometimes even ambiguous ways (Johnston, 1992: 205). Johnston explains the difficult distinction by asserting, "In drawing attention to these issues, one is, in fact, touching upon a long-standing, yet unresolved problem in social and political theory about the nature of the public-private divide" (1992: 215).

For purposes of this study, the distinction between public and private can be explained from the notion of property ownership. One of the key assessments is to determine who owns the property in question. For example, each private security firm in this study is a closely held corporation in which the shareholders are limited to a small number of private citizens. From this perspective, the notion that business is owned by private individuals fits the common assumption of the private sector.

There is no clear line of distinction, however, relative to the "ownership" of an American corporation. In fact, there are two opposing schools of thought. On one hand, some authors argue that since the process of forming a corporation is a privilege granted and administrated by government, the corporation can be considered a public entity. McKenzie cites Adolph Berle, who says the modern corporation "has de facto, at least, invaded the political sphere and has become in theory, if not in fact, a quasi-governing agency" (1994: 125). This public nature of corporations was also asserted by other authors. For example, Lakoff argued that private associations are considered governments when they exhibit, to a significant extent, certain fundamental political characteristics (McKenzie, 1994: 134–135). Conversely, the other school of thought contends that since corporations are owned and controlled by individuals, the corporation must be a private entity (see Savas, 2000, for explanation of such).

In regard to the question of property ownership, additional facts complicate this assessment. For instance, the monies used to pay the private security firms come from property tax revenues derived from property and business owners in the patrol area. In this way, the monies are derived from public sources through taxes. The taxes are collected by the county government, and then disbursed to a not-for-profit community corporation, which is overseen by a committee appointed by the local alderman. Based on these facts, it is clear that there is considerable interplay between what is commonly viewed as public and private sectors.

Even if it is assumed that the security firm is owned by private share-holders, which is debatable given the assertions by McKenzie — the larger question is left unresolved. That is, who owns the provision of services? Can the taxpayers in the area properly declare such ownership? Can the community based not-for-profit, or even the governing committee, declare itself the owner of such services? While these are rhetorical questions, they are the core of the property ownership notions raised above.

These issues, and others, illustrate the conceptual ambiguity between public and private property. Simply put, there is no straightforward dis-tinction. Significantly, most American legal codes define public places as those to which the public has access, as of right, or by invitation (John-ston, 1992: 206). However, many "public places" are owned by someone or some entity. For instance, many large facilities frequented by the gen-eral public, such as entertainment, sports and concert stadiums, are pri-vately owned by individuals and shareholders. Owners of such property, of course, retain the right to exclude persons from entry. Here the issue of public-private is particularly blurred. This assertion leads to the inevitable question: how do we define or differentiate public property from private property? *Black's Law Dictionary* (fifth edition) defines a "public place" as

> a place where the general public has a right to resort; not neces-sarily a place devoted solely to the uses of the public, but a place which is in point of fact public rather than private, a place visited by many persons and usually accessible to the neighboring public. Also, a place in which the public has an interest as affecting the safety, morals, and welfare of the community. A place exposed to the public, and where the public gather together or pass to and fro.

This definition provides a baseline for this research. Notice that a public place is defined as one where the public has an interest in affecting the safety, morals and welfare of the community. Consider the concept of "king's peace" in this light. It is clear that an overriding desire is to foster law and order. In this way, the use of privatized policing relates to public safety. Consequently, public safety is connected with what is deemed pub-lic property.

Since public safety is a consideration in any property, whether pub-licly or privately owned, it can be argued that there is little need to worry about the distinction between public and private property. The use of pri-vate police on public streets can be considered a counterbalance to the concept of the king's peace. In the assertion of king's peace, it was govern-ment's influence which was extended. With the use of private policing on public streets, it is the corporation's influence which is being extended. In both cases, however, the quest is for public safety — or for law and order. With this in mind, the concept of privatization must be considered in context, with certain definitions and elements related to its usage. We need to examine exactly what is meant by the term "privatization."

Privatization Definitions and Elements

Before we deal with the issues related to the privatization of policing, two caveats must be addressed. First, since privatized policing is related to the larger concept of privatization, the issues inherent in privatization must be considered in this light. Privatization can be broadly characterized to illustrate the dichotomy between two competing theories, one being government based and the other market based. Each such viewpoint would be applicable to the privatization of most, if not all, public services—from garbage collection to private policing.

This is not to say, however, that certain aspects of privatization would be universally true in all settings. The validity of the perceived benefit often depends upon the particular service provision, the specific setting, or even the subjective viewpoint of the individual assessing its merits. It is important to note that this research does not, nor will not, make any normative assessment as to the merits of either side of the debate. It is beyond the scope of this book to become enmeshed in the merits of privatization from an economic standpoint. Nonetheless, the basic issues relating to privatization are clearly relevant and must be understood.

Second, an intellectual distinction between public and private must be provided. While it may be difficult to clearly distinguish what constitutes "private policing," there must be an acknowledgment that an entity that could be called "private" exists, both in terms of the nature and location of the services, and of the service providers themselves. As will be shown below, the privatization literature provides various mechanisms to distinguish public from private.

With these caveats established, in its broadest terms, privatization could apply whenever a public function is combined with elements of the private sector (Shenk, 1995: 22). Another broad definition is that privatization involves increased governmental reliance on the private sector, rather than on governmental agencies, to satisfy the needs of society (Clemow, 1992: 344). Similarly, Miranda defines privatization as "service delivery arrangements that increase the use of the private and nonprofit sectors in service production or decrease government responsibility in service provision" (1993: 432). Both Finley (1989: 8) and Clemow (1992: 44) assert a similar definition, which is explained by introducing the application of market forces to functions previously provided only by government. These broad definitions were echoed by Savas, who states that "privatization can be broadly defined as relying more on the private institutions of society and less on government to satisfy people's needs" (Savas, 2000: 3).

Another way to understand the concept of privatization is to break it down into distinctive elements. These elements, as explained by Donahue, are as follows (1989: 38):

Figure 1

Privatization Elements

Production<————————————————>Provision

Government<————————————————>Firm

In this breakdown, the elements of production and provision represent a functional analysis, while government versus private firm represents a structural analysis. Functions relate to what goods or services are provided — in other words, the provision. Structure relates to the entity which provides the goods or services— in other words, the producer. Kolderie (1986) explains that the purest form of public sector activity is where government does both the production and the provision. Conversely, the purest form of private sector activity is where private firms do both the production and the provision. Between the two extremes are the more common mixtures— either the production or the provision is derived from private firms (Kolderie, 1986: 285). In this case study, the provision is patrol services, while the production of such is derived from private security firms.

With these broad definitions in mind, we need to go deeper into the concept of privatization. Kolderie's explanation of these key components, while helpful in describing the distinction between the production and provision of services, does not explain why the distinctions are relevant. They are relevant because the distinction is based on the classic choice between two basic dimensions, financing and performance. This is consistent with assertions made by Donahue (1989: 7). The question relative to financing focuses on who (or what entity) should pay for the goods or services. Should private firms pay, or should government pay? The performance question focuses on who (or what entity) provides the goods or services. Should they be provided by private firms, or the government? At its core, the provision of goods or services for compensation by an individual or entity are deemed either "government jobs" or "government contracts"

(Donahue, 1989: 37). At this level, privatization can be reduced to one simple question: Who does the work?

Savas (2000) takes a market-orientated approach to privatization. He breaks out privatization into four broad categories of goods or services, specifically: Individual, Toll, Common-Pool, and Collective. A brief summary of each category is as follows:

> *Individual*: This entails the delivery of goods and services based on free market forces. In this analysis, consumers demand the goods, businesses recognize the demand and produce the goods, and sell them to willing buyers at a mutually acceptable price [Savas, 2000: 50].

Examples of the above include food, clothing, and housing.

> *Toll*: These goods and services can be supplied by the marketplace, but also can be supplied by government. However, because consumers can be excluded, users have to pay in order for producers to supply the goods. Sometimes these goods can be natural monopolies, where the cost per user decreases as the number of users increases [Savas, 2000: 50–51].

Examples include cable television, electric power, water distribution facilities, or other utilities.

> *Common-Pool*: These goods and services pose a supply problem because there is no need to pay for them, and no effective way to prevent their consumption. As such, it is not unusual that such goods be squandered — even to the point of exhaustion — as long as the direct possession of the free goods does not exceed the value of the goods to the ultimate consumer [Savas, 2000: 51–52].

Examples include fish, whales, or elephant tusks.

> *Collective*: According to Savas, these goods and services pose the greatest problem within society because by their very nature, they are used simultaneously by many people, with no one effectively excluded from such usage. As such, each individual has an economic incentive to be a "free rider," that is, to use the goods without paying and without regard for sharing in the effort required to supply them [Savas, 2000: 53–54].

Examples include street cleaning, fire protection, and protective patrols.

These broad categories of goods and services are particularly insightful when one considers the collective goods problem articulated by Savas. His concern was based on how society pays for such. In essence, the payments are either voluntary or coerced contributions. The question can be reduced to the method in which the goods or services are derived. For example, citizen patrols designed to augment law and order would be viewed as a voluntary collective action for the provision of public safety services (Savas, 2000: 53). The "payment" may not be in the form of money. Instead, payment could be in the form of contributed services. However, such voluntary services are extremely difficult to sustain over time. They also present "free rider" problems in that many people, arguably even most, will not contribute their fair share of the voluntary services (Savas, 2000: 53). In this way, collective goods represent a considerable societal dilemma. Savas views the collective goods (or services) problem in a classic market analysis. The demand for services, such as patrol services, would be simultaneously desired by many (or all), yet no one (or no entity) has a direct incentive to pay for the goods or services.

Because of this collective goods problem, in this case study, the service is derived from a coerced contribution plan, whereby every property owner in the protected area (called "special service district") must contribute a prorated portion of their property taxes to pay for the patrol services. With this arrangement, all property owners pay for the patrol services. There is no "opting out" of such payments, short of selling the affected property. Based on such, it is fair to contend that not all property owners are happy to contribute to the patrol services. Indeed, some may not even want the patrol services.

Another useful analysis used to distinguish between private and public comes from Benn and Gaus (1983). These authors provide a continuum to illustrate the respective level of privatization in any setting or arrangement:

Figure 2

Public–Private Continuum

Private		*Public*
Closed<——————— ACCESS —————————>Open		
(How Open)		
Individual<——————— AGENCY —————————>Government		
(Who Owns or Who Acts)		
One/Few<——————— INTEREST —————————>All/Many		
(How many Concerned or Affected)		

In this analysis, the key is to answer three inquires dealing with Access, Agency and Interest. The answer to these questions would enable the researcher to determine whether the particular function or activity should be deemed private or public. The closer a particular function or activity is to *private* on the continuum, the more likely it will be deemed to be private, and vice versa. Using this continuum, the patrol functions of this book's case study, Marquette Park in Chicago, can be assessed to determine whether they involve public or private matters.

Related to Access, the security patrols would be quite open in that they are conducted on public streets, alleyways, parks, and businesses used and frequented by the general public. Therefore, according to the continuum, the patrols would be deemed *public*. This conclusion coincides with the definition of "public place" presented earlier. Consequently, even in the most restrictive definition of public, the patrols must be deemed to occur on public property.

Related to Agency, the basic distinction is whether the agent acts privately — on his or her own account or publicly — as an officer of a political entity (Benn and Gaus, 1983: 5). In this case, the security firms who conduct the patrols are owned by a small number of private individuals. Generally, those who act or perform the patrol function are also private citizens, not sworn police officers. Further, the patrol services are paid for by private property owners (although administered by city and county government). Conversely, these services are administered by a publicly appointed commission on behalf of the City of Chicago. Nonetheless, the preponderance of the evidence substantiates that the patrol services are private.

Related to Interest, the basic distinction is determined by the status of the people affected by the arrangement (Benn and Gaus, 1983: 5). The private patrols — potentially at least — may provide for certain improvements of the crime rates or the environment. They also may result in unintended consequences, such as constitutional violations. In any event, it is safe to assert that the patrols may affect all or many of the people living or traveling within the area where they operate. Consequently, these patrols would likely be deemed public.

Based on these factors, these patrols are a mixture of both private and public functions. Does this make the patrols private or public? This is an unsettled question. Are the patrol officers deemed public actors, thereby making constitutional provisions applicable to their actions? The answer to this question will largely be determined by their specific functions. This study illustrates a basic contention asserted by Donahue, who maintains that the "border between public and private realms is at once ill-defined, shifting, and disputed" (1989: 222).

In addition to the distinctions described above, the legal concept known as Agency can help define what is public and private. In this concept, the "principal" is the public, and the "agent" is either a governmental agency, such as a police department, or a private security firm (Morgan, 1992: 252; and Donahue, 1989: 38). In the principal-agent relationship, the principal delegates or contracts out certain functions to the agent, who is then required to perform on behalf of the principal. There is a duty or a standard, known as a "fiduciary duty," attached to the actions of the agent. This duty is essentially an obligation to adhere to the interests of the principal. In essence, the duty is not to do anything which would conflict with the best interests of the principal.

As may be implied from this duty-bound relationship, it is not perfect. For example, the principal does not have complete control over the agent, and the agent usually only has partial information about the interests of the principal (Donahue, 1989: 38). This creates, according to Donahue, a "fundamental problem of mutual responsibility in human society" (1989). This is so because individual interests overlap, but are not identical. According to Donahue, the solution of such potentially inconsistent interests requires a carefully designed structure of accountability. The goal is to ensure that those who act on behalf of citizens do so in a way that makes them accountable to the citizens (Donahue, 1989). This is difficult to achieve.

This realization creates the "root social challenge" of accountability to which cultural devices such as the law, ethics, and the market are meant to respond to and resolve. Given the problems inherent in agency theory, Donahue believes that "there is no reason to believe that a private form of organization will always, or even usually, improve accountability" (Donahue, 1989). This issue of accountability, therefore, is a critical component within privatization literature. Indeed, the level of accountability exhibited in the private patrols bring up questions of constitutional violations. This will be explored in detail later.

Privatization Provisions and Issues

From a market or economic perspective, advocates of privatization essentially argue that the use of private firms will result in lower costs for the same — or better — service derived from government (Wessel, 1995: 45; Donahue, 1989: 50; Tolchin, 1985: 1; Clotfelter, 1977: 876; Miranda, 1993: 432; Carlson, 1995: 72; Benson, 1990: 21; Morgan, 1992: 251; and Clemow, 1992: 344). These authors maintain that private firms are able to pay lower wages (at least partially due to non-unionized labor), and are more able to terminate inefficient workers. Consequently, private firms can deliver better quality service at a lower cost. Admittedly, this may not be universally true. However, there is substantial evidence that labor costs (including benefits, training, etc.) have a direct relationship to service quality (see Benson, 1990: 186; Donahue, 1989: 83; Linowes, 1988: 244; and Wessel, 1995: 45). The logic is this: if labor costs are high, then service quality would be high (or better). To be sure, this assertion is somewhat speculative or, at least, not always true.

While this notion may not be definitive, there is ample evidence to support the assertion that private firms can deliver more efficient services for less cost. For example, a study commissioned by the Department of Housing and Urban Development revealed that municipal services are 50 percent less efficient than private contractors (Donahue, 1989: 138). The cost savings associated with this finding were due to:

1. More flexible use of labor.
2. A richer array of incentives and penalties.
3. More precise allocation of accountability.
4. Less constraint on process, more focus on results [Donahue, 1989: 40].

Without getting too deeply into the economic merits of this argument, proponents of privatization assert that market competition forces private firms to be more efficient, especially when many similarly situated companies are ready, willing and able to provide such services (see Morgan, 1992: 251; Donahue, 1989: 166; and Benson, 1990: 236). Conversely, the absence of competition within the public sector allows for complacency, with little incentive to provide better service at the lowest cost possible.

Of course, the fact that services are privatized does not guarantee that market forces will lower costs and increase service quality. Opponents of privatization argue that reduced labor costs are illusory. Bilik (1992: 339) argues that any cost savings are illusory because they are achieved through hiring less qualified and less trained personnel, providing inadequate benefits to employees, using hiring practices which focus on part-time employees, and even using creative accounting methods. These, he says, reduce or negate the benefits derived from privatization. Even the cost of contract bidding and administration must be assessed, as it adds to the "bottom line," and may even invite corruption (Hebdon, 1995: 11–12; Donahue, 1989: 147; and Chanken and Chaiken, 1987: 23). In short, some authors cite the common proposition that without adequate competition, the ill effects of monopolies will result (Shenk, 1995: 22; Clemow, 1992: 348; Schine, et al., 1994: 39; Bilik, 1992: 340; Donahue, 1989: 127; and Hebdon, 1995: 6).

Others argue that even if cost savings are true, the result is a negative effect on larger public policy interests (Johnson, 1992: 25; Tolchin, 1985: 1; and Hebdon, 1995: 13). For example, both Bilik (1992: 339) and Clemow

(1992: 346) believe that poorly paid private employees undermine the wage and benefit standards achieved in this country. Shenk (1995: 16) also argues that private firms have less clear guidelines and standards on employment practices, thereby providing a less consistent service to the public. The use of private firms could even create the illusion that government is a private money pit for their economic ends (Shenk, 1995: 20). Consequently, Donahue argues that "evidence is overwhelming that where competition, negligence or the nature of the service itself undercuts competition, the benefits of privatization shrink or vanish" (1989: 218).

Going beyond the direct economic assessments, some authors assert that service quality will suffer, regardless of cost, due to the higher turnover rates and lower pay in the private sector (Bilik, 1992: 339; Tolchin, 1985: 1; and Cunningham, et al., 1991: 3). Their reasoning is that private firms cannot offer the same consistency of service due to their higher turnover rates. With this logic, the more times a new hire has to be trained and acclimated to the job, the less consistent daily service will be. Further, since public employees are generally better paid, the logic is that the better paid employee is more qualified and skilled at the job. Conversely, public employees may be less motivated due to their relative job security, and their comparatively higher pay may merely be a reflection of the power of their unionized position. Regardless of the truth of these opposing viewpoints, it is safe to assert that the use of privatized service providers does not necessarily result in either lower costs or better service quality.

While it's debatable whether one system is better than the other, the fact remains that the use of privatization in this country indicates that many types of goods and services should or could be considered. Much of the interest, at least on the surface, relates to the desire to trim government costs. Former Indianapolis Mayor Stephen Goldsmith once stated, "We have been trying to drive down the cost of doing business; the need to slim down is more urgent than ever" (Shenk, 1995: 17). Despite inevitable economic swings, the issue of governmental service provision — and its associated costs— will not go away. Many authors believe that in any economic environment, government officials will inevitably seek less costly ways to provide necessary public safety services (see West, 1993; Palango, 1998; Tolchin, 1985; Benson, 1990; and Reynolds, 1994).

Public-Private Police Characteristics

The clearest distinction between the two modes of policing is the fact that public police officers are duly sworn by officials of government. For our purposes, public police officers include sworn employees of local, county, state or federal government entities. In contrast, private police are individuals who are employed by private firms or other organizations without governmental affiliation.

However, this distinction is not always as clean as it appears. In most states, private security personnel are licensed and regulated by the state. Some state and local governmental units even grant "special police" status to private security personnel. Like the sheriff, or in earlier times, the constable, modern private police personnel are sometimes given this special police status, which provides broad arrest powers similar to public police officers. In Marquette Park the patrol officers are not vested with special police status. Nonetheless, the governmental involvement is substantial. Each private security firm was hired by a local community association, overseen by political appointees, contractually regulated by city government, and was paid by tax revenues collected by county government. Consequently, this case study provides an excellent example of the difficulties in cleanly distinguishing between the two groups. As asserted by Johnston (1992), "In the real world of policing and security, there is rarely, if ever, a clear exclusivity between the public and private provision of such services."

As inferred from Johnston's assertion, any factual analysis between private and public police may be somewhat arbitrary and artificial. However, certain authors have neatly categorized the two groups. For example, Carlson identifies five specific categories:

> *Philosophical:* Private officers/guards lack moral authority that only government can give to law enforcement.
> *Legal:* Private officers/guards are hobbled by the law, with only limited powers of arrest, usually restricted to the commission of crimes within their presence. However, some private officers/guards with "special police" status have nearly all powers of public police, including authority to make arrests and carry guns.
> *Financial:* Private officers/guards can perform certain tasks more cheaply.
> *Operational:* Private officers/guards are more flexible, can be assigned to specific locations, and spend nearly all their tour on the beat with fewer arrests, little paperwork, and rare court appearances.
> *Security/Political:* Private officers/guards give citizens more control over their own safety by augmenting police efforts, helping to maintain order when police are spread thin. Also, private policing encourages citizens to follow community standards in a way that police officers cannot or do not [1995: 67].

These categories illustrate that there are many facets in the distinction between public and private policing. These categories can all be applied to the case study of Marquette Park. Relative to the legal issues, the individual security personnel from the firms associated with this study do not have "special police" status. The security personnel have the same arrest powers as those of a private citizen. Interestingly, this does not greatly limit their ability to make arrests. This is so because in Illinois, as in many states, a private citizen is given relatively broad arrest powers. In this light, the act of making an arrest raises constitutional questions. Certain constitutional protections, such as the Fourth Amendment prohibition against unreasonable searches and seizures, would not apply unless the private police officers were deemed state actors.

Related to these legal questions are the philosophical implications addressed by Carlson. This relates to the fact — or at least a perception — that security personnel do not carry the same sense of legal or moral authority as public police officers. This may or may not relate to the extent of police powers. Indeed, the level of perceived authority could affect how the private officers perform their jobs. For example, if a private police officer directs someone to refrain from loitering, the willingness to adhere to this directive may relate to whether the officer has the authority, either legal or moral, to force compliance. This may not be clear cut, either from a legal perspective or from an individual perspective. Consequently, the level of perceived versus actual authority is extraordinarily important.

The security/political category has to do with the level of control over the functions of the private police, and how responsive the private police are to the needs of the "client." In this case study, one seemingly basic question does not have a straightforward answer. That is, who is the client? The answer may depend on who (or what) is viewed as the recipient of the services. In this sense, who or what receives the patrol services? Is it the property owners who contribute their monies through real estate taxes? Is it the larger community, or any individual who happens to drive through the neighborhood? Is it the sole service provider, or even the governing commission, who maintains some controls or contractual relationship with the security firm? Each of these can be construed as the "client" in the context of the patrol services.

In the community policing model, the public police are deemed more accountable to the interests of the citizens they serve. In this sense, the citizens are the "clients" of the public police. Similarly, security personnel have traditionally been "client focused." This is based, at least partly, on the fact that the client is paying the bill. Consequently, private police must account — at some level — to the desires of the "clients" within the patrol program. This may or may not relate to the performance of specific functions in the course of the patrol services.

Some authors distinguish public and private police by the roles they play or functions they perform. The literature contends there are differences in how public police function as compared to how private police function, and vice versa. The distinctive aspects of these policing functions were set out by Chanken and Chaiken (1987: 21):

Figure 3

Policing Role and Functional Distinctions

Private Police	Policing Function	Public Police
Client<————————————Input ——————————>Citizen		
Crime Prevention<———————————— Role ——————>Crime Response		
Specific< ————————————————Targets ——————————>General		
Profit-Orientated Enterprise<————Delivery System————>Government		
Loss Reduction/Asset Protection< ————Output ————>Enforcement/Arrest		

This figure illustrates that the functions of public and private police vary in a rather dramatic fashion. One of the most profound distinctions regards the "input." For whom is the service designed or intended? For private policing, the bill payer is usually deemed the client. For public police, the citizen or society is the client (Shearing and Stenning, 1983: 500). In our case study, however, the distinction between the "client" and a "citizen" is muddied by the fact that in many instances the client is both a bill payer and a citizen. This is so because the property owners pay for the patrol services, and are also citizens within the protected area. This creates a complex interplay regarding the service delivered by the security firm. Of course, the service is to patrol the streets and properties in the protected area. Because patrol services—in a public policing context— often result in arrests and investigative stops, it is expected that the private police will conduct themselves in a similar manner, thereby resulting in the enforcement of laws or the assertion of legal authority. Consequently, some property owners may be paying for protection, while others may be paying to be *arrested*. While this ironic situation can be analogous to paying taxes to public police, which inevitably results in taxpayers being arrested, the link between the payment and the arrest is less direct, or at least, more of an accepted principle of this country.

In between these two functional extremes outlined by Chanken and Chaiken is the more realistic, yet less acknowledged, commonality between the two groups. McKenzie's analysis of the commonalities—rather than the simplistic distinctions—is noteworthy. McKenzie (1994) explains that a corporation is performing both a private and public function by hiring civilians as security personnel, and equipping them with uniforms, badges and weapons. The responsibility or function of the security officers is to provide for the enforcement of certain laws on the company's property (McKenzie, 1994: 123). In this way, this seemingly private function provides for an external benefit to the larger society, or at least to the citizens who happen to be within the protected facility or area.

Additionally, McKenzie asserts that the governmental responsibility to register private security guards and the mandate of certain training requirements are creating standards similar to those of public police officers (McKenzie, 1994). In this way, the regulatory constraints of government upon "private police" illustrates that this entity may not be completely private. While this regulatory mandate by government is also imposed on many other industries, such as petroleum, automobile, tobacco and liquor companies, to name a few; there is one key distinction. That is, government does not simultaneously perform the same function. Government does not produce petroleum, it does not manufacture vehicles, it does not make and distribute cigarettes and alcohol. Government does, however, perform police patrols. These examples illustrate, once again, that the distinction between public and private is not clear cut, especially as it relates to patrol services.

Most would not hesitate to argue that, at least in theory, the "input" distinction explains a great deal about the service orientation of the two entities. Particularly in the private sector, the need to "please the client" cannot be underestimated. In essence, private security firms tend to view behavior in terms of whether it threatens the interests of the client (Shearing and Stenning, 1983: 500). In any competitive market, however, the determination of what constitutes the "interests of the client" is not always clear nor consistent (Dalton, 1993: 62). For example, it is commonplace in the security industry that clients are concerned only with getting a "warm body" for the lowest cost possible (Dalton, 1993). In this scenario, the ability to "please the client" would rest on whether the pre-determined number of "guards" show up for work, and that the cost for such "service" is at or below market rates. In other scenarios, the ability to please a particular client may involve sophisticated and aggressive security methods, whereby the focus is on providing an extremely secure physical environment and protecting specific personal or physical assets. Much of the current debate stemming from the recent terrorist incidents has centered around the need for effective security measures, not merely providing "guards" who are physically or intellectually incapable, unable, or ill prepared (see, for example, *Chicago Tribune*, October 14, 2001).

Given the wide range of client motivations for security, it is simplistic to assert that the only goal or the critical input to the security firm is to please the client. However, the ability to please or even discern the motivation(s) of the client is a critical determination of any firm. This is so because the goal, or input, drives how the security firm performs its duties or functions. A client could desire aggressive and extensive security, resulting in practices being markedly similar to the duties or functions of public police. Such a role could entail aggressive enforcement of criminal laws through proactive law enforcement, and crime prevention techniques such as order maintenance.

In essence, the underlying question is the motivation or the desire of those who hire private patrols. Are the privatized patrol officers expected to "act like the police," thereby enforcing laws and public order? This ever-increasing role of private security on public streets is where significant constitutional and public policy concerns arise.

Another important aspect of the traditional functions set out by Chanken and Chaiken regards the "output" of the service. The traditional (though not necessarily historical) output for private policing is that it focuses on loss reduction or asset protection.[1] The role of private police (or private citizens) changed from a desire to address and prevent crime within the community as a whole to a more focused desire to protect specific business and property owners (Benson, 1990: 125). This latter focus has become the "traditional" view of private security. However, there is ample evidence that the role of private security may be shifting back to its historical roots. Private policing could renew its enforcement orientation, thereby asserting arrest powers—currently, largely the exclusive realm of public police.

Finally, perhaps the most important issue relative to the function of private police versus public police is the delivery system. For private police, the delivery system is profit-oriented firms or corporations. With public police it is government. This distinction is critical. The key question is whether constitutionally guaranteed protections against unreasonable searches and seizures apply. Historically, such constitutional protections did not apply to private police (see Nemeth, 1989; and Chanken and Chaiken, 1987). However, courts are now apt to extend constitutional protections to include actions by private police, provided those actions have a connection to government or with sworn police personnel. Many questions still remain, however, since courts have not developed a consistent theme or standard.

Consequently, the overlap between the respective functions of private and public policing, coupled with the mixing of their conceptual distinctions, illustrates the significance of the constitutional and public policy issues raised in this book. The nuances of these issues may be better understood by assessing the respective functions of each group.

What is the proper function of private police? Should private police be relegated to private property and private accounts? Should they be a supplement for the public police? Is it necessary or proper for private police to replace public police? These questions result in many diverse answers. Some authors assert that the private sector will bear an increased preventive role, while public police will concentrate more heavily on violent crimes and crime response (see Cunningham and Taylor, 1984; Benson, 1990; and Johnston, 1992). Regardless of how these questions are ultimately answered, these two entities seem to be increasingly overlapping, sometimes to the point that they are indistinguishable. Johnston has stated that "conceptions regularly deployed in the social control literature, such as 'blurring of the boundaries' do little more than confuse the issue, since they tacitly assume the existence of definable boundaries which can at some point be subject to 'blurring'" (1992: 215).

While acknowledging that these role distinctions are somewhat arbitrary, a broad definition may help to explain the functional attributes of private police. From a privatization perspective, Finley (1989: 3) asserts privatization occurs when "security is produced or delivered when safety/ security actions are taken that reduce unsafe/insecure behaviors." This view of privatization would encompass production of security services in almost limitless ways, from citizen volunteers to private police, from fences and gates to sophisticated electronic surveillance. In this sense, the concept of privatization is much broader than the use of security guards to "police" specific environments.

In the case of Marquette Park, the private police patrols act as a supplement to public police. A key question is whether the private police function in a similar manner to the public police. If there are similarities, what functions do the private police tend to focus on? Does the performance of these functions impact constitutional protections? Are there any public policy implications related to this privatization arrangement? Before these questions are directly assessed, it may be helpful to understand why these questions may be particularly relevant in contemporary America. As is often the case, the significance of contemporary circumstances can be illustrated by tracing their historical development.

IIII

Historical Developments in Private Policing

In developing this historical overview, it may be valuable to first consider the concepts of "police" and "policing." The former is a relatively modern concept, while the latter has ancient historical roots. Both words are derived from the Greek word "polis" (Johnston, 1992: 4). The word "polis" is also the root for the terms polity, politic and policy. As such, the term "policing" originally had a broader socio-political function, rather than merely a formal legal one (Johnston, 1992). Johnston observes that the word "police" came into use around the mid–18th century. At that time, this term — for the first time — referred to specific functions of crime prevention and order maintenance (Johnston, 1992). Given its linguistic origins, the term "police," which refers to governmental policing personnel, ignores the historical basis of policing.

Origins of Policing

The concept of a publicly funded entity designed to serve and protect society is a relatively recent historical development. In fact, the first publicly organized police force did not occur until 1829, in England, under the sponsorship of Sir Robert Peel (Nemeth, 1989: 6; Miller, 1977: ix; and Reynolds, 1994: 3). Prior to the formation of public police, the concepts of self-help and self-protection were considered the foundations of law enforcement and public order (Nemeth, 1989: 1; and Shearing and Stenning, 1983: 493). Historically, private citizens have provided for their own safety and the protection of others. In this historical context, the role of kings began to change. In earlier times, the king was primarily concerned with conducting warfare. This changed when leaders began to see law enforcement, or in broader terms—the justice process—as a cash cow (Reynolds, 1994: 2; and Benson, 1990: 29). This realization facilitated the expansion of government's role into the internal justice process through the expansion of the king's peace into larger and larger public areas.

As the power of the king evolved, many offenses that were previously regarded as intentional torts (wrongs subject to civil action) became increasingly deemed as crimes against the king's peace (Johnston, 1992: 2). As Reynolds observes, "whereas the spoils of tort law belonged to the victims, the spoils of criminal law went to the king" (Reynolds, 1994: 2). Consequently, the incentive to expand the king's peace was clear. If individuals were declared to be criminals, their property could be subject to confiscation by the king, with corporal or capital punishment being instituted (Johnston, 1992: 2). In this way, the king could collect property or revenue from the "criminal." At the same time, the criminal would be punished (or even executed) for deeds against the king, his sovereignty, and his people.

The expanding role of kings into the sphere of criminal justice was furthered by the Norman conquest of England in 1066. King Henry I in 1116 decreed that certain offenses would heretofore be deemed against the king's peace. In this decree, the king declared arson, robbery, murder, and other felonious and violent actions as "crimes" (Reynolds, 1994: 2). Certainly this decree does not seem unusual in light of 21st century norms. At the time of the decree, however, it was another large step in the direction of the king's sovereignty over the internal justice system. King Henry II went even further. He replaced the private, decentralized civil law with a public, centralized and politicized criminal law (Reynolds, 1994).

The latter decree particularly affected the aggrieved citizen. The impact centered on who was to be compensated—whether financially or physically—for the injury caused by the act (i.e., crime or tort). Victims attempted to have an offense considered a civil tort, since that was the only way they could collect financial compensation. Conversely, the king had an incentive to declare the act a crime, thereby deriving financial benefit. By doing so, the king sought to secure his monopoly over the prosecution of criminal law, thereby generating more and more revenue for his coffers (Reynolds, 1994).

It is important to note, however, that the ever-increasing expansion of the criminal law was not without justification. Advocates who favored increasing sovereignty of the king believed it would reduce the incidence of retribution by private citizens, as well as provide for a legitimate sanction by the government (Nemeth, 1989: 2; and Benson, 1990: 12). The sanctioning of criminals by the state was deemed to be legitimate in the sense that it removed the need for the victim (or his or her family) to retaliate against the offender. In this way, the state (or king) would avenge the harm done to the victim on behalf of all the people. As such, the retribution involved the power of the state, not simply of the aggrieved or the family of the aggrieved. In return, the duty to maintain crime prevention and control was transferred to the king. Of course, many private citizens were happy to transfer this duty. This is because the costs, resources, and efforts previously devoted to the task would also transfer to the king (Reynolds, 1994: 3).

Notwithstanding this gradual transfer of authority to the throne, the burden of law and order rested on the citizenry for a large part of recorded history. To accomplish the control of crime during the Middle Ages, the protection of the town or community was provided by citizens through the use of the "hue and cry" (Nemeth, 1989: 2). In effect, hue and cry was a call to order or attention. This was designed to help an individual who had observed a criminal act. Upon such a call to order, able-bodied men would respond to lend assistance when criminal actions arose, or when a criminal was to be pursued. This ancient system of crime protection is remarkably similar to the "observe and report" function of private police, absent the pursuit and capture of the criminal. The theory behind observe and report is that the security officer should act as a deterrent to crime. In the event that he or she observes a crime, the function of the security officer is to gather information about the criminal (or the crime), and then immediately report such to the public police. This function of observing and reporting by private police is expanding for reasons not unlike the motivations behind the expansion of the king's peace in medieval times. Similarly, the hue and cry system necessitated citizen involvement in the policing of medieval society, and required all able-bodied men to contribute to the protection of their community (Spitzer and Scull, 1977: 19).

Over time, however, a more defined system was established. This system, known as "watch and ward," entailed the use of a more formalized method of crime prevention, headed by "shire reeves" who were appointed by the king (Nemeth, 1989: 3). The shire reeves, in turn, appointed constables to deal with various legal matters. Both the shire reeve (later shortened to sheriff) and the constable became the forerunners of modern sworn law enforcement officers (Nemeth, 1989). This system served to further extend the legitimacy of public officers into the realm of crime prevention and control, with the appointment of individuals directly reportable to the king.

Despite the deficiencies in the system, the American colonies adopted the watch and ward system. Partly due to those same deficiencies, some early American towns supplemented this method with night watches conducted by either soldiers or by citizens appointed by the local government (Reynolds, 1994: 3). These night watches often proved to be ineffective. Indeed, Miller noted that the "night watches" were the butt of longstanding jokes, including "while the city sleeps, the watchmen do too" (Miller, 1977: 4). Further, as would be expected from ill-trained, ill-equipped groups of men, they often lost control and violated laws and created violence in the quest to institute "law and order." With rising crime and the inability of the unpaid, ill-trained and ill-equipped constables to combat it, private persons, especially businessmen, developed their own means of protection (Nemeth, 1989: 3; Benson, 1990: 74; and Warner, 1968: 10). Consequently, as is common in contemporary society, businesses hired private persons to provide security specifically for their company.

The resultant public outcry against rising crime and vigilante type actions was one of the reasons leading to the formation of publicly accountable police officers (Nemeth, 1989: 11). These public outcries grew louder with the advent of organized criminal gangs that plagued American cities in the 1830s (Reynolds, 1994: 3; Warner, 1968: 78; Benson, 1990: 64; and Clotfelter, 1977: 868). Some authors asserted that the emergence of municipal police forces were a direct result of the growing levels of civil disorder within society (Spitzer and Scull, 1977: 21; Miller, 1977: 7; and Warner, 1968: 78). Indeed, Miller emphasized that in 1834, known as the "year of riots," New York legislators decried the need for order (1977: 8). Of course, this outcry for order translated into more "security" forces, which helped bring about the institution of municipal police departments.

Advent of Public Police

The emergence of public police, as with any societal initiative, was not without its problems and detractors. Some argued that a full time police force was too expensive for taxpayers, with the traditional methods of sheriff-watch being much cheaper (Warner, 1968). Beyond this economic criticism, other concerns came from a deeper level. Disputes arose which centered on the more philosophical, or at least political, concern that government should not have a monopoly on policing (Johnston, 1992: 24; and Miller, 1977: 3). The typical criticism related to fears of excessive police power (Miller, 1977: 3). To many citizens, the cop on the beat represented an "ominous intrusion upon civil liberty" (Miller, 1977). To others, the concern for security overrode the integrity of constitutional provisions. Thus was launched the tension between the desire for security and the desire to maintain constitutional protections. Of course, this same concern is echoed in modern America relative to public policing. It is also raised by some who oppose private policing.

There are other similarities to the early days of public policing. For example, some viewed the institution of police departments as a system of favoritism for the wealthy (Chanken and Chaiken, 1987: 21). This concern created intense class conflict, whereby one man's law and order could be construed as another man's oppression (Miller, 1977: 4). The concern, often echoed in America today, was that the enforcement of laws and the maintenance of order disproportionately impact the poor in favor of the rich. Indeed, many argued that the use of "police powers" could result in an oppressive, anti-democratic society (Miller, 1977: 13). This criticism is similar to the concerns raised about the potential for a "dual system" of policing in contemporary America. Opponents of private policing assert that the rich will be able to afford private police forces for their protection, while the poor will be relegated to the public police — who will not or cannot provide adequate protection. Interestingly, arguments on both sides of these issues echoed those from earlier times, when the king expanded his powers and sovereignty into public places through the concept of the king's peace. Of course, the proponents of public policing won out in the implementation of this important policy initiative.

The founders of public policing also grappled with criticism related to operational or competency concerns. Again, such concerns are remarkably similar to today's criticisms voiced against the widespread use of private police. According to Benson, after Parliament gave Sir Robert Peel authority and financing to form the London Metro Police Department in 1829, there was substantial opposition from the public. This opposition was at least partly based on the fact that in just two years, from 1829 to 1831, fully 3,000 of the 8,000 public police officers were fired for "unfitness, incompetence or drunkenness" (Benson, 1990: 74). Many in contemporary America level the same criticism against private security personnel as "want-to-be" police officers, thereby inferring that they are not capable of working for police departments (for a critique of such, see DuCanto, 1999: 14). Indeed, this criticism survives today because sometimes it has a grain of truth attached to it. In any case, it may be reassuring to the security industry that the public police were also subject to the same criticisms.

Additionally, in the early years of public policing, New York City police officers were criticized as more "private entrepreneurs than public servants" (Spitzer and Scull, 1977: 20; and Miller, 1977: x). Wilson also asserted that detectives in 19th century Boston served essentially private interests (Spitzer and Scull, 1977: 20). Wilson drew the analogy of detectives to modern day tort lawyers, who operate on a contingency basis. Since the main concern of many crime victims was restitution, detectives would be evaluated and rewarded based on their ability to recover stolen monies and property. As such, Spitzer and Scull explain, much of policing took on the character of a contractual arrangement negotiated between clients (or victims). The clients sought protective, investigative or enforcement services, while the agents (i.e., police) supplied such services in return for a fee, reward or share of recovered goods (Spitzer and Scull, 1977).

Notwithstanding the abuses attributed to public policing, or possibly because of such, the need for private police did not end upon the emergence of public policing (Shearing and Stenning, 1983: 493; Benson, 1990: 75; and Einhorn, 1991: 16). During the mid–1800s, it became obvious that the newly created public police agencies were unable — or unwilling — to provide for the security needs of the business and commercial sectors of the country (Nemeth, 1989: 6–7). During the same time frame, the western part of the country had few government employed police officers (Reynolds, 1994: 3). These circumstances, coupled with the fact that criminals did not then nor do they now respect jurisdictional boundaries, created a difficult burden upon small, ill-equipped municipal police departments. This was especially problematic for the newly developing mobile commercial enterprises, such as the railroad industry, which greatly needed protection (Nemeth, 1989: 6–7). Of course, there were no federal law enforcement agencies with sufficiently large resources and jurisdictional boundaries to service these enterprises. Finally, the incidence of labor unrest, especially in the steel, coal, and railroad industries, created a substantial focus on security by these business owners (Nemeth, 1989).

Not surprisingly, this need for security created a great drain on already overextended municipal police departments (Spitzer and Scull, 1977: 21). In order to serve this growing market, which was not being served by the public police, Allan Pinkerton formed the first contracted private security firm in America (Spitzer and Scull, 1977). This occurred in 1850, at a time when many municipal police departments were in their infancy. Consequently, even as public police departments were being formed, the growth of privately paid security personnel was developing. These dual service providers continued to fuel the debate between public and private police in early American cities. One example of the contentions being raised was found in a Detroit newspaper. The paper addressed the cost and class factors related to public and private policing. It stated that "privatized policing was left to the wealthier and densely populated portions of the city, [with] the care and expense of protecting their own interests in some measure at their own exclusive costs" (Einhorn, 1991: 148). This same assertion is still being advanced today by certain authors who warn of the implications inherent in a dual system of policing (see Johnston, 1992; Zielinski, 1999; and Kaplan, 1994).

Despite the deficiencies of the public police, by the end of the Civil War, private policing was eclipsed in both importance and numerical terms by government organized, salary-based, tax supported public policing (Spitzer and Scull, 1977: 21). This development toward the growth of public policing continued for a variety of reasons.

First, the feasibility of private controls continued to erode, both in urban areas and in the western part of the country. The result was the cost of crime control began to be increasingly absorbed by the state (Spitzer and Scull, 1977: 23; and Warner, 1968: 137). As one can imagine, the costs of crime control, especially in large businesses such as the steel, coal, and railroad industries, were enormous. These businesses, as well as other smaller commercial enterprises, were eager to transfer at least some of these costs to local or state governments (Einhorn, 1991: 146; and Benson, 1990: 64). In this way, these special interest groups sought crime prevention services from public police. They would benefit from these services without having to contract with private security firms (Spitzer and Scull, 1977: 24; and Benson, 1990: 75). This proved to be a great incentive to certain business owners, who may have provided some benefit — albeit informal or even illegal — to government officials who facilitated the development of public policing. Einhorn notes that local aldermen even sought to deputize private watchmen, "who would be much more serviceable to their employers ... if vested with police powers" (1991: 148). Clearly, people understood that the ability to provide protective services was enhanced by the power of government.

The second reason for the growth of public policing was based on various operational and cost effective arguments. As police departments grew in size and stature, their organizational effectiveness and functional responsibilities also increased (Spitzer and Scull, 1977: 23). The effectiveness of public police was essentially based on economies of scale. Conversely, private police were limited in their resources, or by the client's ability to pay. In order to achieve any degree of crime prevention and social order, private security firms "policed" areas of the town or within a specific business property. Even assuming that they had sufficient resources to protect the property, there was limited — if any — protection provided to surrounding property. In this sense, the "protectors" (i.e., the private police or their clients) had significant economic and personal interests in the places they policed (Einhorn, 1991: 148). Their interests coincided with those of the property owner, who hired the security personnel.

On the other hand, local police, being servants of the public, had a broader or more generalized interest in addressing crime prevention. They had little regard for ownership of specific property or the interests of a particular property owner. Accordingly, at least in theory, public police were viewed as the protectors of the entire municipality, not merely the protectors of certain businesses or certain property owners. Police sought to adhere to the role of law enforcement and order maintenance within the larger community, while security firms focused on the protection of specific property owners, or the profits and assets of a particular business. Faced with these economic constraints, private police increasingly sought to serve a specific need within the marketplace, with their services designed to protect particular business clients or property owners (Spitzer and Scull, 1977: 24). Conversely, public police increasingly were seen as protectors of the people, and of the town or the city, generally.

The final and arguably the most important reason for the advancement of public police was based on the "rule of law." As with the desire to expand the king's peace, this argument had a familiar refrain. In essence, those who advocated the establishment of public police argued that the enforcement of the law and social order was best left to the sovereignty (Benson, 1990: 15; and Miller, 1977: 21). The legitimacy of government, particularly regarding the use of force and of powers of arrest, had a deep-seated historical premise.

The desire to restrict policing to government personnel is consistent with the concept of sovereignty within American government. The argument can be summarized as follows. Since the people elect government officials, and police officers are duly sworn representatives of elected officials, then the enforcement of laws by public police personnel is a natural extension of democratic principles (Miller, 1977: 20). Miller cites de Tocqueville, who argued that Americans entrusted their public officials with broad discretionary power because they elected them, and if dissatisfied, they could remove them (Miller, 1977). Of course, this rationale was further advanced by the assertion that social order was preserved by the "rule of law, not of men" (Murphy and Pritchett, 1986: 600). This rationale resonated in our constitutional democracy. In this way, many advocates for public policing, including business owners and industrialists, sought to separate their desire to protect their own economic interests from the legitimate legal or constitutional arguments offered in support of public policing (Spitzer and Scull, 1977: 23).

These perspectives, based on economic benefits and on political or philosophical tenets, were powerful arguments for the advancement of public policing. As a consequence of such, the notion of law and order changed from being the responsibility of the people. This was replaced with the dominant viewpoint that it is the responsibility of government to protect its people. With this transformed belief system solidly established in today's America, many citizens do not realize how dissimilar it was to earlier times. For good or for bad, many will have the opportunity to witness another profound change in how this society is policed. This change, indeed, has already begun.

Private Policing Statistical Data and Analysis

Recent data reveals substantial growth in the private security industry. Much of the data generated about the security industry is derived from two major research studies, entitled the Hallcrest Report and Hallcrest II. These studies were conducted to assess the relative growth of the security industry in relation to public policing, including policing agencies at the local, state and federal levels. These studies reflect what is sometimes termed as the public safety industry. Consequently, one of the major goals of these studies was to quantify the respective resources and personnel within both the private and public sectors.

Before we look at the data from the Hallcrest studies, there are some definitions to consider. The term "security" or the "security industry" broadly describes the provision of security services. These services may include security alarm services, security consulting, detective or investigative services, and residential and commercial patrols, including both contracted or proprietary (in-house) security firms (see Patterson, 1995, and Cunningham, et al., 1991). Contracted firms service a variety of clients and environments as vendors in contractual arrangements. Conversely, proprietary security refers to security personnel who are employees of a corporation, where its primary business is not security, such as Motorola, I.B.M., Microsoft, or others (Dalton, 1993: 27). Of course, public policing refers to governmental entities, such as municipal police departments, county sheriff departments, and state and federal law enforcement agencies. Chanken and Chaiken (1987) use the term "police support services" to refer to the kinds of activities that private firms can perform under contract in support of the broader role of public police agencies.

The Hallcrest studies reveal that in 1981, the security industry spent approximately $21.7 billion, compared to the $13.8 billion spent on public policing. In 1991, these expenditures rose to $52 billion for private security, compared to $30 billion for public policing (Cunningham, et al., 1991: 1–2). In the year 2000, private security spent approximately $104 billion, while public policing spent only $44 billion (Cunningham, et al., 1991). This ratio of dollars reveals that about 70 percent of all money invested in crime prevention and law enforcement is spent on private security (H.R. 2996: 1; Carlson, 1995: 66; and Cunningham, et al., 1991: 2). Further, statistics reveal an annual growth rate for private security to be about double the growth rate of public policing (Cunningham, et al., 1991: 2). Through the year 2004, private security is expected to grow at a rate of 8 percent per annum (Bailin, 2000: 12). As a consequence of the September 11, 2001, terrorist attacks, certain security firms predict revenue growth to be in the range of ten to twelve percent per year (Perez, 2002: 4). Indeed, these figures illustrate that private security is one of the fastest growing industries in the country (Zielinski, 1999: 1). Most of this growth was prior to September 11, 2001.

The number and ratio of employees in both sectors further reveal the predominance of the security industry. From 1964 to 1991, employment in private firms increased by an astonishing 750 percent, with the number of firms providing security and investigative services increasing by 543 percent (Benson, 1997: 1). Other estimates maintain that there are approximately 10,000 private security firms which employ about 1.5 million security personnel, nearly triple the 554,000 employed by public policing (Cunningham, et al., 1991: 1; Zielinski, 1999: 1; and H.R. 2996: 1). In New York City alone, there were about 460,000 employed in the private security industry (Cunningham, et al., 1991: 1). Again, this was prior to 9/11. Further, in El Paso, Texas, private police to public police ratios are estimated to be 6 to 1 in favor of the private officers (DuCanto, 1999: 8). By any account, these data reveal a substantial variance between the two entities. Recent census data shows that the number of full time sworn police personnel is estimated at 663,535, representing an increase of approximately 40,000 from census data accumulated three years earlier.[5] This increase, however, pales by comparison to more recent security industry estimates, which contended that there will be two million people employed by security firms from the year 2000 (Zielinski, 1999: 1).

The growth of private security can be illustrated by two huge international firms, both of which dominate the security industry in America. Securitas, a Swedish based firm, had revenues of $5.8 billion with a net income of $115.2 million in 2001 (Perez, 2002: 4). This firm employs

220,000 people worldwide, with 124,000 in the United States. Since 9/11, they have hired about 10,000 more guards to serve U.S. accounts (Perez, 2002). Similarly, Group 4 Falckas, a Danish firm that recently acquired a large U.S. firm, Wackenhut, had revenues of $2.81 billion dollars, with a net income of $3.7 million dollars in 2001 (Perez, 2002). This firm employs 58,000 guards worldwide, with 38,000 in the U.S., of which about 3–5 percent are directly attributable to 9/11 (Perez, 2002). By any account, these are impressive numbers, both in terms of revenues and of personnel employed. Based on expected additional terrorist incidents, these numbers will likely grow — possibly substantially. The Chief Operating Officer of Wackenhut, Alan Bernstein, complained that they could hire another 5,000 guards immediately if the labor force was prepared to work for his firm (Perez, 2002).

Going beyond the explosive growth of the security industry, the ratio of public police officers to reported crimes has seen an equally dramatic change. In the 1960s, there were about 3.3 public police officers for every violent crime reported. In 1993, there were 3.47 violent crimes reported for every public police officer (Walinsky, 1993: 39). In effect, these statistics illustrate that each public police officer in contemporary America must deal with 11.45 times as many violent crimes as police from previous eras (Walinsky, 1993). Walinsky notes that if this country were to return to the 1960s ratio of police to violent crimes, about 5 million new public police officers would have to be hired by local governments (1993: 40). To be sure, this will not occur.

Even with this disproportionate statistical relationship, Justice Department data reveals that the economic costs of public policing increased from $441 million in 1968 to about $10 billion in 1994. This represents a 2,100 percent increase in the cost of public policing, while the number of violent crimes exploded 560 percent from 1960 to 1992 (Walinsky, 1993). In this sense, as crime rates increased, the monies used to "combat" crime also dramatically increased. One obvious question begs to be answered: would any additional monies spent on public policing result in a reduction of crime? Based on this short historical and statistical overview, the answer appears to be negative. One thing is certain. These statistics reveal that the relationship between the amount of crime and the amount of money spent on public policing has been substantially altered over the last generation or so. During this same time frame, private security has grown dramatically, and is now firmly established in the provision of public safety services throughout this country.

As dramatic as these statistics may seem, numerous authors assert that the security industry should not be assessed only in raw data. Indeed, the sheer and undeniable growth of the industry can be viewed by its involvement in businesses, homes, and communities throughout the country (Zielinski, 1999: 1; Carlson, 1995: 66; and Goldberg, 1994: 11). This involvement stems from such diverse services as alarm systems, security guard services, and investigative and consulting services, to name those most common. The impact of the security industry may even be more substantial than what the data suggests. For example, James K. Stewart, the former director of the National Institute of Justice, stated, "We are witnessing a fundamental shift in the area of public safety. It's not a loss of confidence in the police, but a desire to have more police" (Tolchin, 1985). Indeed, there are appropriate comparisons being made of the security industry in relation to the advent of public policing in the mid–1850s. The significance of this assertion was emphasized by Chris Vail, who compared the current state of private security to the advent of public police. He stated that "this is a significant time for the private security industry. People are just beginning to realize its potential. I see private security in 1996 and 1997 much like what public law enforcement was in the 1850s" (Spencer, 1997: 1).

Numerous authors have argued that there is a need for more police, or at least more protective services (see Dilulio, 1995; Walinsky, 1993; Cunningham et al, 1991; Spitzer and Scull, 1977; Benson, 1990; Clotfelter, 1977; West, 1993; and Seamon, 1995). Other authors were more critical of the ability of the public police to provide an appropriate level of protection (see, for example, Benson, 1990). Similarly, another author observed, "People want protection, and what they cannot get from the police, they will get from private security companies" (Kolpacki, 1994: 47). Thus, private policing will be, as Goldberg states, the "wave of the future" (1994: 12).

Due to the nature of the industry and of the complexities encountered in objectively defining the "policing" concept, the exact size and scope of the security industry must be viewed with some skepticism (Nalla and Newman, 1991: 543). Even the authors of the Hallcrest Reports admit that there are problems with the validity of the data, since they were compiled from sources that relied on different sampling methods and classifications (Cunningham et al., 1991: 1). Whatever the exact numbers within the industry, however, the data is so disproportionate that there can be little doubt that private security is now *the primary protective resource* in the nation (Bailin, 2000: 12; and Cunningham, et al., 1991: 1). As evidenced by the above authors and statistics, one could hardly argue against the notion that crime prevention and protective services will increasingly become the domain of private security. This statement is strongly echoed by Lawrence Sherman, who stated:

Few developments are more indicative of public concern about crime — and the declining faith in the ability of public institutions to cope with it — than the burgeoning growth in private policing ... rather than approving funds for more police, the voters have turned to volunteer and paid private watchers [Benson, 1990: 201].

IV

Policing in Contemporary Circumstances

If it is true that there is a trend toward the growing use of private policing, then the natural follow-up question is, why is this occurring now? As the proponents of privatization assert, there are a number of pragmatic reasons which justify the use of private policing. The elements and issues presented in Chapter II provide the intellectual or economic basis for private policing. Also, the literature on privatization helps to explain the trend in pragmatic and socio-economic factors. What can be drawn from the privatization literature, coupled with crime research, are certain circumstances which may contribute to the trend toward privatization of police services. These factors can be broadly stated as:

- Economic and operational constraints
- Order maintenance techniques
- Crime (or the fear of crime)

It is important to qualify, however, that the presentation of these factors does not imply their direct causal relationship to privatized policing. Instead, these factors provide the contextual framework which converges to facilitate the widespread use of private policing. Consider how these factors influenced the advent of public policing. Broadly speaking, the factors are similar. As illustrated in the historical overview, the factors that drove the development of public policing included crime, economic considerations, and order maintenance techniques.

It may be that independent factors, such as political or economic considerations—as described by some proponents of privatization—are the direct causal link to private policing. This contention, however, does not

46

withstand critical analysis. First, those who assert that privatized policing is somehow intruding on the realm of the public police lacks historical context because private security has been around for many years. In fact, private policing clearly pre-dates public policing. Second, those who attribute privatized policing to a purely economic argument also miss the mark because economic and budgetary constraints have always existed in one form or another. Third, those who assert purely political arguments fail to observe that political discourse and expediency has been present for centuries. Fourth, one may also argue that crime (and the fear of crime) has been around throughout the history of mankind. According to many of the authors cited in this book, however, the effect of crime in contemporary America is arguably more pronounced than at any time in recorded history. With these qualifying statements raised, we see that certain factors coincide with the emergence of private policing in contemporary society.

Economic and Operational Issues

The relative cost of salaries is a significant factor in any discussion of financial and economic matters. Indeed, labor costs and benefits have a substantial price tag. Accordingly, when the focus is simply on economic and financial matters, private policing is relatively attractive and seemingly cost effective, as compared to public policing.

From a purely financial perspective, alternative service providers, such as private security firms, provide certain savings. For example, the Bureau of Labor Statistics conducted a compensation survey and found the cost of hourly pay for security personnel ranges from an average of $6.82 in Tampa/St. Petersburg Metro area to $12.82 per hour in Denver (IOMA, May, 2000). These figures are consistent with the compensation of the security personnel in this research. The private officers were paid $10.00 per hour for the patrol services. Conversely, public police cost 2.79 times as much as private police in 1979 (Benson, 1990: 261). More recent data reveals that it costs at least $100,000 per year per police officer when salary, benefits, and overhead expenses were calculated into the equation (Reynolds, 1994: 2).

An explanation of the rise in personnel costs can be attributed to the seemingly ever increasing cost of public policing. As evidence of such, during the period of 1967–1973, the average salary for state and local police increased 56 percent (Clotfelter, 1977: 875). During the same period, the average salary for employees of private protective firms increased only 34 percent (Clotfelter, 1977). Further, Miranda found in his research on City of Chicago expenditures that the single largest rate of increase was for personnel (1993: 433). Personnel costs included salaries or wages, pensions, and fringe benefits. These costs, adjusted for inflation, increased 63 percent over the ten year period (Miranda, 1993: 435). Two groups—police and fire—represent about 55 percent of the total city work force (Miranda, 1993). Therefore, the economic costs of just these two groups are substantial. Similar economic constraints have been reflected in other research. For example, it is estimated that about 90 to 95 percent of police budgets go to personnel costs (Spitzer and Scull, 1977: 25). Consequently, if these statistics are true, then the vast proportion of the expenditures of policing—and of municipalities—is to pay salaries and benefits of public police officers.

These statistics raise the logical question. Can this pay structure be sustained? While the answer is yet to come, I believe that municipal budgets will not be able to support such proportions. There are other authors who support this assertion. Savas asserts that over a twenty-five year period, the number of public police officers in New York City rose from 16,000 to 24,000. However, the total annual hours worked by the entire force actually declined (Savas, 2000). He noted that the entire increase in the city's police force (fully 50 percent) was devoted to personnel benefits, such as shortening the work week, lengthening lunch periods and vacation time, and providing more holidays and paid sick leave (Savas, 2000). Can this benefit structure be sustained? My answer, again, is negative.

Beyond the strict dollar costs of public enforcement, a number of authors have addressed certain operational issues that tend to drive up the costs associated with public safety services. Savas cites a New York City example in which inefficient staffing was actually legitimized by state law. In essence, the law required that each police shift must have an equal number of personnel assigned to it (Savas, 2000). Savas observed that this law was enacted despite the fact that crime statistics show crimes are not equally distributed in each shift. Similarly, Robinson uses a comprehensive formula to determine that 70.8 percent of police duty time is "out of service," with only 29.2 percent of their duty time in visible patrolling (1994: 20). The implications of these statistics are evident when compared to the recommended optimal proportions by the National Institute of Justice. N.I.J. recommends 35 percent out of service time, and 64 percent patrol time (Robinson, 1994: 19).

Additionally, in his study of police efficiency, Blumberg argued that approximately 80 percent of police resources are utilized in "social worker, caretaker, baby-sitter, and errand boy" activities (Benson, 1990: 98; and

Reynolds, 1994: 2). Partly as a result of this situation, the Toronto Police Department reports that more than 60 percent of all calls to the police are handled by "alternative response" units, which could include private policing acting as a supplement to public police departments (Palango, 1998: 2).

These statistics were supported by another study, conducted by the Police Foundation. This study found that instead of watching to prevent crime, motorized police patrols are often merely waiting to respond to crime (Benson, 1990: 134). The study found that about 50 percent of police duty time is spent simply "waiting for something to happen" (Benson, 1990). While police officials claim this time is devoted to "preventive patrols," systematic observations seem to show otherwise. Such observations reveal that such time was largely occupied with conversations with other officers, personal errands, and sitting in parked cars on side streets (Benson, 1990). While some of these activities may be necessary, the compelling conclusion of these studies is that municipalities will not be able to afford the status quo.

These studies also infer that policing has been traditionally very reactive, as opposed to private security, which has taken a more proactive approach to crime (see Cunningham and Taylor, 1984; Benson, 1990; and Johnston, 1992). One reason cited for the different approach has to do with the incentives tied to the two groups. Private police — at least theoretically — are more prone to "please the client." Given this propensity, the desire to prevent problems— and crime — is a major focus of their work. Conversely, since public police are expected to produce arrest statistics, they have less incentive to "prevent crime" (Benson, 1990: 132). Instead, their incentive has been traditionally geared to wait for crimes to be committed, then make the arrests of the offenders (Benson, 1990).

This issue of police resources in relation to crime or crime prevention has been a dilemma for many police administrators. One problem relates to the longstanding desire to reduce "response time" to calls for police service. This desire has been deemed to be illusory. A study by the Police Foundation found that cutting response time makes little difference in whether a criminal is apprehended. This is so because citizens often take too long to report crime, or are unaware that the crime is occurring (Benson, 1990: 132). If the police are not called to the crime scene in a timely manner, then response time has no effect since the criminal is often long gone.

Even beyond the relative effectiveness (or ineffectiveness) of response time, there are other problems with this focus. To be sure, response time may be helpful to police administrators relative to staffing and objective crime data. However, according to Robinson, the focus on response time creates a dilemma. On one hand, police officers are expected to be visible, in order to act as deterrence to potential criminal actions. At the same time, police officers are expected to respond to calls for assistance and other service oriented functions. These functions interrupt the patrol function. The more calls for assistance are handled, the less time remains for patrols and visibility. Further, the more calls for service that the police handle, the longer their response time is likely to be. This is especially true if the particular officer is already tied up on an assignment when an "in-progress" crime is reported. Consequently, there is a direct conflict between the two goals (Robinson, 1994: 6). In this sense, private police may be able to supplement the public police in the performance of these goals by responding to certain service oriented calls, thereby allowing public police officers more free time to respond to serious crimes and in-progress calls.

The dilemma for law enforcement officials in budgetary and fiscal matters is also illustrated by alarm response. Alarm response is a term which refers to police being dispatched to burglar, fire, or panic alarms. These alarms come from commercial, industrial, and residential facilities. One of the key problems is the high rate of false alarms. Studies show the false alarm rate is often as high as 95 percent (Benson, 1990: 99; Olick, 1994: 20; and Cunningham, et al., 1991: 2). The significance of these statistics is further evidenced by the fact that alarm responses account for 10 percent to 30 percent of all calls for police service (Cunningham, et al., 1991: 2). Consider that in the 1980s, only 2 percent to 5 percent of residences had alarm systems. This figure increased to 10 percent in the 1990s (Litsikas, 1994: 70; and Cunningham, et al., 1991: 2). It was expected to double again around the year 2000 (Cunningham, et al., 1991: 2). Consequently, the impact of just one service has substantial implications on the ability of the police to perform their overall mission, to serve and protect society.

The above analysis and statistics reveal that public police are over-burdened with many service-oriented duties, and by the economic costs of the service provided to the public. As illustrated by these examples, private police can contribute to both goals—by patrolling and by handling certain service functions, such as alarm response, currently performed by public police. In fact, private police firms have been contracted by some departments in response to the aforementioned economic and operational constraints.

Chapter VI will show various sites have used private police patrols financed through alternative funding sources to address economic and operational constraints which burden police departments. In each case, the monies used to provide public safety services are obtained from business or property owners. Sometimes the monies are derived from special tax-ing initiatives, while others are obtained more directly by a contract with a property association. Such contracted revenue production requires lit-tle explanation, other than the contracting party is usually a property or homeowner association.

The taxing initiative usually involves the creation of a special taxing district or body, which has its powers derived from a governmental entity, such as state or city legislation (Robinson, 1996: 39). The specially created district or body acts as a political subdivision of the legislative entity which created it (Robinson, 1996). Depending upon the purpose of its creation, the political subdivision could be conferred broad powers—usually to promote economic development or stability—through the assertion of health, safety and infrastructure improvements (Robinson, 1996). The specific source of the monies can be a tax on real property or even a sales tax levy. Since the tax is confined to a certain geographic area, the local property or business owners usually maintain control over the authority vested in the district. This control enhances the accountability on the taxing and revenues derived from the district (Robinson, 1996). Partici-pation in this authority, however, usually requires certain factors. These entail being a property owner, working in or owning a business within the district, or owning stock in a corporation within the district (Robinson, 1996).

Carlson asserts that more communities are certain to follow these examples because "they may have to" (1995: 72). He draws the analogy with medical care in that hospitals were "forced" to give more responsi-bility to nurses due to rising medical costs. Carlson emphasized his point in this way: "Cities may find that sworn police officers whom they must train, pay relatively well and sustain pensions—are too expensive—for fighting and deterring certain types of low-level crimes. To maintain basic civic order, rent-a-cops may be a better deal."

Budgetary and operational constraints will likely be further impacted by the widespread use of "community policing" in law enforcement. Com-munity policing has created additional functions and duties which were largely ignored by enforcement oriented police departments (see Moore and Trojanowicz, 1988; and Trojanowicz and Carter , 1990). These func-tions and duties cost money to administer. The overriding financial ques-tion is how much longer can municipal governments afford to focus on community policing? This is especially important since much of the fed-eral funding for community police officers was designed to "sunset" in the early 2000s. One possible response is for order maintenance to be shifted to other entities, either private firms or public police auxiliary services.

Ironically, the success of community policing in the reduction of crime may provide an impetus to transfer or supplement forces with private police. Crime prevention and order maintenance are the type of functions which have been the forte of private security. For these reasons, the possibility exists that private policing will play an increasingly larger role in the policing of America. The form of such may mirror the community policing model, which is already widely utilized throughout the country.

Finally, from a personal perspective, it is important to note that the analysis presented here is completely based on economic and financial issues. As a former Chicago Police officer, as an attorney for police unions, and as an assistant professor who has the pleasure of teaching many active police officers, I have great respect for the work of police officers. In many ways, it is the hardest job in the world. I certainly do not view the police as being overpaid. Surely, what is the value of being sworn, yelled and spit at, as a matter and course of the job? These may occur before you even leave the police station. Indeed, officers are shot at on a daily basis. Many have lost their lives in the service to their community and their profession. Make no mistake, I do not desire to diminish the service and the sacrifices of any police officer. I can say with complete candor that I respected the work of police officers long before many people finally came to realize their bravery during and after 9/11. The bravery and strength of character of police officers are often unparalleled in this society.

Consequently, the work of the police is hard. This book is not designed to advocate taking bread off their tables. It is not designed to complicate their already difficult jobs. Instead, this presentation is geared toward explaining the economic and financial realities currently existing in public police departments. Many authors, including myself, simply do not believe that the status quo can continue, but that private police officers will supplement municipal police departments more and more. In this way, the services currently provided to the communities could be sustained, and the economic benefits of a privatized service provider can help reduce already strained municipal budgets.

Order Maintenance for a Safer Environment

Order maintenance techniques and their relationship to the physical environment are relevant for several different reasons. Order maintenance — developed and widely utilized in community policing — may prove beneficial in both reducing the incidence of crime, and in reducing the level of incivility or disorder within a given community or jurisdiction. Many criminal justice researchers have come to believe that an area often undergoes a transition from relatively few crimes to one with a high incidence of crime or a heightened fear of crime if order isn't maintained (see Covington and Taylor, 1991; Lewis and Maxfield, 1980; and Kelling, 1995).

The theory of order maintenance is essentially that crime problems initially occur in forms of relatively harmless activities, such as drinking on the street, graffiti on buildings, and youths loitering on street corners. If these activities go unchecked, the level of fear and incivility in the area begins to rise. Left to fester, more serious crimes— sometimes related to the aforementioned activities— such as gang fights or even drive-up shootings may take place. Some serious crimes, however, may be completely independent of these activities. For example, incidents of domestic violence may be unrelated to environmental conditions. Nonetheless, the theory asserts that the presence of disorder tends to reduce the social controls previously present in the area. The result, at least in theory, is increased serious crime. Increased crime, in turn, contributes to the further deterioration of the physical environment and economic well being of the community.

Much of the literature in the 1960s and early 1970s focused on the various conditions in cities, particularly in the "slums" (for several works on this issue, see McLennan, 1970). At that time, much of the literature sought to explain crime in terms of the conditions found in the slums. In these areas of the city, conditions included "physical deterioration, high density, economic insecurity, poor housing, family disintegration, transience, conflicting social norms, and an absence of constructive positive agencies" (McLennan, 1970: 127). Many, if not all, of these factors were deemed scientifically significant by some researchers.

Over time, researchers began to focus less attention on socioeconomic factors, and more on the physical characteristics of the community, or the "environment." The focus on the physical characteristics of the space where crime occurred resulted in a substantial body of scientific research. As far back as the 1970s and into the 1980s, researchers such as Cohen and Felson argued that the completion of a crime requires the convergence in time and space of an offender, a suitable target, and the "absence of guardians capable of preventing the violation" (Cohen and Felson, 1979: 34). This transition to a different research emphasis was explained by stating that the

> focus on criminological research has shifted from a primary
> emphasis on offenders and the derivation of their motivation to

commit crimes, to a broader view encompassing the relative opportunity level of an area as a criminogenic structural condition [Jack-
son, 1984: 173].

This focus on environmental factors was found in a number of studies. For example, in Jackson's (1984: 174) review of the previous research
on this issue, she demonstrated through authors such as Gibbs and Erickson (1976) that the daily population flow in large cities "reduces the
effectiveness of surveillance activities by increasing the number of strangers
that are routinely present in the city, thereby decreasing the extent to which
their activities would be regarded with suspicion." The implication was
that the more people there were in the area, the less likely strangers would
be noticed. In this way, less natural surveillance from community residents may lead to more crime.

Jackson further cited studies by Jacobs (1982) and Rubinstein (1973),
who concluded that "law enforcement agencies are handicapped by
immense communities." Additionally, Reppetto (1974) concluded that the
social cohesion and informal surveillance declines with the large number
of people living in a given area (Jackson, 1984: 176). Both Jacobs (1978)
and Mayhew and Levinger (1976) found that as anonymity increases with
city size, it in turn "increases the ease of crime commission and reduces
the risk of detection" (Jackson, 1984).

Jackson's research, and her supporting theoretical basis, continued to
build the body of research toward the desire to understand, and possibly
manipulate or impact, the physical conditions of a particular environment
in order to prevent the incidence of crime. One such study conducted even
prior to Jackson was by Lewis and Maxfield (1980). These researchers
focused on specific physical conditions within the environment to assess
its impact on crime, and the fear of crime. They looked at such things as
abandoned buildings, teen loitering, vandalism, and drug use. They
believed that these factors draw little attention from the police partially
because the public police have limited resources to effectively deal with
these problems (Lewis and Maxfield, 1980: 187). The researchers noted
that such problems, nonetheless, are important indicators of criminality
within any community.

These factors, termed the "level of incivility," create a sense of danger and decay. The presence of danger and decay, in turn, increases the
perceived risk of victimization (Lewis and Maxfield, 1980: 162). These
authors concluded that people see the problem of incivility as more important than the problem of crime itself (Lewis and Maxfield, 1980: 182). The
presence of incivility may lead to crime, or it may simply *seem* to be dangerous. Of course, some of these factors are not even criminal, but are dis-

concerting nonetheless (Lewis and Maxfield, 1980: 179; and see Liska, et al., 1982: 768, for similar assertions). These studies concluded that policy makers should focus on "neighborhood level" approaches to reducing crime and fear.

This research was then supported and further validated by subsequent studies. Covington and Taylor conducted research into what they term as an "incivilities model." Their argument was people perceive "clues" to the underlying level of disorder in their immediate environment. Upon doing so, they will feel more vulnerable and more fearful (Covington and Taylor, 1991: 232). In this sense, clues serve to warn residents that they are at a risk of being criminally victimized. Consequently, such clues represent incivility within the environment and provide an early warning, or an indicator that the environment may be ripe for serious crimes.

What are the signs of crime? According to Covington and Taylor, there are several indicators or clues. These clues were broken out into two distinct categories: social and physical. Social clues include public drinking, drug use, loitering, and disturbances such as fighting and arguing. Clearly, these activities are disturbing to some people, and dangerous to others. Physical clues include litter, graffiti, abandoned buildings and vacant lots, and deteriorating homes and businesses (Covington and Taylor, 1991). While these conditions may not be inherently dangerous, they create the impression that the neighborhood is declining. This impression, in turn, may foster an attitude that the people in the neighborhood do not care about their homes or their property. As a consequence of such, people may feel that the environment invites criminal activity.

The conclusions of this research were telling. The authors assert that neighborhoods with more objectively observed social and physical incivilities have higher fear levels. Neighborhood level analysis was contrasted against individual perceptions. Findings at the individual level were found to confirm the broader neighborhood level findings— specifically, that individuals who perceive higher levels of incivility would be more inclined to be fearful. Comparatively, those individuals who do not perceive incivility (or perceive lower levels of such) will tend to be less fearful (Covington and Taylor, 1991: 234).

Subsequent research by Fisher and Nasar also supported, and further validated, these earlier studies. Fisher and Nasar studied the effects of "microlevel" clues. Microlevel clues involve a specific place or location. The authors found that such clues relate to fear in three specific criteria:

- Prospect — openness of view to see clearly what awaits you.
- Escape — ease of departure if you were confronted by an offender.

- Concealment — extent of hiding places for an offender [Fisher and Nasar, 1995: 226].

Based on an analysis of these criteria, the authors concluded that "fear spots at the microlevel do exist" (Fisher and Nasar, 1995). Specifically, when in an area that has a lack of prospect, much concealment and lack of escape, individuals are likely to react accordingly. When faced with these conditions, individuals tend to feel a greater exposure to risk, have loss of control over their immediate environment, and are more aware of the seriousness or the consequences of attack (Fisher and Nasar, 1995: 234–235). This conclusion further advanced the concept of "situational crime prevention." The thinking is that by looking at the criminal event itself, and assessing the "intersection" of potential offenders with the opportunity to commit crime, some criminal actions could be avoided. In this way, the commission of a particular crime could be avoided through certain preventive measures designed to reduce the offender's ability (or even propensity) to commit crimes at specific locations. The authors assert that eliminating "fear spots" could be used as a fear and crime reduction strategy (Fisher and Nasar, 1995a).

The conclusions from these studies have been echoed by a number of other authors. The incivility literature is supported by Kelling (1995: 36), who asserts that citizens regularly report their biggest safety concerns to be things like "panhandling, obstreperous youths taking over parks and street corners, public drinking, prostitution, and other disorderly behavior." Each of these factors has been identified as precursors to more serious crime. Indeed, the failure to correct these behaviors often is perceived as a sign of indifference. Such indifference will then often lead to more serious crime and urban decay (Kelling, 1995). Consequently, the intention is to address both the physical and social conditions which foster crime, rather than allowing such conditions to fester into more serious levels of crime and decay.

This focus on prevention has been supported by at least one other study. Roth has asserted that a greater emphasis on preventing violent events is critical (1994: 1). This focus on prevention is again aimed at intervening in the chain of events which ultimately results in the occurrence of a crime (Roth, 1994). While it is impossible to know in advance how or when a criminal act will occur, Roth asserts that every event has a set of risk factors. One of the most important risk factors is "temporal proximity." This refers to how close in time the factor is to the violent event. The key to this assessment entails the specific circumstances that surround an encounter between people. The circumstances of each particular encounter, will either increase or decrease the chance that violence will occur or that harm will take place if it does (Roth, 1994).

Implicit in each of these studies is the desire to prevent crime, or reduce the conditions or factors which foster crime. These conclusions have been embraced by both public police and private security. The key component of these preventive programs, in both the public and private sectors, is order maintenance.

In essence, order maintenance techniques are designed to improve physical conditions within a specific geographic area. This can be accomplished in a number of ways. Such remedies include the rehabilitation of physical structures, the removal or demolition of seriously decayed buildings, and the improvement of land or existing buildings by cleaning and painting. It also includes other environmental improvements, such as planting flowers, trees or shrubs, and various other methods to enhance the "look and feel" of an area. These physical improvements are also combined with efforts to reduce or eliminate certain anti-social behaviors, such as loitering, drinking and drug usage, fighting, and other disorderly behaviors. Of course, the focus is to stop these behaviors before more serious crimes occur.

Viewed in its broadest terms, "security" in this environmental perspective can be as diverse as trash collection to private police patrols. Each such service is designed to improve the conditions within the area. This approach, of course, is consistent with the concept of order maintenance, emphasizing the importance of the environment. When one considers the importance of the environment in the aforementioned research, the need to control physical conditions and public activities stands out. The advent of terrorism will only magnify this environmental focus. For example, any unattended package left on a street corner may prove to be lethal. The importance of an orderly and clean environment cannot be understated. However, such perceived or potential threats are difficult to remedy. Nonetheless, this focus on the environment has been echoed by Kaplan, who views the environment as *the* security issue of the early 21st century (1994: 58).

In public policing, the above order maintenance techniques are encompassed in the concept of "community policing" (see Moore and Trojanowicz, 1988; Kelling, 1995; Palango, 1998; Matthew Robinson, 1997; Seamon, 1995; Kolpacki, 1994; Spencer, 1997; Cox, 1990; and Johnston, 1992). The crime prevention techniques in community policing have been described in many research studies. Moore and Trojanowicz provide a concise analysis of the major tenets of community policing that emphasizes the creation of an effective working relationship between the community and the police (1988: 8). The community is seen as having a greater status, with the police seeking wider consultation and more information from the community. One goal of community policing is to extend beyond the traditional goal of crime fighting to focus on fear reduction through order maintenance techniques (Moore and Trojanowicz, 1988). These goals of crime and fear reduction through order maintenance are in accordance with the environmental theories articulated above.

In the private sector, the focus on prevention, as opposed to enforcement, has traditionally dominated the strategy and tactical decisions of security industry officials (see Chanken and Chaiken, 1987; Shearing and Stenning, 1983; and Cunningham et al., 1991). The similarity of private security techniques and community policing techniques can be narrowed to one core goal. That is, both are intended to utilize proactive crime prevention that is accountable to the customer or the citizen (Kolpacki, 1994: 47). As such, private security has traditionally been "client focused," with its emphasis on preventing crime — not merely making arrests after a crime has occurred. Community policing was implemented to broadly achieve this same goal, and the functions of the two entities have or will inevitably move closer together.

For various reasons, private security is particularly well suited to serve in a crime prevention or order maintenance role. At least partly because of its focus on the property and financial interests of their clients, private security personnel have replaced public police — long ago — in the protection of business facilities, assets, employees, and customers. As explained in the historical chapter, private security personnel did for business what the public police could not accomplish. Specifically, private security firms provided services for specific clients, focusing on the protection of certain assets, both physical and human, as their primary and even exclusive purpose.

As is their practice in environments which are privately owned or controlled, security personnel seek to prevent crime by attempting to predict reasonably foreseeable crime and develop precautions against it (Gordon and Brill, 1996: 5). A substantial body of law has grown around the notion of the environmental aspects of crime. Tort causes of action, known as either premises liability or negligent security, have provided explosive growth and business for personal injury attorneys.

These lawsuits stem from the theory that the business or property owner knew or should have known that a criminal would come along and commit a crime within the property. Assuming this, the victim of the crime can sue the business or property owner (and its insurance company) for the actions of the criminal. The logic of these causes of action is that the owner contributed to the crime, or at least allowed the crime to occur by not taking remedial action. In this sense, the owner, who did not commit the crime, is nonetheless guilty of negligence by allowing the conditions conducive to crime to occur or to fester. The failure to cure the conditions served to "invite" the criminal act.

The larger point is that premises liability and negligent security lawsuits did not exist in the not too distant past. In earlier days, courts would view the actions of a criminal as being a superseding cause, thereby breaking the chain of causation required in a negligence case. The crime was deemed superseding, or at least not reasonably foreseeable, thereby destroying the plaintiff's requirement to show that the defendant (owner) had a duty to protect the victim.

These causes of action are based on two contemporary developments. First, the impact of crime was and still is creating substantial damage in society. In this light, courts were faced with innumerable potential plaintiffs—who were crime victims—looking for a cause of action. These victims usually could not sue the offender, as most criminals have little, if any, resources to contribute to the victim to make restitution. Faced with these financial and human tragedies, courts began to create the logic and reasoning to support these lawsuits.

The second and more important reason is that the lawsuits were intellectually justified by the body of knowledge presented above. In essence, the scientific studies relating to the relationship between crime and the environment were compelling. Research provided a wealth of evidence that criminals do not act arbitrarily and randomly. Despite our moral abhorrence to their criminal actions, it is quite clear that most offenders view the decision to commit a crime as a fairly rationale action. The offender will often weigh the risk of being caught versus the benefit from the crime. If he or she believes that it is a risk worth taking, then the crime will occur. Based on this body of research, it was reasonable to conclude that crimes tend to occur in specific locations or in certain environments. Indeed, this research demonstrated that certain factors may lead to crime. These factors included disorderly conditions, diminished lighting, high prospect for escape, increased ability to conceal the crime, and various other factors related to the criminal decision process. For these reasons, it was not a large step for courts to begin to accept the counterintuitive notion that the property or business owner should pay for the crime of the offender.

One important result of these lawsuits—other than the fact that crime victims had a remedy that previously did not exist—was the fact that property and business owners were motivated to institute security measures within and around their property or business location. This is both a carrot and a stick. The carrot was the belief that property or business owners were providing a safe and secure place to do business, or to live or work in. Certainly, providing such a safe and secure place could not hurt the reputation of the business or the viability of the property. On the other hand, the stick was substantial liability exposure, with seven figure jury awards more common than one can imagine. Further, the negative media exposure stemming from these incidents is substantial, not to mention the reputational and public relations nightmares created by such crimes.

The result of this carrot and stick approach was a growing use of security personnel and methodologies. This certainly boded well for the security industry. Business and property owners started to think and worry about security. They became more proactive in their approach to a safe and secure environment. For security firms, it created a larger and larger market of potential clients. More importantly, it brought security further and further into the realm of the average citizen. Security personnel began to be routinely used at businesses and large corporations, now often focusing on the *protection of employees and clients*, instead of simply preventing them from stealing. In this sense, security became more mainstream — as part of the American workplace, as part of the hospital you visited, as part of the apartment building you lived in.

Consequently, security moved closer and closer to the American people. No longer was it just the public police who serviced the people; now there was another service provider, this one operating out of the private realm. Now private security was protecting the American people. This closeness to mainstream society also increased the scope of the services provided by private police. As premises liability and negligent security lawsuits developed, the liability of business and property owners expanded farther and farther from the "protected facility." The seemingly ever increasing perimeter was the result of court decisions. It was not uncommon for incidents in parking lots to create liability exposure. It is now fairly common for liability exposure to apply to attacks that occur *outside or beyond the perimeters of the property or business*. In fact, lawsuits have been successful when the criminal attack occurred down the street from the property or business. Consequently, while the liability exposure expanded, so did the security perimeter and methodologies. It is now common for security patrols for properties and businesses to extend into the streets and other public areas, in the quest to prevent crime and to provide a safe and secure environment.

Conversely, public police had and still have a much more difficult task incorporating crime prevention into their organizational and societal context. This is based on the broader societal mission to generally enforce laws throughout society, as well as to preserve democratic and constitutional ideals. When one considers that the already overburdened public police are also faced with economic and operational constraints, it is not unreasonable to conclude the role of private security will continue to increase. For these reasons, many have advocated that private police play a larger role in the prevention of crime in areas traditionally and exclusively patrolled by public police (Chanken and Chaiken, 1987: 11; Palango, 1998: 1; and Benson, 1990: 212–213). The use of order maintenance techniques will prove to be an important inducement to employ such patrols.

Crime and Fear of Crime

As demonstrated above, the relationship between crime and fear has been systematically developed in numerous studies (see Smith and Hill, 1991; Lewis and Maxfield, 1980; Liska, et al., 1982; Benson, 1990; and Moore and Trojanowicz, 1988). Some authors have also asserted that crime has led to an increase in fear in certain demographic subsections and in the larger society (see Farnham, 1992; Litsikas, 1994; Walinsky, 1993; and West, 1993). From both perspectives, the conclusions were similar and compelling. In essence, the conclusion was that crime has created a concern, often rising to what could be construed as a fear, in contemporary America. Indeed, Liska, et al., argue that *"fear is a social fact* which varies across sites and situations" (1982: 761).

Research on the relationship of crime and fear has provided certain important insights. Some research focused on the actual incidence of crime, while some addressed the perceptions of the incidence of crime and its effects on people. Both perspectives demonstrate a commonality between crime and fear. In this regard, the operative question is: does the experience of being a crime victim increase the fear of crime? This question was answered in the affirmative by Smith and Hill (1991). These researchers found that victimization experience is significantly related to the fear of crime (1991: 231). To be sure, the researchers assert that the greater amount or level of victimization experience, the more a respondent reports being fearful (Smith and Hill, 1991).

Lewis and Maxfield (1980), however, went further than just measuring the relationship between victimization and the fear of crime. They looked deeper into this relationship by also measuring whether indicators of fear affected the resultant fear of crime. Their conclusion is that the fear of crime is exacerbated by signs of criminal activity. In essence, they assert that signs of criminal activity, such as disorder or incivility, have an impact on people's perceptions of crime (Lewis and Maxfield, 1980: 160; and Kelling, 1995: 36). The authors attributed certain physical and social characteristics as being signs of disorder or incivility (Lewis and Maxfield, 1980: 162). In this regard, incivility is equated with disorder, in that both purport to represent chaotic conditions which result in more serious criminal activity.

The results of their research were telling. They found that it is the *combination* of concern with crime and incivility (or disorder) that affects neighborhood fear levels (Lewis and Maxfield, 1980). They assert that the levels of fear are greatest where there is a combination of extreme concern about crime and incivility. Hence, objective crime rates are mediated by *perceptions* of neighborhood incivility. As such, if incivility (or disorder) is not perceived to be a problem, then it appears that residents can cope with higher rates of crime (Lewis and Maxfield, 1980). This conclusion, as asserted by these authors, has important implications for policy makers. Their recommendations were to deal with both the crime rate *and* the physical and social indicators which lead to the perception of incivility and disorder (Lewis and Maxfield, 1980).

The proposed policy "solutions" of such research were to reduce the level of crime, and to reduce the perception of incivility and disorder in society. While the latter solution dealt with order maintenance or environmental techniques, the relationship between crime and fear can be assessed as follows. Given the recent reductions in the level of crime, the natural corollary question is whether the reduction of crime has resulted in a reciprocal reduction in the fear levels of American citizens. The answer appears to be negative (see Walinsky, 1993; Benson, 1990; and Spencer, 1997). The explanation, however, is very complex and imprecise. Without delving too deeply into a psychological analysis, the following theories may explain why the reduction in crime has not resulted in a corollary reduction in fear.

One of the most compelling theories is advanced by Walinsky. He asserts that even though official agencies report a reduction in crime rates, people cannot do a "memory rinse" (Walinsky, 1993: 40). He explains that it is very difficult for people to forget the horrors and the impact of crime, particularly violent crime. For people who have personally experienced crime, or those within their immediate family, it is very difficult to completely wipe away the effects from one's memory and life. Walinsky argues that the effects of crime are not disjunctive, but instead are cumulative (Walinsky, 1993). As such, the impact of crime has a lasting effect, especially when an individual has experienced numerous criminal incidents, either personally or through their frame of references. This is consistent with the Figgie Report on fear of crime, which states that "most people perceive crime rates as continually increasing and look at any decline as an aberration, a temporary ebb in the inexorably rising tide of petty theft, armed robbery, murder and international terror" (Benson, 1991: 3).

One of the difficulties of doing a memory rinse is related to the level of attention which the media devotes to crime. Certain researchers have asserted that people often form their image of the crime problem from the mass media (Liska, et al., 1982: 761–762). Lurigio stated that "the fear of crime is out of proportion with the crime rate ... partly because the media has fueled the perception of the crime problem" (Spencer, 1997: 1). Further, other security industry professionals assert that television crime reports— particularly local news shows— are a boon to sales (Barron, 1997: 1). Barron echoed this notion through his research of media coverage. He stated that network coverage of murders rose 336 percent from 1990 to 1995 (Barron, 1997). This coverage, of course, does not include extraordinary events such as the O.J. Simpson trial, the Ramsey killing, and the more recent examples of school violence, such as Littleton, Colorado, each of which had substantial hours of television coverage. Additionally, the amount of media coverage in response to recent terrorist incidents was probably unprecedented. Surveys further support these assertions and statistics. Gallup Poll research has shown that citizens consistently believe that crime is increasing in the U.S. and within their own neighborhoods, even though crime statistics may actually be decreasing.[6]

One implication of these statistics, as various authors have asserted, is that private police will be increasingly utilized to combat or respond to crime (see Benson, 1997; Tolchin, 1985; Cunningham, et al., 1991; Spencer, 1997; Meadows, 1991; Walinsky, 1993; and Bailin, 2000). These authors, and many others, have predicted or have shown that private security personnel are being hired in response to the incidence of crime. Chris Vail, the president of Law Enforcement Development, observed that the "growth of the private security industry resulted from a combination of factors: fear of crime, downsizing of public police forces because of limited funds, and the belief that the criminal justice system isn't working" (Spencer, 1997: 1). This assertion is validated by Stephanie Mann, the author of *Safe Homes, Safe Neighborhoods*, who asserted that "people need to take responsibility for their safety.... Citizens are the law and order in a community, not the police" (Litsikas, 1994: 72). Consequently, one can argue that the private security industry is responding to the demand from individual citizens, businesses, and even communities, at least partially, due to the incidence and fear of crime.

Going beyond the growing demand for security, from a purely demographic perspective, some authors assert that the recent reductions in the level of crime will be short lived. For example, McNulty predicted that "in the final years of the decade [1990s] and throughout the next, America will experience an 'echo boom', a population surge made up of the teenage children of today's aging baby boomers" (McNulty, 1995: 84). McNulty uses demographics to explain the effects of such on society. In 1980, the U.S. census reported 10.7 million males in the 15–19 year old age bracket. By 1990, this population segment declined by 15 percent to about 9.2 million (McNulty, 1995a). The downward trend continued until 1995, when America had the fewest number of young men since 1965. By the year 2000, however, the population in this age cohort will have rebounded to more than 10 million. In the year 2010, the number of 15–19 year old males will be 11.5 million, an increase of 30 percent from the 1995 low (McNulty, 1995). The result, according to McNulty, is chilling. He stated that "as today's five-year-old children become tomorrow's teenagers, America faces the most violent juvenile crime surge in its history"(McNulty, 1995).

This gloomy prediction is echoed and expounded on by Walinsky, who points to research by Fox and DeIulio, both of whom draw similar dire predictions. Specifically, Fox predicts a 23 percent increase in 14–17 year old youths (Walinsky, 1993: 52). This increase, coupled with what Dilulio terms the development of a "white underclass," is especially problematic (Dilulio, 1995: 1). This vision of a problematic culture coupled with increased population growth is repeated by Kaplan. In his compelling piece, Kaplan asserts that crime will be increasingly based on "environmental scarcity, cultural and racial clashes, and geographic destiny" (1994: 54). He maintains that "as crime continues to grow in our cities, and the ability of government and criminal justice systems to protect their citizens diminishes, urban crime may develop into low-intensity conflict by coalescing along racial, religious, social, and political lines, resulting in a 'booming private security business'" (Kaplan, 1994: 74). Another prediction, according to Dilulio, is an increase in homicides to approximately 35,000 to 40,000 per year (Walinsky, 1993: 52). This predicted rise in the number of homicides compares to about 23,500 homicides in 1990 (Roth, 1994: 1).

Going beyond crime research and the data related to demographics, the ability of terrorism to create fear and the desire for security cannot be overstated. The relationship between terrorism and fear has been widely developed (Wardlaw, 1982: 36; Davis, 1982: 116; Ezeldin, 1987: 33; Wolf, 1981: 20; and Clutterbuck, 1975: 206). Without getting into the complexities of this relationship, it is clear that one of the principles of terrorism is to foster fear in the affected society (Greisman, 1979: 145; Wolf, 1981: 107; and Clutterbuck, 1975: 206). Indeed, one of the basic principles of terrorism is that the "audience" (society) is the true target, not the actual victims of the attack(s). In this sense, terrorism is deemed to be primarily theater (Wardlaw, 1982: 38).

The impact of terrorism in relation to the perception of fear in society is difficult, if not impossible, to predict. The fear and crime studies discussed above have largely focused on "ordinary crime." Of course, even ordinary crime creates fear. Terrorism is designed to create fear, but at a much deeper level. The intent is to break the "inertial relationship" which binds the citizen to the government (Wardlaw, 1982: 10; Waugh, 1982: 85; Crenshaw, 1983: 23; and Clutterbuck, 1975: 286). This disorientation is often coupled with the disruption of the stableness of daily life (Wolf, 1981: 282; Knauss, et al., 1983: 77; Greisman, 1979: 138; and Young, 1977: 289).

At this level, terrorism upsets the framework and images which people depend on (i.e., trust and security). This creates more anxiety and uncertainty, due in part to the unpredictability of violence. People can become so paranoid and isolated that they are unable to draw strength and security from their usual social supports, causing them to rely entirely upon their own resources. Ultimately, Greisman contends, the watchword for the stricken masses becomes, "Don't wait to be hunted to hide" (1979: 41). This impact of terrorism is summed up in a pointed assertion by Graham (1971: 181), who states that "terrorism destroys the solidarity, cooperation, and interdependence on which social functioning is based, and substitutes insecurity and distrust." Clutterbuck uses the descriptive term "climate of collapse" to refer to the cycle of violence and fear in which the political balance begins to favor the terrorists, instead of the government or the police (1975: 206). This potential impact would create substantial demand for additional and more sophisticated security — including the use of private patrols on public streets.

Strategies designed to address the impact of crime can and must be implemented. Certain policy initiatives, both from policing and from other areas of government, may negate the predicted increases in crime — or deal with the effects of terrorism. However, the ability of society to counteract the large increase of youths, who traditionally have been most crime prone, is problematic, at best. And the ability of society to effectively combat terrorism is still uncertain. What is predicted is that the government cannot implement the necessary remedies to deal with these issues (including the attendant fears) without the contribution of the private sector. The role of private police and security methods is predicted to increase along with rising fears created by crime or terrorism. In any event, the movement toward more privatized public safety services has been forwarded — albeit slowly and silently — across this country. To better understand the implications of privatized patrol services, it may be valuable to consider the legal issues surrounding private policing.

V

A Legal Overview
of Private Policing

This chapter delves into the legal and constitutional aspects of private policing. The analysis of these issues will entail a three part process. The first is an overview of case law that shows how constitutional provisions have applied to actions by private security personnel. The second involves a similar analysis of the legal authority of private security personnel. Finally, the third section analyzes the legal issues relevant to the case study.

The significance of this legal and constitutional overview can be explained in terms of both the factual guidance derived from the cases, and from the implications of private policing. The cases demonstrate how courts analyze the facts and the law related to the use of "police power" by private security. The term "police power" is another way of describing legal authority, including searches, seizures and arrests. To better understand the significance of the use of police power by private security, it is helpful to establish what the law is on this issue in order to set the stage for the case study of Marquette Park. These cases provide a scientific basis for the research, coupled with the legal analysis to develop the appropriate methods of the case study.

Constitutional Issues

Private policing presents a host of problematic issues relating to certain constitution protections. The implications are broad and far reaching. One way to introduce these implications is to describe the government's duty to provide security or protection to society. As previously discussed, the historic roots of policing stemmed from the notion that citizens had the obligation to maintain law and order. This notion was consistent with the ideas of the framers of the constitution, who assumed that law abiding people would largely be responsible for their own safety (Reynolds, 1994: 1). The constitution does not provide any obligation on the part of government to protect citizens from crime. Indeed, absent the Second Amendment's right to bear arms provision — which some assert gives citizens the right to own firearms, thereby being consistent with the notion that citizens should be responsible for their own safety — the only language in the constitution dealing with providing protection is directed at foreign countries.

Approximately fifty years after the birth of this country, public policing was introduced as a major societal initiative. As stated in Chapter III, there were many unanswered questions related to public policing. How would the police be controlled? Who would the police answer to? What were their obligations relative to maintaining law and order? If the police failed to provide law and order, would they be responsible to society, or even to individual citizens? These questions—and others—resonated in early America.

As public policing began to take hold in this society, certain legal decisions carved out the duty of the government as it relates to the safety and security of its citizens. In a famous U.S. Supreme Court case entitled *South v. Maryland* (1856), the court held that government does not have a specific duty to protect individuals (Reynolds, 1994: 1). The court refused to create this duty, as it would "impose a crushing economic burden on government" (Reynolds, 1994). Instead, the court held that government had a general duty to enforce laws, but not to protect any particular person. Significantly, the *South v. Maryland* court held that

> there is no constitutional right to be protected by the state
> against being murdered by criminals.... The constitution is a char-
> ter of negative liberties, it tells the state to let people alone, it does
> not require the federal government or the state to provide services,
> even so elementary a service as maintaining law and order.

This decision provided the intellectual principle that has been extended to contemporary times. The principle states, in essence, that the government is not responsible for the safety of its citizens—as safety relates to criminal activity. Accordingly, citizens are required to secure their own safety independent of government. This basic principle, whereby government is not responsible for the safety or security of individual citizens, has not changed. Absent the duty of a third party, such as a corporation or a property owner, the burden is on each individual to provide for his or her own safety and security.

This requirement to secure individual safety has been made much easier in modern society (Savas, 2000). Savas explains that "economic factors are making people less dependent on government for goods and services, and more accepting of privatized approaches to their needs." The advent of large, privately owned and funded security forces has helped make this assertion ring true. When massive companies like Securitas and Group 4 Falckas employ thousands of private police officers and operate with substantial resources and revenues, there can be little doubt that the market has the ability to provide protection services to individuals, companies and even communities.

The ability of individuals, companies and even communities to provide for their own safety, however, is not without its implications. One of the more obvious concerns regards the Fourth Amendment prohibition against unreasonable searches and seizures. This prohibition establishes one of the most basic rights of citizens, and arguably, one of the most powerful restrictions on police authority. The Fourth Amendment provides:

[t]he right of the people to be secure in their persons, houses, papers, and effects, against unreasonable searches and seizures, shall not be violated, and no warrants shall issue, but upon probable cause, supported by oath or affirmation, and particularly describing the place to be searched, and the persons or things to be seized.[7]

Many authors have acknowledged that the Fourth Amendment generally does not have the same application to security personnel (Chanken and Chaiken, 1987: 21; and Zielinski, 1999: 3). In this sense, security personnel may not be required to adhere to the prohibitions contained in the Fourth Amendment. This is of great concern to many people. Simply stated, if security personnel are deemed to be private citizens, then this constitutional prohibition would not apply to their actions (Shearing and Stenning, 1983: 501–502). This is so because the constitution was specifically limited to apply only to the government, or in constitutional parlance, to "state actors." However, as illustrated earlier, the distinction between private and public is not as clear-cut as it would seem. In fact, courts have applied constitutional prohibitions to private security personnel under certain defined facts or circumstances.

In order to fully understand the application of the Fourth Amendment, it may be helpful to illustrate two possible scenarios. On one hand, consider the possibility that private security personnel can disregard the constitutional prohibitions relating to search and seizure, and still maintain a legally valid arrest. Security personnel can obtain evidence regardless of protections in the Fourth Amendment, and still use this evidence against the defendant at trial. Conversely, if a police officer obtains evidence in violation of the Fourth Amendment, the evidence could not be used at trial. This, at least in theory, creates a dual system. Those "lucky" enough to be arrested by public police would be protected by the constitutional limitations imposed upon the police. Those arrested by private security, however, could be convicted of a crime through the use of evidence obtained contrary to constitutional protections. Most would maintain this is unacceptable.

The implications are clear. Historically, the state has been perceived as posing substantial threats to individual liberty. However, Wilderman contends that private policing has paradoxically increased state control by reducing the civil rights and liberties of citizens (Johnston, 1992: 219). The paradox stems from the fact that most of the attention relative to the protection of civil liberties has focused on the state through the power of the public police. Ironically, private police have the power to undermine the rights of American citizens (Johnston, 1992). This is especially relevant and problematic when one considers the use of police power by private security on public streets. Consequently, the growing use of private security has created substantial concerns for individual rights and freedoms (Shearing and Stenning, 1983: 497; Johnston, 1992: 219; Reynolds, 1994: 5 and Zielinski, 1999: 9). This is at least partly evidenced by the questionable application of constitutional prohibitions.

A remedy to this dilemma is through the assertion of civil lawsuits. According to some authors, lawsuits may be a more potent remedy against private security than they are against public police (Reynolds, 1994: 2; and Benson, 1990: 305). This is so because victims of erroneous arrests can pursue civil causes of action for damages. The jury awards in such cases may be substantial, often involving seven figure recoveries. The threat of these lawsuits—at least theoretically—can serve as a deterrent to illegal arrests or improper conduct by private security personnel (Geyelin, 1993: 1; and Reynolds, 1994: 2). The logic is that market pressures and liability exposure stemming from such lawsuits act as an indirect mechanism to "force" professional and legal conduct on the part of security personnel (or of business and property owners). In this way, liability exposure serves as a stick to force professional conduct on a firm which otherwise may not care about the constitutional rights of citizens.

Additionally, illegal or abusive conduct on the part of security personnel adds nothing to the corporate bottom line (Reynolds, 1994: 2). This means that such conduct would do little — or nothing — to further the financial interests of the firm. Indeed, abusive or unconstitutional conduct may take away from the bottom line, in the form of multi-million dollar judgments. The usefulness of lawsuits as a deterrence may or may not resonate to the dictates of reality. Nonetheless, the possibility that lawsuits could provide a remedy — however effective — will be assessed in the documentary component of the methodology.

Constitutional Case Law Analysis

The cases presented below will set out a relevant sampling of legal decisions relating to private security personnel. The cases will show that the courts have moved away from the broad principle made in *Burdeau v. McDowell* (1921), which definitively established that constitutional prohibitions do not apply to private security. Over time the courts softened this broad notion, and began to allow constitutional prohibitions to apply under certain facts and circumstances. The later cases, however, still adhere to the basic principle that the constitution only applies to state actors.

These cases illustrate the reasoning of the courts, and the trend toward finding a "nexus" between public police and private police. Nexus refers to a combination or connection between the government and individuals who would normally be deemed private citizens. When nexus is established, the courts will find the private security personnel are state actors, or at least have a sufficient connection with governmental authorities to apply constitutional prohibitions. In this sense, these cases show the fluidity of the law, and the court's reaction to the growing incidence of police power by private security personnel. In a number of cases, the court specifically discusses the growing use and scope of private security. These decisions, therefore, are tempered by the reality of private security in relation to the provision of public safety services in this country. While these cases are only a sampling of important decisions, they provide a solid basis to explore the research questions related to private policing, especially as to its impact on constitutional prohibitions, as well as for certain public policy implications.

BURDEAU V. MCDOWELL

The classic case dealing with the application of constitutional prohibitions for private security is *Burdeau v. McDowell*, 256 U.S. 465 (Supreme Court, 1921). In *Burdeau*, the case involved an investigation into fraudulent activities of a company executive. The executive, McDowell, occupied an office, in which he kept personal and company documents. The office was searched by company personnel, while police detectives secured the area. The improperly recovered documents were later tendered to Burdeau, who was a Special Assistant to the U.S. Attorney General. Burdeau indicted McDowell based on information derived from the documents. Significantly, the court determined that if this search was conducted by police officials, it would have violated the Fourth Amendment.

The *Burdeau* court observed that the origin and the history of the Fourth Amendment manifested an intention to act as a restraint upon the activities of sovereign authority. In this way, the Fourth Amendment was specifically intended to limit only governmental officials. Since the documents used to prosecute McDowell came into possession of the U.S. Attorney General's Office without any direct violation by any governmental official, the court reasoned that the constitutional protections against unreasonable searches and seizures were not applicable. This decision, therefore, had the effect of excluding constitutional protections, when the purported violation was done by private security personnel. The *Burdeau v. McDowell* court stated, "We see no reason why the fact that individuals, unconnected with the government, may have wrongfully taken [documents] should prevent them from being held for use in prosecuting an offense where the documents are of an incriminating character."

COMMONWEALTH V. LEONE

Over time, courts began to move away from the proposition established in *Burdeau*. One such case, *Commonwealth v. Leone*, 435 N.E. 2d 1036 (1982), stands for the proposition that private security personnel who are recognized as "special police" by a governmental entity are more likely to be deemed as state actors, thereby making constitutional prohibitions applicable. The term "special police" relates to a special license provided by a governmental entity, which confers arrest or police powers similar to those conferred on sworn police officers.

The facts in *Leone* are not unique. The case deals with the search of the sleeping compartment of a commercial truck as it entered a facility owned by General Electric. The search by the security guard revealed the truck driver to be in possession of a stolen firearm. The security guard then turned over the arrestee and the weapon to the police, who formally charged the defendant.

The court in *Leone* observed, as did the court in *Burdeau*, that the Fourth Amendment and the exclusionary rule apply only to governmental action. The court deemed evidence discovered and seized by private parties is admissible without regard to the methods used. However, the *Leone* court provided an exception to this general principle. The exception includes situations where state officials have instigated or participated in the search. If this exception can be shown, then constitutional protections would apply.

The court struggled with the fact that privately employed security forces pose a difficult problem in distinguishing between state and private action. It articulated its standard in making this distinction. The distinction was related to the primary function and concern of private security, which is the protection of their employer's or client's property. This primary function was contrasted with public police, who are generally more concerned with the arrest and conviction of wrongdoers. The *Leone* court noted an important aspect of this case study when it stated that "private security forces have come into increasing use as supplements to police protection, and perform functions much like those of ordinary police."

The *Leone* court articulated the appropriate legal standard involving searches and seizures by special police. Since special police are commissioned officers by the government, and generally possess authority beyond that of an ordinary citizen, they may be treated as agents of the state, and thereby subject to the constraints of the Fourth Amendment. The court, however, further distinguished special police from sworn public police personnel. The key question for the court was whether the officer acted in accord with the interests of the public or those of his employer. The *Leone* court explained this additional distinction by asserting,

> [t]he guard's private function adds a new aspect to his activities, which we believe is relevant to the proper application of the fourth amendment. The action he [guard] takes on behalf of his employer may be a lawful and necessary means of protecting the employer's property, although it would be impermissible if taken on behalf of the state in pursuit of evidence. When the guard's conduct is justified by his legitimate private duties, it should not be treated as lawless, or "unreasonable" search and seizure.

The court also reasoned that a guard's actions are similar to that of a police officer who intrudes by lawful means upon an individual's privacy, and then discovers unanticipated evidence. Similarly, when a subject is on private property, he or she has reason to expect some scrutiny or interference by the agents of the private party whose property he or she is using or upon. When the guard takes legitimate steps for the protection of the employer's property, there is no cause for the deterrent sanction of the exclusionary rule. Exclusion of the evidence, the court reasoned, would serve only to frustrate prosecution of crimes which happen to come to light in the course of a routine inspection by a security guard. For these reasons, the *Leone* court concluded

> that an investigation by a special police officer privately employed as a security guard does not violate the fourth amendment when it is conducted on behalf of the private employer, in a manner that is reasonable and necessary for protection of the employer's property. If, on the other hand, the officer [guard] steps outside this sphere of legitimate private action, the exclusionary rule applies as it would to any state officer.

The *Leone* court provided further guidance for factual determinations to be made by other courts. These four specific criteria concern whether constitutional protections would be applicable, depending on the purpose or motivation behind the functions conducted by the security officer, and on the environment in which the actions occurred. The *Leone* court stated:

> 1. The guard must have acted under the control of his private employer. If the investigation exceeded his private duties or authorization, he must be considered to have acted in his official capacity. Similarly, if the guard has received instructions from state authorities, on a regular basis or in regard to the particular investigation at issue, his conduct is not protected by his private role.
> 2. The guard's action must be clearly related to his employer's private purposes. An investigation that goes beyond the employer's needs cannot be justified as an incident of the guard's private function.
> 3. The investigation must be a legitimate means of protecting the employer's property, and so must be reasonable in light of the circumstances surrounding it. Reasonableness depends in part on the expectations engendered by the particular setting. If the employer has maintained the private character of his property, those who use it must anticipate and accept supervision. But if the employer has exposed his premises and chattels to semi-public use, the sense of private prerogative to control its users is much diminished. Custom or advance warning may bear upon the propriety of an investigation, but should not be determinative.
> 4. The court should consider the methods chosen and the manner in which they are carried out. Failure to employ available, less intrusive alternatives, may suggest that the methods employed were unwarranted, and an offense to individual dignity is impermissible in almost any circumstances.

UNITED STATES V. FRANCOEUR

In *United States v. Francoeur*, 547 F. 2d 891 (1977), the case dealt with the indictment of three individuals for counterfeiting charges stemming from the use of bogus currency at Walt Disney World. The facts of the case are not difficult. The defendants were observed by security personnel passing counterfeit bills while shopping at various stores within park property. The defendants were confronted by the security personnel, and all were removed to a security office. Once in the office, nine counterfeit bills were recovered. While still being held by security personnel, the defendants were identified by store cashiers. Following positive identifications, the U.S. Secret Service was called and a search warrant was obtained which resulted in the recovery of additional counterfeit bills. The defendants sought to preclude the admission of the evidence based on their assertion that the initial detention and recovery by the security personnel violated their constitutional rights.

The court in *Francoeur* asserted that the Fourth Amendment gives protection only against "unlawful governmental action." Recognizing this principle, the defendants contended that the security personnel of Disney World are in "truth and in fact" government officials. The court disagreed with the defendants. The court held that the amusement park was on 'private property' to which admission is charged. In this sense, no one is permitted to enter the outer gates except by implied or actual consent of the owners. If the owners of the property committed an illegal act against park guests, then there are civil remedies which could be asserted against the owners. The court construed, however, that such illegal conduct would not give the guests protection of the Fourth Amendment or the exclusionary rule which has developed from it. In ruling against the defendants, the *Francoeur* court stated, "[t]he Supreme Court has in no instance indicated that it would apply the exclusionary rule to cases in which evidence has been obtained by private individuals in a manner not countenanced if they were acting for state or federal government."

PEOPLE V. STORMER

In *People v. Stormer*, 518 N.Y.S. 2d 351 (Co. Ct. 1987), the case dealt with another arrest by private security personnel in a confined semi-public area. The defendant was a Sagamore Hotel employee who performed maid duties. The hotel was located on Green Island, which is within the corporate limits of the Town of Bolton in Warren County, New York. The only connection to the mainland is a causeway between the town landing and the Sagamore Hotel on Green Island.

Based partly on the remote nature of the island, the Sagamore Hotel security force had advised the Warren County Sheriff's Department that routine patrols to the island were unnecessary, and that in the future their presence on the island would be required only upon special request. Subsequent to this notice, Sagamore Hotel security personnel were involved in a theft investigation at the hotel. As a result of the investigation, the security personnel searched the vehicle of the defendant, without her knowledge or consent. This search recovered money missing from a hotel room. The defendant was then held by security personnel until she was placed in custody with the Warren County Sheriff's Department.

The defendant sought to suppress the evidence based on her assertion that it was an unreasonable search and seizure, notwithstanding that it was made by a "private" security force.

The prosecution, on the other hand, asserted that the prohibitions regarding unlawful search and seizure "do not require exclusion of evidence because a private individual has gathered it by unlawful means." The court considered these conflicting assertions, and stated: "Given the proliferation in this country of privately-employed security personnel as a supplement to or, as in this case, a replacement for local law enforcement authorities, the privacy rights of a citizen of this State may be increasingly jeopardized."

The court then analyzed the facts of the case and determined that the security personnel were performing a public function. This determination was largely due to the self-contained nature of the property, and that the security force essentially functioned as an autonomous entity.

After finding this "public function" test, the court then had to determine if two conditions were met. The conditions were:

- The "searcher" must have a strong interest in obtaining convictions; and
- The "searcher" must commit searches and seizures regularly in order to be familiar enough with the rules to adopt his methods to conform to them [rules].

After making these assessments, the *Stormer* court held that the hotel's interests could have been vindicated by the confiscation of the money, and the termination of the employee's job. By going further and detaining her for criminal charges, hotel security personnel went beyond simply asserting the hotel's interests. Instead, they asserted society's interests by prosecuting the defendant. In this way, the safeguards provided by the Fourth Amendment were activated. The court held that the seizure of the money was unlawful, and as such, was suppressed as unconstitutionally seized.

MANCUSI V. DEFORTE

In *Mancusi v. DeForte*, 392 U.S. 364 (U.S. Supreme Court, 1968), the district attorney ordered a union to bring certain books and documents to court. The union refused to comply. Instead of pursuing legal remedies, union officials seized the books and documents, and gave them to the district attorney. The evidence was then used against the defendants at trial.

The *Mancusi* court held that the seized materials were inadmissible, as their seizure violated the Fourth and Fourteenth Amendments. This court deemed the constitution applicable. This was so even though the facts were strikingly similar to those in *Burdeau v. McDowell*. In both cases, the evidence was initially seized by private non-governmental personnel, and then turned over to prosecutors. Each court took a different approach. The *Mancusi* court did not have the same anguish over the functions of private security in relation to the constitution. Indeed, *Burdeau* established — definitively — that the constitution does not apply to non-governmental actors. In contrast, the *Mancusi* court did not seem to concern itself about this principle. Instead, it was more focused on the protections provided by the constitution. As such, the *Mancusi* court declared that:

> it is, of course, immaterial that the state might have been able to obtain the same papers by means which did not violate the 4th Amendment. As Justice Holmes stated in *Silverthorne Lumber v. U.S.*, the rights ... against unlawful search and seizure are to be protected even if the same result might have been achieved in a lawful way.

Legal Authority Case Law Analysis

Cases in Illinois state courts relating to legal authority — otherwise known as police power — date back to at least the 1860s. In Illinois, and other states, courts have slowly expanded the authority of private citizens to effect arrests, just like constitutional protections have gradually been applied to private policing. The cases themselves provide an interesting insight into this judicial development. Key cases which illustrate the development of the law are as follows:

DOBBS V. BOARD

In *Dobbs v. Board*, 43 Ill 95 (Illinois Supreme Court, 1867), the court established the authority of an arrest by a private citizen. As conveyed in the court's opinion, the notion of private citizens conducting arrests was not a desired public policy. In fact, it was viewed with much reservation. Instead, the court clearly desired to avoid the incidence of citizen arrests. Notice that the court sought to err on the side of *less force, thereby less potential bloodshed,* when it rendered its opinion. The *Dobbs v. Board* court made the following pointed statement:

> There are, no doubt, cases which hold that private individuals may arrest on probable cause, but there are authorities which hold to the contrary rule. And in the conflict of authority we are left free to adopt the rule which seems to be most consonant with reason and the public interest. And, to prevent breaches of the peace and even bloodshed, we think that a private individual should not be justified [to effect arrest] unless a crime has been committed and the person arrested shall be shown to be the guilty party.

LINDQUIST V. FRIEDMAN'S, INC.

Similarly, in *Lindquist v. Friedman's, Inc.*, 366 Ill 232, 8 N.E. 2d 625 (Illinois Supreme Court, 1937), the court reaffirmed the earlier case decision. Here again, this court determined that citizen arrests were not a desired public policy. The decision reflected the concern of the citizen taking the law into his or her hands. This concern is interesting considering that this country was founded on the notion of self-help and self-protection. However, this mindset is not surprising given the pervasive and deeply established influence of public policing. Clearly, the court was concerned that private citizens (thus private security) could become the officer and jailer, without any involvement of the government. In the hundred years since the advent of public policing, this court seems to have forgotten the historical roots of private self-help and self-protection. This is not to say the court was wrong in desiring constraints on private citizens. It is interesting, however, to note how far the notion of public policing had come in this period of time. The actual court language in *Lindquist v. Friedman's, Inc.*, is instructive:

> In our state a citizen is not permitted to take the law into his own hands and to arrest another upon suspicion or even upon probable cause ... to permit a private citizen, without observing the formal requirements enumerated, to become a *self-constituted officer and jailer* upon mere suspicion of the guilt of the accused person, or even upon probable cause to believe such person guilty, would result in more and greater evils than the possible escape of the few guilty persons occasioned by the delay in obtaining warrants and officers to serve them [emphasis added].

KAROW V. STUDENT INNS, INC.

Over time, legislation in Illinois changed the requirements relating to the legal authority of citizens to make arrests. The new legislation broadened the ability of citizens to effect arrests. The new law allows a citizen to effect arrest when he has reasonable grounds to believe an offense is being committed. This was in contrast to the old law which required that the offense be committed in the presence of a private citizen, before the citizen could make an arrest. It is uncertain why this law was enacted. One can speculate that this broadened power given to private citizens may have been in response to the growing incidence of crime. Whatever the reason, one of the first cases dealing with the new statute was *Karow v. Student Inns, Inc.*, 43 Ill App 3d 878, 357 NE 2d 628 (4th District, 1976). The *Karow* court explained the law as follows:

> The committee comments to section 107-3, state that the section continues the former law as to arrests by private persons except in regard to ordinance violations. A comparison of the old and the new sections clearly reveals a change. The former section prohibited arrests except when an offense was being committed, while the present section, by its very language, permits a private person to arrest when he has *reasonable grounds to believe an offense is being committed* [emphasis added].

PEOPLE V. LAWSON

This expanded ability of private citizens to make a lawful arrest was re-affirmed by the court in *People v. Lawson*, 36 Ill App 3d 767, 345 NE 2d 41 (1st District, 1976). In this case, the court again articulated the authority to make arrests in Illinois. The court in *People v. Lawson* stated: "The law in Illinois authorizes any private person to make an arrest under circumstances such as disclosed here since any person would have 'reasonable grounds' to believe that an offense other than an ordinance violation is being committed...."

Case Study Legal Issues and Factors

The guidance provided by these court decisions are useful in conducting the case study of Marquette Park. The analysis of functional characteristics of private and public policing can be broken down into specific, critical factors. These factors can be broadly described as legal authority to make arrests, and the admissibility of evidence derived from arrests made by private security personnel. Both aspects involve the use of police power by private security personnel.

In their critique of the Hallcrest Report, Nalla and Newman (1991) focused their research on the term "policing agency" which was used in the Hallcrest studies. This term was the operative definition to determine whether a particular function of a security firm should be counted as a proximate comparison with public police. Their conclusion was that the term resulted in an expanded definition of policing, because private security personnel do not engage in the kinds of direct controlling behavior that are traditionally linked with the police (Nalla and Newman, 1991: 537). These authors believed that a different operative definition would be more appropriate. They focused on whether privately employed personnel had an explicit function to "regulate human behavior" (Nalla and Newman, 1991a).

Regulation of human behavior is a broad idea which could encompass a myriad of different functions and occupations. For purposes of this case study, however, this term would encompass any of the three types of functions previously described; that is law enforcement, order maintenance, or traditional security methods. At the core of this case study is the assumption that private security will use such regulatory methods, thereby exerting police powers on public streets in order to affect human behavior.

While there are few black letter legal principles, case law provides insight into key factors within the research design. According to Illinois law — as in most states, a private individual is authorized to make an arrest when there are reasonable grounds to believe that an offense other than an ordinance violation is being committed. According to *People v. Lawson*, 36 Ill. App. 3d 767, 345 N.E. 2d 41 (1st Dist., 1976), the legal definition of an arrest requires three elements. They are as follows:

- Authority to arrest
- Assertion of that authority with intent to arrest
- Restraint of the person to be arrested

As this definition reveals, effecting an arrest can be broadly construed. Notice there is no requirement that an arrest be made by a public police officer. Nor it there any requirement that the person be handcuffed or be given their Miranda rights. These are common misconceptions. Instead, the key components of an arrest can be made by either public or private police officers. Broadly speaking, anyone can effect an arrest in Illinois for any crime other than an ordinance violation, which only public police officers can do. Private citizens— thus private police — have the legal authority to arrest for all other crimes.

Police powers can be defined as the assertion of an arrest, as well as conducting any search and seizure. In practice, however, it is difficult to separate an arrest from a search and seizure. This is because effecting an arrest almost always entails some corresponding search of the person or property of the arrestee. The search may also result in some seizure of property or contraband from the arrestee. Conversely, there are numerous situations in which a search (and even a seizure) could occur without an arrest being made. In these situations, it is a common police practice to conduct certain investigatory searches of individuals who for one reason or another are not arrested. The decision to forego an arrest can be based on the fact that there is no evidence to support the arrest. It may also be based on tactical reasons or even the discretion afforded any police officer. Notwithstanding the myriad of factors which go into any such encounter, the term "police power" is used to describe the act of making an arrest, and depending on the circumstances, conducting searches or seizures which result therefrom, or are independent of such.

There are subtle distinctions, however, between the use of police powers, and whether constitutional protections would apply to actions of police officers. This depends on whether private police officers have the legal authority to effect an arrest in a given situation — and whether the arrest holds up in court on constitutional grounds. These are often two distinct questions of law. The first issue involves legal authority. As described above, the legal authority to effect an arrest is not substantially different for either public or private police officers. In Illinois — as in most states — public or private officers generally have the legal authority to arrest. As such, for the purposes of this research, the legal authority to effect an arrest by the private police officers will be inferred. Consequently, the typical concern related to police powers that must be assessed is the constitutionality question.

The constitutionality question is more factually driven. As the court cases show, it is an unsettled question whether constitutional protections would apply to the actions of the private police officer. The answer is largely dependant upon whether the private police officer(s) is deemed a state actor, by the particular facts in a given situation, and by the principles established in case law. The courts have provided some guidance as to the triggering of constitutional protections. The typical trigger is to assess whether there is a "nexus" or connection between the public and the private police.

The assessment of nexus requires an analysis of the function and situation surrounding the use of private policing. An analysis of the case law can supply the following guidance:

- The amount of interaction, communication or involvement by the private and public police.
- The level of governmental involvement in the licensing, contracting, and the legal status (i.e., "special police") of the private policing program as compared to the relative autonomous nature of the private firm.
- The environment or the nature of the area to be patrolled by the security firm, with the more isolated the area, and the more controls placed on freedom of movement into and out of the area, the more likely the officer will be deemed "private."
- The propensity of the security force to use "police powers" (or assert criminal charges). The more commonly these occur, the more likely the officer will be deemed as a "state actor" because the functions are "public" concerns, such as crime control and criminal prosecutions.

The answers to these questions are subjective. For operational purposes, however, certain factual assumptions address each of the above stated criteria. In the Marquette Park study, most of the evidence shows a lack of sufficient nexus relative to the first criteria — the level of interaction, communication, and involvement between the public and private police. While there is some evidence of interaction, the level appears to be limited. Interactions between the private and public police were generally limited to only necessary communications, such as processing prisoners. While there were some pointed exceptions, such as tendering information on drug dealers to tactical police officers, the extent of such communication seemed infrequent.

In regard to the second criteria, the extent of governmental involvement was rather substantial. While there were no "special police" powers conferred, governmental involvement was illustrated many other ways. Specifically, the state of Illinois regulates and licenses all security guard firms. Each contractor of security guard services is required to possess certain personal attributes and experience to be eligible to take the licensing examination. The licensing examination is developed and administered by the state through the Department of Professional Regulation. Further, employees of security firms are required to undergo twenty hours of training for unarmed personnel, and forty hours of training for armed personnel. In addition to these state regulations, the City of Chicago was directly involved in the implementation of the patrol services at Marquette Park. This involvement included a ballot referendum, passing a council resolution following the vote on the referendum, the facilitation of property tax dollars to pay for the services, drafting contract documents to support such services, and the appointment of a commission by the local alderman to oversee the operation of the patrol operation. This substantial level of involvement by government would be deemed a nexus.

Similarly, in regard to the specific site environment, the private police patrols clearly operate on the public domain. The patrols roam the streets, alleys, public parks, and businesses commonly used by the general public, such as food, liquor, video, and drug stores. The patrols also go into apartments and private residences when called by the owners or tenants to do so. These examples are strikingly similar to the operation of public police. Even the entry into private residences, is done in furtherance of their public safety function. Consequently, the facts outlined here also would result in a nexus.

Finally, the fourth criteria regarding the use of police powers—the functional analysis—is a key determination. In essence, the question regards factual circumstances which will be detailed in the case study of Marquette Park.

These court cases illustrate an important overview of the state of the law relating to private policing. To be sure, many legal issues impact the functions and roles of private policing. Unfortunately, little is known as to exactly how private police perform their functions—particularly as they relate to constitutional prohibitions. These issues are developed and analyzed in the case study.

VI

Privatization Environments

The use of private security patrols on public streets—though relatively new and unusual—is not unprecedented. In fact, certain municipal areas have implemented privatization initiatives similar to the one at Marquette Park to enhance public safety. Indeed, few would argue against targeting crime and reducing its impact upon society. Given the concern for crime demonstrated in this book, it seems perfectly reasonable to implement such innovative privatization arrangements. This chapter will present some examples of privatization arrangements, wherein private police play a role in providing public safety services.

As Moore and Trojanowicz assert, there's no question that police are responsible for managing crime and its effects. No other *government* agency regards itself as specifically responsible for crime. Without question, the police are responsible for these matters, not only as an important approach to crime prevention, but also as an important value-creating activity in its own right (Moore and Trojanowicz, 1988: 12). However, if the police will not or cannot prevent crime at sufficient levels to satisfy business, property owners, and even communities; then one logical "solution" is to hire private security firms. As Carlson emphasized, private security firms can help restore community life, allowing people to worry less about crime and spend more time building families and neighborhoods (1995: 72).

The scope and specific arrangements of these initiatives vary widely. In rare cases, private security has *replaced* the police department within a given jurisdictional area. In most privatization initiatives, however, some level of "partnership" or some supplement with local police agencies form the basis for the arrangement. In this sense, Savas (2000: 3) recommends that the term partnership be used because people tend to view it in a less contentious manner. Partnership was defined by Savas (2000: 4) as "any arrangement between a government and the private sector in which partially or traditionally public activities are performed by the private sector."

These partnership arrangements have a particular logic, especially when one considers the characteristics of public and private policing. Both entities have many similar goals. This commonality of goals may also foster cooperative efforts within the two groups in the "spirit of public safety." These cooperative efforts were called "parallel objectives" by Patterson (1995: 33). From an economic perspective, these arrangements are referred to as accommodation and cooperation (Chanken and Chaiken, 1987: 9). This occurs when public police personnel informally rely on private security personnel to carry out tasks they prefer not to undertake. In return, public police provide some needed service, such as expeditious response to calls for assistance (Chanken and Chaiken, 1987). Cunningham noted most public police officials welcome a fuller partnership with private security if contracting would free up their officers for crime fighting (1991: 112). Consequently, this mutual relationship has been characterized in the following manner:

> Partnerships between security and law enforcement groups will
> likely continue to be forged ... creating an increasingly formidable
> coalition fighting crime and favoring joint solutions to issues
> affecting private security and law enforcement, the public, and the
> business community [Kolpacki, 1994: 47].

The examples presented below describe privatized policing arrangements which have been or are currently being employed. These examples help to provide context to the case study site (Marquette Park). The arrangements described below demonstrate that the site of the case study is part of a larger trend. Also, the case study can be contrasted against privatization initiatives in other areas of the country.

There are several ways in which private security is used in contemporary America. The distinctions relate to the location and the provision of services. Location can range from purely private environments to clearly public environments, such as public streets, parks, alleys, and businesses frequented by the general public. Sometimes, however, this is not an obvious determination. For example, is a gated neighborhood with a fenced perimeter within a larger municipal area a public or private environment? While this answer is debatable, we can consider it a private environment because even though the area is part of a larger community, the perime-

ter fencing effectively provides the level of separation to make the neighborhood "private."

The provision of services is easier to categorize: Either security personnel are used to supplement public police, or they are used to replace
public police. Admittedly, there are many situations between these two
extremes. For example, the level of involvement by a particular private
security firm may vary widely. In some cases, the private firm has only
ancillary involvement in public safety. In other arrangements, private security personnel may be engaged in proactive and tactical enforcement techniques, designed to search out and arrest criminal offenders. However,
in most examples, including the site in this case study, the typical provision is that the security firm will act as a supplement to public police. The
question remaining is the level of supplement that the security firms provide.

There is little information as to exactly what a security firm does in
any given arrangement. Most research on these privatized arrangements
does not address how the private police officers do their job. Instead, the
focus is on the result — whether it relates to crime rates, occupancy rates
of commercial properties, improvements in the physical appearance of the
community, or other similar indicators of a "successful" privatization
arrangement. Hence, this case study goes deeper. It looks at what functions the private police officers actually perform, and makes some assessment as to the constitutionality of their actions.

Current Firms and Environments

Accurate statistical information on the current level of privatization
of public safety is difficult to pinpoint, as there is no reference source
which collects information on these arrangements. Nonetheless, from a
general perspective, there are private security firms operating in both private and public environments, sometimes as a supplement to, and less
commonly, in place of, public police. As a means to introduce these examples, it may be helpful to think about the roles of private police and those
of public police. Remember that much of the traditional literature on policing distinguishes public police as being focused on "law enforcement,"
while private police focus on "observe and report." Partly due to the impact
of community policing, these traditional roles appear to be changing.

Sometimes it is difficult to distinguish the work of the public police
from the work of the private police. One would not expect to learn that
private police are serving in a tactical role, aggressively enforcing crimi-

nal laws. This is, in fact, what is occurring in certain places. For example, Intelligarde International, a Canadian based firm, stands out as an example of a paramilitary private security force. The firm bills itself as a "hard nosed American style organization" that will clean up crack houses, patrol dangerous ghettos, and handle other risky assignments *once undertaken by local police* (Palango, 1998: 2, emphasis added). Notice the emphasis on services which were once undertaken by local police — these are functions one would deem to be the job of the "police" rather than a security service. While this is clearly a marketing tool, even the assertion of this impression creates some value in the market. It also illustrates the Company's desire to engage in law enforcement activities, traditionally the domain of police agencies.

On the other hand, critics have argued that Intelligarde International "is pushing law enforcement in a new direction" (Palango, 1998). The Ontario Coalition Against Poverty (O.C.A.P.) stated that "Intelligarde likes to push the limits ... we know that security is a legitimate concern in neighborhoods, but in our minds, Intelligarde is the biggest threat to security" (Palango, 1998). This statement demonstrates the ideological distinctions, the tension between liberty and security. In this instance, the "security" concern is with the continued viability of constitutional protections.

This proactive — even tactical — approach to security is also occurring in this country. For example, a Fort Lauderdale based company, GSI Tactical Response, provides patrol services in certain areas for residential communities, including alarm response (Olick, 1994: 20). The company provides these services within specific communities, or overlapping several neighborhoods to enhance their cost effectiveness. In this way, the patrols were to provide crime prevention and enforcement services to residents within the "protected zones," as a supplement to the local police. The philosophical and economic approach to this service was echoed by Stan Teets, who is president of Personal Protective Services, Inc. He stated that "security is going to take over the majority of enforcement for most major cities. We can go in and patrol a part of the city more effectively than a police department for less expense" (Bole, 1998: 11).

Another tactical oriented firm is Critical Intervention Services (C.I.S.). This security firm exemplifies the "hard nosed" approach mentioned earlier. The firm markets itself to low income, high crime housing developments. The owner has stated that "we dress to intimidate the bad guys, we're not here to play games" (Bole, 1998: 20). This firm actively functions as a law enforcement agency. Indeed, some argue that they use a "Gestapo-like" approach to security. As an illustration of the approach taken by C.I.S, the following equipment and attire are typical of its security personnel:

- All Black Dress
- Spit Polished Combat Boots
- Bullet Proof Vests
- .357 Magnum Pistols
- Mace
- Two-way Radios
- Heat Detecting, Night Vision Scopes
- Sound Boosters
- Attack Dogs

The company boasts that crime has dropped by an average of 50 percent in the more than fifty Florida apartment complexes it patrols (Boyce, 1996: 20). While the "ninjas" have limited arrest powers, their duties include monitoring the actions of drug dealers, issuing trespass warnings to intruders, and prodding landlords to issue eviction notices (Boyce, 1996). David Walchak, when he was president of the International Association of Chiefs of Police (I.A.C.P.), commented that he would "*be concerned if they tried to exercise that type of authority on public streets*" (Bole, 1998: 20, emphasis added). This leads to the logical question. What would prevent firms who provide these services from doing so on public streets? Indeed, it is already happening.

Other companies "at the forefront" of private security includes Special Response Corporation (S.R.C.) and the Asset Protection Team. The advertisements for these firms illustrate how they view their mission. The S.R.C. ad features a uniformed security "agent" wielding a riot shield beneath a headline which proclaims, "*A Private Army when you Need it Most*" (Zielinski, 1999: 4). Similarly, the Asset Protection Team ran an ad which features a "jack booted security agent" equipped with a riot shield, club and helmet. The brochure "guarantees" guards will arrive with all the personnel necessary to "handle all levels of violence" (Zielinski, 1999: 5).

As these examples illustrate, many security firms are providing services which complement, and even exceed those of local law enforcement. This fact has raised concerns. Indeed, one of the most compelling is to the amount of cohesive power imposed by private security firms. Of course, the constitution was designed to limit the use of cohesive power by government. The question remains as to whether constitutional protections would apply to private security personnel. Suffice it to say that the use of private security has generated criticism related to constitutional concerns.

Despite such criticism, private security firms silently and continually expand their influence in contemporary America. The following examples illustrate the privatization of public safety.

Private Environment: Supplement

There are many examples of security arrangements operating in private communities, and acting as a supplement to the public police. In these instances, the "protected communities" are often separated by perimeter fencing coupled with private security patrols within the area. For example, thirty-five neighborhoods in Los Angeles have asked local governmental permission to separate from the surrounding communities by installing gates and hiring security firms (Farnham, 1992: 43). In suburban Detroit, the 2,300-home East English Village Association hired a private security force to supplement patrols of local police (Farnham, 1992). The reasoning behind this decision is illustrated by a statement from the president of this property association: "We figured if we wanted to keep this neighborhood stable, we couldn't stick our heads in the sand and say the police should take care of it. We realized there's only so much they can do" (Farnham, 1992).

In another private community, the property association in the Frenchman's Creek development in Jupiter, Florida, hired a "mini-swat team" (actually called S.T.O.P.— Special Tactical and Operations Personnel). This specially trained tactical team "roams the grounds every night dressed in camouflage face paint to stay as unobtrusive as possible and give them the edge on any intruder" (Cruickshank, 1994: 13). This "tactical team" stays sharp by conducting exercises with equipment which includes high-tech night vision gear, and infrared body heat detectors to distinguish a human body from the surrounding vegetation (Cruickshank, 1994). The security force also includes a marine patrol, and enforces speed limits by ticketing violators (Cruickshank, 1994).

Public Environments: Replacement

The most dramatic examples of private policing are those cases in which the public police were actually replaced by private security firms. Currently, these instances are rare, and have largely proved to be problematic. Despite the problems, the fact is certain municipal governments— and the citizens thereof— decided to "fire" their police departments, and replace the sworn police officers with security personnel. This is a controversial decision, indeed.

The town of Sussex, New Jersey, fired its police officers in 1992, following a drug scandal (Reynolds, 1994: 1). The town of Reminderville, Ohio, did the same. The police officers in both towns were replaced by private security guards who patrolled the town in blue "police-like" uniforms. The security personnel were armed with .9mm semi-automatic weapons, radios, batons, and handcuffs. In essence, the security personnel maintained the appearance of public police, but provided their services at a lower cost (Geyelin, 1993: 1; and Reynolds, 1994: 1). While the towns saved money, the "experiments" were terminated after considerable pressures from public police organizations, and from complaints by residents that the security personnel were not adequately enforcing the laws (Reynolds, 1994: 1; Geyelin, 1993: 1; and Tolchin, 1985: 27). Notwithstanding the fact that these arrangements ended, certain troubling issues remain.

According to Geyelin, the consequences are far reaching from both a legal and social perspective. Of course, federal and state constitutions limit police powers, with certain limitations and immunities attached to the use of police powers (Geyelin, 1993: 1; and Reynolds, 1994: 2). As noted by Geyelin, however, while the security personnel look like police officers, "they have no more than citizen's power of arrest, and have no authority whatsoever to question, detain or search a suspect without risking a lawsuit" (Geyelin, 1993: 1). However, some government entities have the authority to award "special police" powers to private security personnel. This enhanced level of authority was not exercised by either Sussex or Reminderville, nor were special powers acquired in Chicago's Marquette Park private patrols.

Unlike the Sussex and Reminderville arrangements, the Chicago Police Department continued to provide police services to the Marquette Park community, which would be characterized as a supplemental arrangement. Conversely, Sussex and Reminderville represent replacement arrangements, thereby being the outer limits of a movement in policing — the privatization of public safety (Geyelin, 1993). Notwithstanding the fact that the replacement of public policing by private security personnel has not been sustained, such examples manifest a host of constitutional and public policy implications.

Public Environment: Supplement

The more common approach in privatization of police services is when private police act as a supplement to public police. This is the approach taken by the Marquette Park patrols in this case study. For reasons to be addressed later, it is this aspect of privatization of police services which is most likely to take hold in this county. In fact, there are a number of examples of this arrangement. For example, in Oceanside, California, a private security firm called Bel-Air Patrol provided armed police-type patrols to town residents. The security patrols work closely with the Oceanside Police Department via radios, scanners, and cellular phones (Geyelin, 1993). The depth and extent of the services offered by Bel-Air are substantial. In its marketing brochure, the firm touts its services in the following manner:

> Our community patrol service tours your community. Patrol routes are carefully planned and reviewed for maximum security coverage....
> Armed patrol officers are highly trained to identify and discretely deal with any threat to your safety. We patrol communities to insure neighborhood safety and privacy from intruders....
> A highly visible patrol vehicle is assigned exclusively to your community providing continuous driving patrol within designated boundaries. This vehicle patrols only the streets of *your* community and *does not* leave your area to patrol or respond to alarms outside your community. With your *dedicated* patrol service, you and your community are assured of a *quick response* to any emergency call [Emphasis in original].

While much of the above language can be dismissed as mere marketing jargon, there are certain assertions made in the brochure which illuminate the implications of private policing. Specifically, the assertions which focus on any *threat to your safety,* and the references to *your community, dedicated patrol service,* and *quick response to any emergency call* appeal directly to the concern for crime, and to the natural human desire for safety and security. It is understandable that the firm would focus on these concerns. It is also understandable that individuals would desire safety and security. These views are not problematic in and of themselves. The problem, however, involves the larger constitutional and public policy issues surrounding these well-founded concerns. Indeed, these concerns have been raised in other arrangements. An overview of other supplemental arrangements will describe the relevant issues in more detail.

Grand Central Partnership

The Grand Central area within the city of New York consists of more than 6,000 businesses, comprising upward of 51 million square feet (Carlson, 1995: 67). To put this into perspective, the total square footage is roughly equal to the entire downtown area of Los Angeles. Each property owner is taxed an additional 12.5 cents per square foot. In 1994, this tax raised $6.3 million for the Grand Central Partnership. All of the tax revenue is returned to the district management association, which administers the program and hires a security force (Goldberg, 1994: 12). A spokesperson for the association emphasized that the program requires "layers of cooperation" with various city planning commissioners, assessment and tax officers, and the city council (Carlson, 1995: 68; and Goldberg, 1994: 12). The revenues and cooperative efforts with city officials provide many diverse services. Included in these goods and services are:

- Private street sweepers and trash collectors
- Garbage cans, street lighting and flower boxes
- Multilingual tour guides
- "Drop-in Centers" to feed and shelter the homeless
- Uniformed security guards

Clearly, the scope of this project goes beyond the traditional functions of security. However, the concept of "security" entails more than physical protection. As described earlier, the notion of security often includes the perceptions of people, the physical environment, and the inherent desire for order and safety. This is why the partnership sought to change the overall environment. This is the same approach used in the community policing model within public policing (Kolpacki, 1994: 47). The distinction is that Grand Central Partnership (G.C.P.) was accomplished with the use of private policing personnel by specific taxing initiatives, and arguably, at a much lower cost. But has it worked?

Carlson asserted that G.C.P. "helped transform the area around the train station from a chaotic mag of threatening streets into one of the safest sections of Manhattan" (Carlson, 1995: 67). Prior to the implementation of the privatized services, the *New York Times* described the area as "chaotic and forbidding, often filthy and sometimes dangerous" (Carlson, 1995). The New York City Police report that the arrangement has had a substantial statistical impact. After the first two years of operation, crime in the area was down 20 percent. In the third year, crime declined 36 percent. This result was called "phenomenal" by an assistant chief of police. After the fifth year, reported crime was down 53 percent (Carlson, 1995).

The reasons for the reduction of crime are varied. Some maintain that the guards perform tasks in a cost effective manner, and are more flexible (Carlson, 1995: 67; and Patterson, 1995: 33). Cost savings entail lower wages and more consistency of services. The consistency is derived from the security employees spending nearly all allotted time "on post" or "on beat." Conversely, police officers spend a much higher percentage of their allotted time making arrests, doing paperwork, testifying in court, running errands, etc. Further, the flexibility of this contracted arrangement allows for the property owners to assign guards to specific locations, without having to leave to answer service calls, as is required of the public police.

Other more concrete reasons for the reduction of crime were offered by two G.C.P. staffers. Gerald Panza, a retired N.Y.C. detective who now runs operations at G.C.P., asserted, "Police are involved with other matters, they cannot concentrate on the quality of life crime when they have major crimes." He continued, "We are the eyes and ears of the police department ... they appreciate our work because we try to solve some problems ourselves, without police intervention" (Carlson, 1995: 72). This assertion was echoed by William O'Conner, who stated, "We don't do homicides, we don't do rapes, but we do other quality of life things. We do the work the police have trouble getting [to] because they are so busy" (Carlson, 1995).

Unmistakably, both of these statements reflect an order maintenance focus. Statistics also demonstrate this focus. This can be shown, at least partly, by the workload handled by the security personnel. In 1994, the security personnel responded to 6,916 incidents, with only 624 requiring police assistance and only 122 resulting in arrest (Carlson, 1995). This serves as an indication that the security personnel handled more than 6,000 incidents without the involvement of New York City police. Theoretically, at least, this freed up the police to concentrate on other matters. One result of this cooperative effort is that police are able to focus on more serious crimes, with the bulk of the service and order maintenance duties shifted to security personnel. This is the model that I contend will take shape in contemporary America.

The required background characteristics and training for the private security personnel are substantially less than those of public police. The criteria are as follows (Carlson, 1995: 69):

- At least 18 years of age
- No recent felony convictions

- Reasonably upstanding and sober citizen
- High school graduate
- Preference for military service
- Pass psychological examination
- Pass a drug screening test

The training of the security personnel takes about seven days. The training curriculum focuses on legal issues (Carlson, 1995). Follow-up training, usually on "use of force" issues and security procedures, occurs weekly. Once hired, discipline is strictly enforced. According to Carlson, absenteeism or lateness, sloppy dress, smoking in public, and even minor rule violations are not tolerated (Carlson, 1995). Further, the security personnel wear distinct uniforms, intentionally designed to resemble New York City police. They — like the police — also wear radios and bullet proof vests.

Notwithstanding the cooperative efforts, training, and favorable statistics, many people — including police officers — are not totally convinced of the merits of this arrangement. The following statement sums up their reservations: "In the eyes of the police, guards [security personnel] seem to occupy a confusing gray area between public official and private citizen that many cops find disconcerting" (Carlson, 1995: 70).

This perception, however, is not universal. There is ample evidence that private citizens and property owners do not seem as concerned with issues such as government sovereignty and legal niceties. In fact, many believe that the issue is *security and safety*, not these "esoteric" issues like the government and the law. Surveyed business owners, such as Joel Oks, did not know what he paid for the security and, like many other property owners, he did not seem to care. Mr. Oks claimed that whatever the amount, the protection received is well worth it (Carlson, 1995). Still another property owner stated, "Before the security guards, there were no cops. Muggers would snatch a purse right in front of the store, and they would be laughing, not even running away.... They can't do that now. Without guards, it's like a jungle out there" (Carlson, 1995: 72).

This sort of reasoning validates the assertion in incivilities literature that crime or fear of crime is the overriding concern of these supplemental programs. Dan Biederman, during his tenure as president of the Grand Central Partnership, related this to the order maintenance function: "When a citizen sees prostitutes, graffiti, rough talking panhandlers, and poorly maintained buildings, he concludes that things are out of control and he foregoes use of that street" (Blyskal, 1996: 44).

Interestingly, much of the critique of this site also dealt with security concerns. There seemed to be less concern for the esoteric issues like the constitution. Hence, once again, the tension between personal security and constitutional rights typically errs on the side of security. Significantly, the articles cited here were published years prior to the 9/11 terrorist attacks. One can reasonably speculate that the desire for security is much more pronounced now than at the time the articles were published. Given this reality, the question that naturally follows is, what initiative arrangements will take place in the future? It is my opinion that these supplemental arrangements will be commonplace, possibly including more aggressive patrol techniques similar to the "tactical" approach described earlier.

CENTER CITY DISTRICT

Another example of supplemental security in a public environment is within the city of Philadelphia. In 1991, the city council approved the Center City District (C.C.D.), a private not-for-profit group responsible for administering the Business Improvement District (Seamon, 1995: 93). Seamon noted that in 1989, downtown Philadelphia was the site of significant police activity. The Central Police District, which serves the downtown area, reported 37 percent of its workload coming from this area (Seamon, 1995). Coupled with this rate of crime were the growing number of vacant commercial properties, unregulated vendors, homeless citizens and trash accumulating on the streets and sidewalks. This privatization arrangement was designed to address these incivilities.

The district covers eighty square blocks, with 2,087 property owners each paying a property tax surcharge equal to 5 percent of the current city real estate levy (Seamon, 1995). In 1994, their budget was $6.6 million. The budget is allocated to the following privately contracted services:

- 53 percent allocated to street cleaning and trash pick-up
- 33 percent allocated to public safety
- 7 percent allocated to administration
- 7 percent allocated to marketing

These budgetary allocations again illustrate that in order to impact crime, the concept of security must be broadly defined. Of course, the broad nature of the concept reflects the environmental and order maintenance focus. Seamon emphasized that a successful privatization program requires city officials, police authorities and security managers to work together in a way that promotes trust and creates bonds between the public and private sectors. Each party also must have a clear understanding of their respective role (Seamon, 1995). In accordance with these goals, C.C.D. set up its daily operations to foster collaboration. As such, the police assigned to C.C.D. and the security officers (called Community Service Representatives or C.S.R.s) share joint headquarters, and locker facilities, conduct joint roll calls and are regularly addressed by police detectives on current crime conditions (Seamon, 1995).

Statistics released by the Philadelphia Police Department reveal that from 1993 to 1994, crime decreased by 6 percent in the C.C.D. area. Comparatively, during the same period, crime increased by 1 percent within the Central Police Division. Data conducted in 1993 revealed that of the 2,000 persons surveyed, fully 78 percent felt that the central city (area encompassing C.C.D.) was more safe, or as safe, as the year before (Seamon, 1995).

The C.C.D. security force consists of 45–50 officers, with a training curriculum touching a wide number of areas. The training ranges from problem solving techniques, customer service, and hospitality aides to police procedures, use of force, radio communications, first aid, C.P.R., and victim assistance (Seamon, 1995; and Connors, et al., 2000). The minimum standards also include two years of college, an age of at least 21 years, and the completion of a background investigation (Seamon, 1995). The security personnel within this district have higher standards than typical guards within the security industry.

The duties of the security personnel consist of unarmed, uniformed service, acting as a supplement for police, as a public "concierge" and as neighborhood "watchers." They are equipped with radios which are interconnected with the police. The security personnel also use a computerized crime mapping system designed to enhance crime prevention methodologies. Unfortunately, the specific functions of the security personnel were somewhat vague.

DOWNTOWN ST. LOUIS

In a similar privatization arrangement, the St. Louis Metropolitan Police Department and a private security company have entered into a supplemental relationship in which private uniformed security personnel patrol the central city. The private security force is operated through a special tax district which was initially created in the late 1950s. The tax district encompasses all of downtown St. Louis, and is administered by Downtown St. Louis, Inc., a private not-for-profit chamber of commerce. Property owners within the district pay a tax surcharge, which is collected by the city and state, then redistributed to the district (Mokwa and Stoehner, 1995: 94). The revenues are used to pay for the following services:

- Market the area's attractions
- Provide special events
- Provide private security

The focal point of the tax revenues was to "guarantee" business owners their own security protection (Mokwa and Stoehner, 1995). The business district is divided into 12 different beats, with a particular allotment from both security and the police. The security personnel consist of a patrol force of 6 to 30 officers, depending upon the time or particular event. The St. Louis Police Department allocates 10 patrol vehicles and 30 foot patrol officers to the downtown area. Also, some off-duty police officers serve on the security force. Partly because of the interrelationship between the security force and the police, the security personnel have the same powers of arrest as police. Security officers wear uniforms, and walk their beats—using reasonable force when necessary to stop a crime (Mokwa and Stoehner, 1995).

The selection and training criteria are more varied and sophisticated than in previous examples. For example, the selection criteria includes factors such as an outgoing personality, knowledge of the St. Louis metro area, two year's prior experience in the security industry, a psychological test, and several personal interviews. The training consists of a 16 hour course designed and administered by the St. Louis Police Department. The training stresses police policies and procedures. The security firm also conducts a 16 hour course focusing on a public relations curriculum. When the training is completed, the security officers are licensed by the St. Louis Police Department, and are given arrest authority by the city's police board (Mokwa and Stoehner, 1995). In this sense, the private police officers are vested with "special police" powers.

This supplemental role of private security has been credited with a reduction in the rate of crime. Mokewa and Stoehner assert that this partnership has "proven successful" (1995: 94). The limited statistical evidence provides some support for this assertion. The total number of crimes in downtown St. Louis declined almost 10 percent in one year (from 306 in 1993 to 276 in 1994). Further, auto theft rates dropped 31 percent in the same year (Mokwa and Stoehner, 1995). Consequently, these statistics bring to light the fact, or the impression, that privatization arrangements contribute to the reduction of crime.

GREATER GREEN POINT MANAGEMENT DISTRICT

The Greater Green Point Management District (G.G.P.M.D.) encompasses a twelve square mile section within the city limits of Houston, Texas. This district has a mix of residential and commercial properties. Between 1980 and 1990, the population within the district grew substantially. Coupled with the population increase were a dramatic rise in crime and a general deterioration in the conditions within the district (Robinson, 1996). Statistics collected by the Houston Police Department revealed that from 1986 to 1991, crime increased 25 percent and calls for service increased 46 percent. At the same time, the number of officers assigned to the area decreased 22 percent (Robinson, 1996).

At least partially due to these factors, local property owners within the district petitioned the state legislature to create the Greater Green Point Management District. The state legislature approved the district in 1991. A tax levy of 10 cents per $100 of the assessed property value was established against each parcel of real property (Robinson, 1996).

The district is administered by a 22 member board of directors appointed by the governor. Included in the board is an executive director who is in charge of operations, and a security manager who is in charge of security and public safety. The security manager caused a comprehensive public safety program to be implemented based on surveys conducted by the district administrators. The findings of the survey revealed that business owners were in "absolute terror" due to the growing crime problem (Robinson, 1996). Among other results was the realization that police call response ranged from 14 to 15 minutes for emergency calls, and almost 2 hours for non-emergency calls (Robinson, 1996). These figures created a substantial and compelling need for more responsive services. The solution was to enact a series of initiatives aimed at reducing crime and improving the conditions in the district.

The initiative included hiring additional police officers, and supplementing these officers with private security personnel. The district was to pay all costs and salaries associated with the increases in public safety personnel. The costs for such amounted to approximately $400,000 per year. Further, the district opened a new police substation, which was donated by a large shopping mall (Robinson, 1996). The police and security personnel were stationed at this facility.

These initiatives—and others—were said to have contributed to a significant reduction in crime. The crime rate in the district dropped 25 percent in the year following the implementation of the initiatives. Further, the occupancy rate of business units within the district rose to one of the highest in the City of Houston (Robinson, 1996). In short, the arrangement was deemed to have contributed to the betterment of the overall environment in the city.

GEORGETOWN

Another example of the success of privatization is the Georgetown section of Washington, D.C. This model differs from the aforementioned in that the security was paid for by residential property owners. About 100 homeowners paid $160.00 per year (equal to 44 cents per day per household) to hire one security guard to patrol a six block area (Carlson, 1995). After one year, residents found their streets transformed. Statistics revealed a 55 percent decrease in burglaries and a 50 percent reduction in robberies (Carlson, 1995). The decrease in crime was so dramatic and substantial, other neighborhoods within Georgetown began hiring guards. Within a year about 90 percent of Georgetown neighborhoods hired security guards (Carlson, 1995).

STARRETT CITY

In the case of Starrett City, the supplemental use of private security is not confined to rich neighborhoods or central business districts. The Starrett City housing development in Brooklyn is a classic model of the benefits of privatization. The development is about 60 percent white, 40 percent black, with 90 percent of its residents receiving government rent subsidies (Carlson, 1995: 70). The development is located in the 75th precinct, which has consistently one of the highest murder rates in New York City (Carlson, 1995: 70; and Walsh, et al., 1992: 163).

The private police officers were hired by the management company which administers the development. By the late 1980s, 60 private police officers were employed, with about 40 armed. Each private police officer has the status of "special police" with full arrest powers. In total, these private police personnel handle about 10,000 service calls each year (Carlson, 1995). The average salary is $31,000 per year, about 70 percent of an average police officer's salary.

Carlson observes that twenty years after hiring security, Starrett City remains as safe as any affluent neighborhood. In 1994, the community of 20,000 people reported only 24 car thefts, 12 burglaries, 6 aggravated assaults and no reported rapes (Walsh, et al., 1992: 165). In the same year, Carlson (1995) noted that the complex reported just 67 robberies, compared to 2,548 reported in the neighborhood just outside its boundaries.

In New York City proper, there were 84 felonies reported per 1,000 residents, while Starrett City reported just 7 felonies per 1,000. Similarly, in the 75th Precinct, a residence was 38 times more likely to be burglarized than in Starrett City (Walsh, et al., 1992). Significantly, there is no boundary in terms of fences or any other physical barriers separating Starrett City from the rest of the 75th Precinct. The only real "physical" distinction is the security guards. The difference between the neighborhoods is so pervasive that a Starrett City security supervisor described the complex as "an oasis in a vast wilderness" (Carlson, 1995: 70).

This is apparently a widespread belief among Starrett City residents. In a survey conducted by Penn State University, almost 90 percent of the residents said that they felt "somewhat or very safe" living in the complex, whereas only 40 percent felt similarly secure outside its boundaries (Carlson, 1995: 70). The survey further revealed that 90 percent of the residents believed the complex would not be safe without its private security, and over 50 percent said they would leave the area if the private police left (Walsh, et al., 1992: 168). Another indication of the residents' commitment to private security, 78 percent said, if assaulted, they would call security before calling the police (Walsh, et al., 1992). In fact, the complex receives only part-time coverage from two police officers. This is so even though the complex accounts for about 16 percent of the population in the 75th police precinct (Walsh, et al., 1992). The authors concluded that without private policing, Starrett City would not be a secure residential environment (Walsh, et al., 1992).

These examples provide compelling illustrations of the effectiveness of privatization. They illustrate the continued and growing need for cooperative efforts between private and public police. These examples, indeed, demonstrate that such cooperative efforts have been successful in combating crime. In this sense, these examples show that security and police create a natural combination of talent and resources. The mission of crime prevention within the security industry, coupled with the ability of the police to arrest and prosecute offenders, provides a dynamic combination of skills and resources. Consequently, the present focus on community policing may act as a precursor toward the widespread establishment of privatized public safety services.

Nonetheless, a difficult and uncertain transition lies ahead. Functional, constitutional, and public policy considerations remain problematic, as one can see in the following case study.

VII

Marquette Park:
A Case Study

Given that this book is designed to assess the functional and constitutional implications of private police patrols on public streets, the exploratory case study focuses on a particular research site to better shed light on this phenomenon. Prior to presenting the case study, a couple of caveats must be discussed.

First, this research focuses on a case study of a community within the City of Chicago. This community is unique because it is the only area within the city, or even in the state, which provides private patrols on public streets. As described in the previous chapter, there are only a handful of similar sites throughout the country (i.e., Grand Central Partnership, Central City District, and Starrett City). This site was selected because it is representative of similar arrangements like those just mentioned, and its location allowed in-depth study without the constraints of travel.

Most research dealing with this subject is devoid of any data analysis—other than basic crime statistics and demographics. Most research addresses the topic purely in a theoretical manner—usually discussing in broad terms the legal or political implications of the phenomenon. These works do not test any particular hypotheses. They simply discuss—albeit important—legal and political concerns raised by the use of privatized public safety. This case study seeks to go beyond the theory centered pieces, to provide a deeper analysis of the phenomenon.

Those studies with a data analysis component, however, address this phenomenon from an analysis of crime and survey data. These studies seem only concerned with narrow questions such as the impact of privatization on crime rates in the protected area, or the perception of citizens as to the effectiveness of the private patrols. While these are important considerations, these studies fail to address certain basic questions related to the use of privatized patrol services. That is, what specific functions do private patrol officers perform, how do they do so, and are their actions consistent with applicable constitutional protections? These larger issues have been addressed in a number of publications; however, they were done from a theoretical perspective — without data to support the well founded concerns of constitutional and public policy implications (see Shearing and Stenning, 1983; Johnston, 1992; Reynolds, 1994; Zielinski, 1999; Shenk, 1995; Hebdon, 1995; and Maghan, 1998; for examples of research addressing these larger questions). This case study takes a different approach. It is designed to test some of the concerns raised in these theory-based works, using data beyond crime rates or surveys.

The second caveat is that a development of an empirical analysis of private policing is potentially a very costly endeavor. One obvious way for a researcher to address the functional and constitutional questions raised in this study would be to conduct an analysis of several existing sites. As illustrated from the previous chapter, such a study is possible in that there are similar arrangements that can be compared and contrasted. For example, in many of these sites, private officers patrolled the community in conjunction with the local police department. These arrangements were similar to this case study site. That is, private patrol services were paid from property taxes. Their services were designed to provide an additional protection from crime. Additionally, the private officers were said to focus their attention on order maintenance. However, there is not much information as to how the patrols were performed. Specifically, there is no hard data on what functions the officers actually performed, how they performed these functions, and whether they performed them in a manner consistent with the constitution.

Fortunately, the site selection of this study was both convenient and illustrative of similar arrangements. While this research could have been conducted at any number of sites (i.e. Grand Central Partnership, Central City District, and Starrett City), this would be an extremely expensive endeavor, particularly since ride-alongs were used to collect data in this study. The time and logistical constraints related to the use of ride-alongs, and even for interviews, is substantial. Of course, the convenience factor, while important in terms of financial constraints, does not justify the selection of the site. The key issue related to this site is whether the conclusions derived from the data can be generalized to describe the larger phenomenon. Given the similarities to private patrols in other cities, this case study could be used to replicate generalized conclusions about private policing. This would be particularly relevant for other sites which use private security firms to supplement the local police in a clearly public environment.

Finally, as with any small sample research, there are reliability questions which naturally come to mind (see Fenno, 1978; Diesing, 1971; King, et al, 1994; and Dexter, 1970). Reliability involves the use of specific measurement instruments and observations. I was very careful to limit error or bias, particularly in the participant observations. This was accomplished — at least partly — through the desire to make the respondents feel as natural as possible as they performed their job.

Community Characteristics

The case study site consists of Marquette Park Special Service Area #14 on the southwest side of Chicago. The boundaries of the special service area are from 67th Street on the north to 74th Street on the south, Kedzie Avenue on the west and Bell Street on the east. Included within the area is approximately one half of Marquette Park, which is part of Chicago's vast park district system. Hence, the name of the special service district — and the neighborhood — reflects the name of the park district.

The neighborhood consists of a mixture of single family residences, two and three story apartment buildings and strips of businesses largely confined to the main arteries. The main arteries are found on Western and Kedzie avenues and on 67th, 69th and 71st streets. Many of these businesses serve as hangouts for young people in the area. Some of these youths appear to be gang members. Partly because of this perception, many of the business owners are fearful of their presence. Others seemed to cater to them, either for business or possibly for protection. Indeed, the presence of loiterers, particularly gang members, was a key concern within the community — and of the patrol program.

The largest concentration of apartment buildings is on the east side of the neighborhood. These apartment buildings are often poorly maintained or neglected to some extent. Most of the single family houses are generally better kept, yet some were showing signs of disrepair. The majority of the deteriorated homes were found on the east side of the community.

The streets are similar to a typical Chicago neighborhood, with trees on the parkways between the street and the sidewalk. Most streets are one-way, except the main thoroughfares, such as Western, California, Sacramento, and Kedzie avenues. In short, the area is typical, in terms of urban setting, of any neighborhood within the city. One possible exception to this assertion is the park — Marquette Park — which is one of the largest, or the largest, in Chicago.

The special service area is part of the 8th Police District, which is based at 3515 West 63rd Street. The District Commander at the time of the study was James J. Molloy. This police district is broken into 16 different beats, and is one of the largest districts — both in terms of land area and population — within the City of Chicago. According to the 1990 census, the 8th District has a total population of 207,481. Of the total population, there are 163,554 white residents; 22,135 African-American residents; 2,333 Asian-American residents; and 33,666 Hispanic residents.

As of this writing, the demographics for the 2000 census have not been broken down into district level of analysis. Therefore, at this time the current demographics within the 8th police district are not available.

Crime statistics within the 8th District reveal a moderate level of crime as compared to the city as a whole. For example, in 1998 the number of reported criminal sexual assaults numbered 113, an increase of 13.0 percent from the previous year. Reported aggravated assaults numbered 1,285 in 1998 and increased 5.4 percent, while known murders numbered 31 in 1998 and declined 26.2 percent, reported robberies numbered 1,016 in 1998 and declined 7.2 percent, reported burglaries numbered 2,656 in 1998 and were down 2.9 percent, and reported motor vehicle thefts numbered 2,213 in 1998 and declined 10.3 percent.

Implementation and Administration of the Private Patrols

The special service area is essentially a separate taxing entity within the City of Chicago. The district was established in 1995 to provide private security patrols. The decision to hire private security patrols was done, at least partly, to stabilize the community. At that time, there was substantial evidence that residents within the community were moving from the area. This flight of longtime residents — in a community with generational ties dating back to the early 1900s and even earlier — created the desire to stop, or at least slow, the demographic changes within the area.

Prior to seeking council resolution, certain community groups petitioned to have a referendum placed on the ballot. At issue was whether property owners desired to increase their real estate taxes for the purpose of hiring private security patrols. These private patrols would supplement the police department to reduce crimes and to minimize the conditions which foster crime, thus stabilizing the community.

There are certain requirements for the creation of a special services district such as this. First, a referendum had to be held to determine if the residents within the affected area desired the creation of the district. This was done. The referendum was successful. After the referendum passed, the matter was referred to the city council. The establishment of the district was accomplished pursuant to a resolution passed by the Chicago City Council. The council resolution provided the legal authority for the Cook County Collector to levy and collect real estate taxes from property owners within the district, established as Special Services District #14.

The city council provided a three year renewal provision for the special service district. This provision allows community residents to maintain an ongoing decision making process relative to the private patrols. It provides for a semi-formal hearing where residents can express their support of or opposition to the private patrols. This case study includes the results of a hearing on December 5, 1997. Pursuant to procedural requirements, public notice of the hearing had to be published. The notice said that if a petition is signed by at least 51 percent of the electors residing within the boundaries of the proposed area *and* by at least fifty one percent (51 percent) of the area's landowners, then the district would be disbanded and the service tax would not be levied on real property in the district. Of course, the service tax is designed to provide security services, including necessary administrative expenses related to the patrols. The notice further provided that the service tax shall not exceed the sum of forty-one hundredths of one percent (.41) of the equalized assessed value of taxable property within the area. The hearing resulted in the district being sustained, and the private patrols continued until the expiration of another three year period.

The special service district is administered in the following manner. Once it is established by the city council, the alderman in the affected ward (15th ward) selects individuals for the governing commission. Those eligible for selection to the commission must either be residents or business owners in the community. Once selected by the alderman, the candidate must pass a background check, focusing on whether the individual owes the city for outstanding traffic or parking tickets or utility bills. Clearly, these are not stringent professional requirements. Indeed, it can be argued that the selection process is purely political, with the only real criteria the desires of the alderman. In this way, the "background" checks appear to be designed to avoid political embarrassment, in the event that a commission member owed money to the city. Nonetheless, once these checks are performed, the candidate is then officially appointed by Chicago's mayor. Once appointed, each commission member serves a two year term.

There are seven voting members within the governing commission. Each politically appointed commission member is deemed a voting member. The commission also contains three non-voting members, including the commander of the 8th Police District, and two officials who represent the City of Chicago Department of Planning and Development. These non-voting members are supposed to provide guidance and advice to the voting members of the commission. The governing commission is charged with the oversight of the special services district. This entails preparing a budget, conducting periodic community meetings, and arranging all applicable administrative manners to operate the private security patrols.

The budget to operate and administer the security patrols is ample. The monies within the budget come from the tax levy on real property within the special services district. According to the governing commission, the cost for the average property owner is about $50 to $60 per year. The total budget for each fiscal year is approximately $200,000. Of this figure, approximately $140,000 to $150,000 goes to the security provider, about $5,000 for insurance, $20,000 for legal fees and other professional services, and the remainder goes to office expenses and administrative costs.

The day to day affairs and other administrative manners are handled directly by the "sole service provider," the administrator of the special services district. Since the establishment of the special services district, the sole service provider has been the Lithuanian Human Services Council. This community based organization acts as the intermediary between the community and the governing commission. In this regard, the organization deals directly with the security firm, discussing crime patterns and incidents, as well as performing other operational and administrative tasks, such as obtaining legal counsel and insurance carriers.

The Lithuanian Human Service Council is also charged with hiring and contracting with the security firm. This occurs after the governing commission makes the selection based on a vote of board members. The hiring of the particular security firm is accomplished through two separate contracts. One contract is between the City of Chicago and the sole service provider (the Lithuanian Human Services Council). The second contract is between the sole service provider and the security firm. Contract documents are drafted by the City of Chicago Department of Law. Oversight of the entire process is accomplished by the city's Department of Planning and Development.

The proposal and contract process of selecting the security firm is rather lengthy and complicated. Initially, the sole service provider is required to advertise that it is accepting proposals from firms that might be interested in providing the service. This legal notice published in local newspapers, includes the requirements for any prospective firm who desires to be considered for the private patrols. At the time of this study, they were:

- Must have a minimum of 5 years experience in security field, and the firm must be licensed, bonded, and insured by State of Illinois.
- Uniformed guards (minimum of two per shift) must be assigned to patrol in an automobile.
- Security officers must have successfully completed an outside training program.
- Must provide a late model, full size, four door vehicle equipped with radio dispatching capabilities, Mars lights, alley lights, spot lights, and a designed logo.
- Must maintain a patrol log and provide this information on a daily basis to the contractor.

The security firm's proposal must show that it can meet these requirements. In order to facilitate the contract process, a model proposal was prepared by city attorneys. It provides two important criteria, which need to be addressed more fully. First, the proposal requires a legal representative of the security firm to affirm and warrant it utilizes a training program for its employees. The requirements for such a training program, however, are not addressed in the proposal. Instead, the document simply requires the security firm to describe its training program. It does not require any standards nor does it provide any specific training guidelines.

Second, the proposal outlines three types of functions to be performed by the private patrols. While the specific functions are not stated or defined, they are implied in the language. They are observe and report, order maintenance, and law enforcement. The proposal states:

Security Firm agrees to provide security in SSA (Special Service Area) 14 comprised of mobile patrols (and foot patrols when and where required as designated by Contractor) on the streets and in the alleys of SSA 14; *report any suspected or actual criminal activity to the police; where practicable, detain individuals who are believed to have committed criminal offenses until the police arrive and take charge of the investigation and/or arrest; and sign court complaints and/or appear in court as witnesses as may be required for the prosecution of criminal offenders*[8] [emphasis added].

This language provides the private police officers with a contractual duty to perform a number of functions, including the arrest and prosecution of criminal offenders.

Upon submission of the proposals, the sole services provider, the Lithuanian Human Services Council, prepares the bid documents to facilitate a comparative analysis. The analysis entails laying out certain criteria articulated in the model proposal in a row and column format. The rows break out the respective criteria, such as hourly rate; vehicle, operational and court costs; firm experience and licenses; and other administrative matters. The bid amount, in terms of actual dollars, is the key factor in the selection process. As with other governmental contracts, the contract is awarded to the firm that is qualified to perform the services and that offers the lowest bid. However, any review of the criteria will reveal that the distinction from one firm to the next is largely based on money. This can be seen in the supporting documents, which address cost issues such as holidays, vehicle expenses and operational costs.

Once these bids are prepared and analyzed, the actual selection of the security firm is accomplished by a vote of the governing commission. This occurs at an open meeting called for this purpose. The selection by the commission seems fairly *pro forma* (a formality) since the commission is required to take the qualified firm with the lowest bid. While there may be theoretical disputes as to what a "qualified firm" entails, the criterion for what constitutes qualified is, at best, basic. Worse yet, almost any security firm (or an affiliated company) with five years experience and a state license could be deemed "qualified." Therefore, the selection tends to be determined by the bid amount. This view was confirmed during the study. I was present at the selection of the Majestic Protective Services, Inc., which was awarded the contract based on the lowest bid amount, without any meaningful comment or question by commission members.

The implementation and administration of the private patrols is illustrated in the flow chart on page 109:

The Security Firms

Two security firms were associated with this research during its eight-month span. The two firms operated in the patrol capacity and were studied for four months each. One firm, Majestic Protective Services, Inc., was actually contracted at the commencement of this research. This firm permitted me to conduct ride-alongs, which allowed me to be a direct observer in the study. The research related to the other firm, American Security Ser-

---

Figure 4
Private Patrol Implementation Flow Chart

COMMUNITY PETITIONS REFERENDUM

CHICAGO CITY COUNCIL
Passed Referendum

SPECIAL SERVICE DISTRICT ENACTED

COMMUNITY GOVERNING COMMISSION FORMED

PROPERTY TAX INITIATIVE INSTITUTED

Upon passage of the referendum, and the enactment and
formation of the Special Service District, the Property Tax
Initiative and the Community Governing Commission,
the city required certain contracts to be drafted and executed.
The contracts were drafted by attorneys from the City of
Chicago, by and between the following parties:

CITY OF CHICAGO

SOLE SERVICE PROVIDER

SECURITY FIRM

---

vices, Inc., was limited to the analysis of documentary evidence, including four months of daily reports.

Both of the security firms executed the same type of contract documents, designed to provide the same service. Specifically, the contract documents with the City of Chicago and the Lithuanian Human Services Council (sole service provider) state that the security firm shall provide "security services" in the Marquette Park Special Service Area. While the term "security services" was not defined in the contract documents, the use of security services can be broadly construed to include anything from arrests to street cleaning and garbage collection. At this case study site, however, the functions of the security providers were limited to patrol services. As such, pursuant to contract terms, the service provision provided by the two firms was supposed to be identical.

The operation of each firm, as reflected in the contracts and reporting documents, appear to be roughly similar. Generally speaking, each firm reported to the same commission and sole service provider, each firm hired individuals who wore similar attire, and each firm was charged with the contractual duty to patrol the streets and properties of the Marquette Park neighborhood.

Based on observations and interviews, the attire wore by patrol officers of both firms appeared consistent. Specifically, each individual officer was armed with handguns and other police equipment, such as handcuffs, flashlights, radios, and bullet proof vests. Each officer wore "civilian dress" clothing, which looked almost identical to the attire wore by Chicago Police tactical officers. The vehicles were also similar, usually unmarked Ford or Chevrolet makes and models typically used by police departments. An exception to this typical mode was one vehicle used by Majestic Protective Services, Inc., which was marked with the words "Marquette Park Patrol" on the front doors. In all other ways, the firms, at least in terms of physical and symbolic appearances, were almost identical, both in relation to each other and with tactical police officers of the Chicago Police Department.

Research Questions and Techniques

This case study is designed to assess the functions of private police officers as they patrol the research site, and investigate whether their functions conform to constitutional prohibitions. The reasoning behind this analysis is related to the most basic question: *What* are these individuals doing in their patrols? Essentially, the functional alternatives can be confined to three broad categories of public safety. They are law enforcement, order maintenance, and traditional security functions (i.e., observe and report). In this sense, the research methods employed in this study (i.e., ride-alongs, interviews and document analysis) will assess these broad functional categories.

The law enforcement function involves serious criminal activities, which would involve an investigative, enforcement or arrest situation. This category includes crimes such as weapons offenses; assisting police or actually apprehending criminals; and responding to victims of violence, including, rapes, thefts, robberies, assault and battery, and the like. The crimes in this category involve enforcement functions that are traditionally the domain of public police. These functions, however, are not confined to the public police. Consequently, this case study examines whether private patrols of public streets will include the involvement of private police officers in law enforcement functions.

The order maintenance function entails incivility activities, such as loitering, public drinking, drug usage, street disturbances, graffiti damage and other ordinance violations or less serious crimes or misdemeanors. Previous research shows that the presence of such disorderly conduct and conditions tends to lead to more serious crimes. Indeed, the use of order maintenance techniques have been shown to be an effective way to combat such behavioral and environmental factors that may lead to more serious crimes. Of course, order maintenance techniques are also an important component of community policing.

Consequently, this research assesses whether order maintenance techniques, made popular in community policing, will be predictive of the functional approach used by private police patrols. Based on the reasons described earlier, private police are likely to perform a similar function as public police in such an environment. This is, at least partly, due to the similar nature and characteristics of community policing, and in relation to the nature and characteristics of private security. The common characteristics include the desire to please the client, and responsiveness to the decision makers. Private security patrols are likely to focus on the needs of the taxpayers (their clients) within the special service district. Since public police departments have traditionally been less attentive to such incivility matters, it was predicted that the private security patrols would focus their attention on the behaviors and conditions which manifest such incivilities.

In contrast to both law enforcement and order maintenance, traditional security functions, termed "observe and report," entail routine matters such as premise and business checks, locking park gates, and other deterrence or client service functions. These are typical services which private security has traditionally provided in private properties and environments. Their duty is to "observe" and then immediately "report" such to the public police. The rationale is that the security personnel are the "eyes and ears" of the community (or the client), with the public police being the enforcers of law and order. On private property, these functions are designed to ensure safe premises, and provide a certain level of deterrence from crime.

The question in the context of this research, however, is whether private police will perform a similar function while patrolling public streets. While it was expected that this traditional security role would be part of the private police patrols, it likely would entail a more limited percentage of their functions. This statement is based on the notion that the property owners did not volunteer to spend their own money to provide security services to local businesses. Consequently, since the contract documents required security patrols, it is unlikely that a client oriented security firm would devote much time to traditional security services.

Based on the analysis presented above, this study will assess three different, but related, propositions. First, the private police officers in this site should be deemed as "state actors." Second, of the three functional categories described above, these private police officers will employ order maintenance techniques as their most common and pervasive function. Third, the employment of private police officers patrolling public streets will result in incidents in which they violate certain constitutional prohibitions, as a direct consequence of their involvement in law enforcement and order maintenance functions.

In assessing each of these propositions, a key distinction between private and public police is the nature of the authority vested in their roles. Police officers are sworn law enforcement officers, while most of the personnel involved in this case study are not sworn peace officers. This distinction is critical. While the legal authority to effect arrest is not greatly different, the level of training, knowledge of the law, report writing, and the depth of understanding relative to police behavioral and operational issues are substantially different.

The research techniques used in this case involve "ride-alongs," formal interviews of key participants, and an extensive document analysis. The purpose of these research techniques is to assess how the private police officers function in their job, and whether such functions may result in constitutional violations—or at least raise serious constitutional questions. A brief explanation of each such technique shall follow.

This case study commenced with a series of ride-alongs while the private police officers performed their patrol duties and functions. With this vantage point, I had the opportunity to directly observe the actions of the private police officers as they performed their job: patrolling the streets and properties of the Marquette Park neighborhood. With this observational technique, I was able to utilize each human sense to assess and understand the substantial data derived from each encounter. I also had a direct vantage point to assess the decision making process of the private police officers, which was facilitated by exposure to communications, both verbal and non-verbal, from each participant during the patrols.

Such observations allowed me to partake in the most subtle aspects surrounding the phenomenon of private policing, including the expressions, tone of voice, body gestures, attitudes, and statements of the participants. While these observations were usually impossible to directly record, such insight provided excellent contextual flavor for this research. In this way, such observations enhanced my ability to understand the relationship between the participants, as well as the actual and perceived role(s) of the private police officers. The participants included, but were not limited to, private and public police officers, crime victims, witnesses, complainants, and even criminal suspects. Consequently, these ride-alongs provided the opportunity to observe each of these participants during numerous incidents.

It should be noted that riding around in the patrol car is a very familiar experience. I spent seven years as a street police officer, five of those as a tactical officer in a gang crime unit. At the time, the gang crime unit was probably the most active enforcement unit within the Chicago Police Department. During these years, I spent countless hours patrolling the streets of Chicago. Almost all of this time was spent in high crime areas on the south side, sometimes in the very neighborhood where the private patrols took place. Consequently, I know the neighborhood, and I am very familiar — and comfortable — in this patrol function.

In essence, patrolling is a people watching endeavor. Most of the time is spent looking at people, analyzing circumstances, and making judgments (or reading gut feelings) about seemingly innocuous events. While sitting in a patrol car, one of things you do is look for people's reactions when they see "the police." Do they look into your eyes? Do they make any gesture, even the slightest indicator to demonstrate that they have sometime to hide or that they do not wish to talk to the police? Does the pedestrian turn and go the other direction when the patrol car turns the corner? When you see a car in an alley, or double parked in front of an area where teens are loitering, does that trigger any suspicions? Many of these seemingly innocuous circumstances raise suspicions to a good street cop.

These and many other "innocent" things occur on the street, every day and everywhere. Most such things are, in fact, innocent. Many people are fearful or resentful of the police and do not want to be noticed by them. So they do not look at them. When they noticeably avoid looking at the police, then this is an indicator that they *may* have something to hide. This can be a source of tension to both the citizen and the police. Of course, officers are not mind readers so they should stop and talk to the person. If this is done respectfully, it is usually sufficient to alleviate the suspicion of the police officer, and the fear or resentment of the citizen. Obviously, this can also result in conflict or difficult encounters. But it must be done — that is it should be done — if the police care about stopping crime and the citizens care about living in a neighborhood where criminals are actively sought out by the police.

Similarly, many people park their cars in garages which are only accessible from the alley. Alleys are also the locations of drug dealings, armed robberies and garage burglaries. It is difficult, or even impossible, to know the difference unless you stop and talk to people there. Numerous other examples can be illustrated. Think of any action that you have taken on a street, coming out of a store, or from an alley, which may have seemed peculiar. This is what a good street cop will look for. Of course, if you are 55 or older, the likelihood that you were committing some illicit activity is far less than if an 18–30 year old male made the exact same peculiar action. Based on statistical crime probabilities, there are substantial differences in these two examples. This, in a nutshell, is the nature of patrol.

The observations from the case study provided substantial information for observation and analysis. To record the data, particularly in fluid and sometimes dangerous situations, I kept a running log of the type of incidents in which the private police were involved. The data obtained from these incidents were often kept in liberal but discreet notes. My technique was to ask the respondent officers if they would mind if I made a "few notes." In each case, they stated it was all right to do so. However, I never made a big deal of the note taking. I simply kept a running log of incidents during the ride-alongs. I usually noted key phrases to trigger the event in my memory — and then later completed narrative reports, using these notes to jog my memory. For example, in one ride-along, a respondent noted that his supervisor was disliked by the 8th district police officers. In order to develop this conversation, I noted the term he used in the conversation, "bad paper," on my notepad.

The use of this log (or notepad), however, was usually discreet. In order to maintain an atmosphere of trust, and to provide for natural responses and conduct, I worked hard to try to blend into the environment. Often this required me to be silent and simply observe the incident, or to listen to the words and characterizations of the participants. Other times, I would ask pointed questions or make certain statements to facilitate conversation with the officers. Sometimes when the context was appropriate, I would ask the officers direct questions, and write their responses on my notepad. In every instance, however, I sought to limit any artificial or contrived responses, including impacting conduct which is not in accord with their normal job style and functions.

During the course of each ride-along, I would also list relevant incidents, making some assessment as to functionality, and whether such actions were grounded on proper constitutional procedures. I would transfer and develop this data — and any other appropriate notation — into a narrative form immediately after the completion of the ride-along so the recollection of the events would be more accurate. The narrative was a descriptive explanation of each tour. It presented and discussed the relevant data derived from the ride-along (or the informal interviews). These data sources were also used to provide a contextual understanding of the case study and the respondents. The desire was to provide an explanatory component of the private patrols, complete with relevant observations, quotations, and analysis.

I conducted informal interviews during the quiet moments of the tour. I typically used informal, open ended questions to facilitate a fluid conversation flow. The interviews were designed to elicit certain relevant information from the officers, such as their background, training, and approach to the job. Further, questions gauging the knowledge of their authority — and limitations — as it relates to the power of arrest, and search and seizure were probed. I also inquired about actions or decisions in particular incidents which occurred during the tour. For example, I would inquire why a particular decision was made, what was the perception of the participants, and what was their understanding as to their authority to intervene or resolve a particular incident. In this sense, the interviews were compared to the observations noted in the ride-alongs. Their responses could then be assessed to determine whether the behaviors of the respondents conform to their stated attitudes and knowledge. Consequently, the process can be assessed on a continuum of "observed" to "expected."

Another research technique was to conduct formal interviews with key individuals involved in the security patrols. These individuals included representatives of the security firm, the sole service provider, and of the oversight commission.

Each of these interviews took place in an off-site setting, and consisted of open ended, structured questions designed to elicit specific facts and perceptions related to the private security patrols. The questions were tailored to answer the two broad research questions. What are the functions of the private police officers? Do their actions conform to constitutional standards?

It must be noted that this research technique involved the assessment of communications contained in the interviews. Of course, it is difficult to determine from interview questions whether constitutional violations would occur from the private patrols. However, *an understanding* of the constitutional questions can be derived from these interviews. In this sense, the technical legal determination becomes somewhat irrelevant. Instead, the question can be answered to the extent that the key participants exhibit a level of concern or thoughtfulness for the constitutional issues raised by the private patrol program. Indeed, the responses to these questions exhibit either concern for the issue, or not.

Evidence of concern will be determined by more than just rhetoric. Another way to test this question is whether or not policies and procedures have been developed to address the constitutionality of the functions performed by the private police officers. The failure to develop such policies and procedures can be used as a key indicator to determine that constitutional implications may have been overshadowed by more pragmatic concerns, such as financial, political, and administrative issues. The failure to implement such policies and procedures, consequently, would leave the resolution of constitutionality decisions to the patrol officers themselves.

It is important to emphasize that most of these patrol officers are not sworn police officers. They possess little or no training or experience in the nuances of legal authority and constitutional law. In fact, to meet Illinois licensing requirements, private security officers are only required 40 hours of training. Of these hours, only 8–10 involve any constitutional, or search and seizure, training. Consequently, the failure to implement policies and procedures would indicate that, at best, there are no protections to prevent constitutional violations.

I also devoted substantial attention to analyzing documents derived from the security patrols. The documentary analysis involved the following:

- Daily incident and security reports
- Police arrest and case reports
- Company policy and procedures
- Contractual agreements
- Legal documents including complaints, motions, etc.

These documents provide substantial data as to the nature of the security patrols. Specifically, the policies and procedures, and other internal documents and memorandums derived from the security firms, provide critical information and inferences. What do these documents say about the functions of the patrol officers? Do they provide specific guidelines to be used by the security officers? Further, as related above, do policies and procedures address appropriate guidelines to be used as directives for constitutional concerns? In essence, these documents provide insight into the level of sophistication of the security firm. In general, the more substantial and comprehensive the documents, the more standardized the performance of the patrol officers is likely to be. Conversely, the failure to articulate defined policies and procedures illustrates that the security firm does not function as a professional policing organization. The failure to provide such guidance may result in a loose or undisciplined security force.

Since accountability within the security firm is closely related to the constitutional question raised in this research, the procedures and policies related to accountability will be compared to those established by the Chicago Police Department.

As a comparative example, the Chicago Police Department has instituted significant procedural requirements related to citizen complaints about the police. Depending upon the nature and severity of the complaint, there are three different entities which can conduct the investigation: the Office of Professional Standards (which is a citizen review organization), the Internal Affairs Division (which consists of sworn police investigators), and a supervisor within the accused officer's unit of assignment. In any case, the investigation typically entails the interview of the complainant, relevant witnesses, and the accused officer. The investigative interview of accused officer requires certain legal rights, including the right to be represented by counsel, notification of charges, etc.

When the investigation is completed, the investigator makes a recommendation relative to the determination of guilt. This recommendation is then reviewed by supervisors in the investigative unit, and is distributed through the chain of command within the police department. After this review is completed, the investigative case file goes to the Advocate Section within the police department for further review. Cases which have a determination of guilt (called a sustained finding) are then critiqued and prepared for a hearing before the Complaint Review Panel. This panel hearing is an internal procedure in which the accused officer, who is represented by a member of the police union, is given the opportunity to plead his or her case before a three person panel of police officials of varying rank. After this hearing, the decision of the panel is then forwarded to the Superintendent of Police for a final administrative determination.

Following this final administrative decision, the accused officer can appeal any suspension over five days to the Chicago Police Board. The police board is a citizen entity of the police department, whose members are highly regarded in the community. Hearings in the police board are rather formal, with the city represented by the corporation counsel office, and the accused officer usually represented by a union attorney. The hearings are conducted before a Hearing Officer, who is an attorney acting on behalf of the police board. Decisions from the police board can be and often are appealed to the Chancery Court of Cook County. Either party can appeal to this court under the Administrative Review Statute (735 ILCS, Sections 5/3-101 to 5/3-112). Adverse decisions from this court can be appealed to the Illinois Appellate Court, and later to the Illinois Supreme Court.

As evidenced by the process described above, the procedural remedies and protections are substantial — both for the accused officer and the
citizen complainant. In comparison, the procedural guidelines established
by the private security patrols will be examined as a means to assess the
level of accountability for misconduct on the part of the security personnel. Any such procedures used by the private security firm will be considered in assessing whether constitutional violations may or may not have
occurred.

The most important aspect of the documentary analysis comes from
daily reports. Daily reports are completed by private police officers during each shift to document each and every incident in which the private
police officers were involved. In each such report, I coded every incident
recorded to determine the category of the incident and to assess the particular functions of the private police officers. That is, whether law enforcement, order maintenance, or traditional security (observe and report)
functions were involved.

Briefly, in reviewing and coding the daily reports, I subdivided these
reports into two groups, one for each security firm in the study, so data
from one firm could then be compared and contrasted against data from
the other firm. I then further broke down the data into either a law
enforcement function or an order maintenance function.

The law enforcement functional category is further broken down into
subcategories, which are based on particular types of crimes or activities:
Weapons Offenses, Batteries, Robberies/Thefts, Alarm Response, Criminal Property Damage, Assist C.P.D., Others, and Arrests.

Each of these law enforcement functions entails various types of criminal activity in which the private police officer was either involved in the
response or used some "police power." This requires some explanation. The
analysis of each daily report — in most cases — simply showed the type of activity each officer "worked" on. The term "worked" in this context does not
necessarily mean that the officer did anything relative to the particular
activity. It may only represent that the officer responded to a call. It does not
mean that he or she took any police action relative to the call. For example,
a line item on the daily report may note "shots fired" at a specific location,
with the officers responding to that location. The activity derived from the
call is largely dependent on whether the call was "bona fide," that is, the incident actually occurred. Stated another way, the call may have been broad-
cast on the radio or reported on the phone, but the incident may not have
actually occurred. If the report was false, then the "work product" of the
private police officers would be little more than driving to the location,
and possibly touring the area to assess what, if anything, actually occurred.

The aforementioned example is very typical of the activities of street police officers, particularly tactical officers. Much of street police work is either responding to calls—deemed reactive, or initiating activity related to suspicious situations or circumstances—deemed proactive. Much of both reactive and proactive police work results in the conclusion that no crime has occurred, or that the particular individual has not violated any criminal law. In police parlance, those cases deemed to be factually false are known as "unfounded" incidents. Unfounded essentially means the alleged crime did not occur. As illustrated by the discussion on the economic and operational aspects of police work, this is a very common product of patrol work.

However, the fact that a particular "incident" is deemed to be false or unfounded does not have any qualitative distinction in police work. Indeed, the fact that a police officer was involved in an activity that is deemed to be unfounded does not in any real sense limit the importance of an appropriate response to the call in a reactive case. Similarly, if the contact is based on a proactive initiative, the officer asserting his or her police powers must do so in an appropriate manner. In either case, the assertion of the police officer into the situation is what he or she is paid to do.

As such, even though the vast number of "incidents" in which police officers involve themselves may be unfounded, the assertion into the situation, nonetheless, is what police work is about. Consequently, while many of the incidents listed on the daily reports were deemed to be unfounded, the involvement by the private police officers—regardless of how minimal—is counted as part of their job, thereby counted toward a particular functional category.

The order maintenance category was also further broken down into subcategories, which are based on particular types of activities, commonly characterized as "incivilities" (see Covington and Taylor, 1991). In this regard, the order maintenance function includes these subcategories: Street Disturbances, Public Vice Activities, Loitering, Suspicious Persons/Vehicles, Noise/Music Complaints, and Other Public Activities.

Of these alternatives, the most obvious assertion of "police powers" involves law enforcement. As described earlier, the term police powers involves the assertion of legal authority to effect an arrest, or even more commonly, to conduct some interview or a search or seizure. The involvement of private police officers in public streets, and into law enforcement matters, would logically entail a greater propensity to "act like a police officer." In this sense, this is clearly an exercise of police powers, whether or not an arrest was made.

Even order maintenance functions also inevitably involve the assertion of legal authority. For example, the admonishment of a person loitering or drinking on the public way requires a certain amount of legal authority. While this is usually a rather routine admonishment, the private police officer must have the legal authority to require a citizen to refrain from certain actions. A simple statement to "stop drinking" or "get off the street corner" requires a certain degree of legal authority.

Conversely, the traditional security function category, termed observe and report, requires little, if any, police power, as this function does not involve any involvement of the private officer. Such incidents will be merely noted and totaled. For purposes of this case study, therefore, the assertion of police powers would consist only of either law enforcement or order maintenance functional categories.

This analysis was designed to aid in the assessment of the functions of the private police officers. Specifically, the question of which function is most prevalent can be assessed using these data sets. Further, the data can also result in a relatively accurate assessment to determine whether the private police officers would be deemed state actors, as well as an assessment of the constitutionality of their actions. Such analysis also involved reviewing other reports, including any case and arrest reports stemming from a specific incident. In reviewing such reports, I drew some conclusions as to the nature of the involvement, and whether the incident entailed any inferences of constitutional violations.

As mentioned earlier, however, the answer to this constitutionality question may not be definitive. Of course, a definite assessment may not be apparent on the face of a report. As stated in the legal overview chapter, this determination is essentially a two part test. Initially, courts would look to the facts related to the function of the private police officer to determine if the private police officer should be deemed a state actor. This determination may be made on the facts related to the data collection, and on the nature of the private patrol program. In this sense, the case law illustrates that the facts in this study *may* suggest that the private police officers are state actors.

Once these facts and circumstances are assessed, certain reasonable conclusions can be drawn from the available evidence. Such evidence would include the nature and type of functions in which the private police officers are involved, the language used by the officers in their reports, and even the facts articulated in the reports. These factors coupled with the raw statistical data can provide a basis for determining that, in certain instances, a constitutional violation may have occurred. This assessment of constitutionality, however, does not merely involve the data and the reports. Such assessments can also be based on the observations made and information gleaned from the ride-alongs.

Another factor was used to assess this constitutionality question. Litigation checks were done to assess whether lawsuits were filed against either security firm in either state or federal court. In the event any such lawsuit was filed, information obtained from the case could be used to assess whether any constitutional violation may have occurred. However, it is important to note an appropriate caveat. The fact that a lawsuit was filed does not necessarily mean that a constitutional violation has occurred. Nonetheless, in the event that a lawsuit was filed from a particular incident, the merits of the complaint viewed in light of the factors mentioned above may serve to further validate any such conclusions of this case study.

Aside from the value of this analysis, the daily reports present an excellent opportunity to assess the internal validity of the study. The data derived from the documents also could be compared to my observations on the street, and the information obtained from the interviews. In this way, I had the opportunity to observe the private police officer perform the patrol functions, and then compare the recorded data on the daily reports to other similar incidents.

For example, when patrol officers remove a loiterer from a street corner, how is it typically accomplished? Similarly, how does the data contained in the daily reports compare to the typical tour of duty experienced in the ride-alongs? Does this information reconcile with the information obtained from the interviews? Consequently, these different data sources provide some level of triangulation, whereby information from each data set can be compared and contrasted against the information derived from other data sources to enhance the reliability of the conclusions derived from this study.

Finally, one other factor related to this study should be noted. As an Assistant Professor in Law Enforcement Management, a police union and security firm attorney, and as a former Chicago Police officer, I have studied, taught and litigated these issues for over twenty years. In this light, I observed the work of the private police officers from the perspective of an individual who has experienced similar incidents, and who has performed similar functions. The observations gleaned from this research can be contrasted with or compared against personal and professional knowledge about police functions, including what constitutes a legally appropriate arrest, and a constitutionally proper search and seizure. This is not to say that my opinion is definitive. Instead, it complements the stated research techniques and provides context to this case study.

Case Study Results

The data analysis will begin with the document analysis, followed by a narrative explanation of the information derived from the ride-alongs and from the interviews. When appropriate to add context, or to further describe facts obtained from the data, there will be some overlap in the presentation of the study results. I sometimes cross-reference these methods in order to discuss or contrast findings for a specific incident or issue.

DOCUMENTARY RESULTS

This analysis is largely based on the daily reports completed by the private police officers; coupled with arrest, incident and case reports, related to certain relevant incidents or issues. The data sought to answer the three research questions: whether security personnel are state actors, what their functions are, and whether they violate constitutional protections. Regarding whether security personnel should be deemed "state actors," the facts derived from the documentary review would answer this question in the affirmative. This conclusion is based on the following analysis.

First, the data reveals that both security firms conducted the majority of their work in the order maintenance function. In total, both security firms conducted 68.1 percent of their work on either law enforcement or order maintenance. This percentage was based on the total number of incidents listed in the daily reports. These 2,486 incidents represented the total times the private police officers provided any service to the community. Of these 2,486 incidents, fully 1,695 (68.1 percent) were directed at law enforcement and order maintenance functions.

This amount of work directed toward the dual public goals of enforcing laws and maintaining order would likely be deemed as predominantly public. This level of public function coupled with the other facts previously discussed, such as the funding source, the relationship and interaction with the government, and the public environment in which the functions are performed, show that the private police officers are, indeed, state actors. Each of these factors suggest that the private police officers were serving a *public function*, in a *public environment*, paid for by tax revenues collected by *public bodies*, and being subject to the administration of *public officials* named by the local aldermen. Consequently, I am quite confident that this finding, based on the data and the facts, would result in a court declaring the private police officers as state actors.

Second, as to the predominant function of the private police officers, the data supports the finding that both firms perform order maintenance functions as their predominant role. Both firms participated in 1,282 incidents involving order maintenance. Of the 2,486 total incidents, 51.5 percent of their work was directed toward this function. As such, this one functional area constituted the majority of the work of both firms. In table form, the data is as follows:

Table 1

Patrol Program Functional Totals

Function Totals		
Traditional	791	31.8%
Law Enforcement	413	16.6%
Order Maintenance	1282	51.5%
Total Incidents	2486	100%*

*percentages are rounded

This data was further broken down into a comparison between the two firms. This breakdown would be illustrative for a number of reasons. Initially, this level of analysis may reveal certain characteristics or factors of each firm which could be useful for explanatory purposes. Next, the comparative data from each firm could be used to further evaluate the respective work product of each firm — to assess *how* each performed the patrol function. Finally, such a comparison may provide additional context and flavor to this exploratory study.

American Security Services conducted 54.2 percent of its work on order maintenance, while Majestic Protection Services conducted 49.3 percent. Both figures further validate the public actors and functional research propositions. The data in table form for each firm are as follows:

Table 2

Firm Functional Totals

Function Totals	American Security		Majestic Protection	
Traditional	437	38.4%	354	26.2%
Law Enforcement	84	7.4%	329	24.4%
Order Maintenance	617	54.2%	665	49.3%
Total Incidents	1138	100%*	1348	100%*

*percentages are rounded

This data was analyzed even further into subcategories for additional explanation, flavor, and context. The breakdown illustrated two rather distinct approaches taken by each firm. While both firms devoted the majority of their work to order maintenance, each firm varied its approach toward either law enforcement or toward traditional observe and report functions. This distinction was not predicted. It may reflect certain tendencies of Majestic Protection Services to view itself as a tactical police unit. In any case, the data in table form showing subcategories for each function is as follows:

Table 3
Firm Functional Totals with Subcategories

Function	American Security		Majestic Protection	
Traditional	*Number/Percentage*		*Number/Percentage*	
Premises Check	278	63.6%	346	97.7%
Park Closing	36	8.2%	0	-0-
School Special Attention	123	28.1%	8	2.3%
	437	100%*	354	100%
Law Enforcement	*Number/Percentage*		*Number/Percentage*	
Weapons Incidents	14	16.6%	56	17.0%
Battery Incidents	14	16.6%	47	14.3%
Robbery/Theft Incidents	22	26.2%	55	16.7%
Alarm Responses	9	10.7%	78	23.7%
Criminal Property Damage	13	15.5%	10	3.0%
Other Incidents	12	14.3%	83	25.2%
	84	100%	329	100%
Order Maintenance	*Number/Percentage*		*Number/Percentage*	
Street Disturbances	143	23.1%	169	25.4%
Public Vice Incidents	44	7.1%	67	10.1%
Loitering	270	43.8%	196	29.5%
Suspicious Persons/ Vehicles	84	13.6%	109	16.4%
Noise/Music Incidents	41	6.6%	7	1.1%

(Function)	(American Security)		(Majestic Protection)	
Other Incidents	35	5.7%	117	17.6%
	617	100%	665	100%

*percentages are rounded

The results of the data analysis for American Security Services are as follows. In the four month period, the total number of incidents was 1,138. Of these incidents, 437 were for the traditional security function. In this regard, approximately 38.5 percent of their total work involved the observe and report function, traditionally viewed as the primary role of private security. While this is a significant percentage of their total work, it leaves the preponderance of their activities in areas involving law enforcement and order maintenance.

Of this 437, the traditional security function was further subdivided into three specific activities. These activities were premise checks (i.e., buildings and businesses), closing the park gates at Marquette Park, and conducting "special attention" at the local schools (one public grammar school and one private high school). The total breakdown for each was: premise checks, 278 (63.6 percent); park closings, 36 (8.2 percent); and school special attention, 123 (28.1 percent).

Law enforcement incidents totaled 84, which results in a percentage of 7.3 percent of the total work devoted to this function. Further breaking down this data, of the 84 total law enforcement incidents, there were 14 Weapons related incidents (16.6 percent); 14 Battery incidents (16.6 percent); 22 Robbery/Theft incidents (26.2 percent); 9 Alarm Responses (10.7 percent); 13 Criminal Property Damage incidents (15.5 percent); and 12 (14.3 percent) Others (5 involved assisting the Chicago Police Department, 6 were for trespassing, and 1 was for a criminal warrant).

As to order maintenance, the total number of incidents was 617, which results in a percentage of 54.2 percent of the total work devoted to this function. Further breaking down this data, of the 617 total order maintenance incidents, there were 143 Street Disturbances (23.1 percent); 44 Public Vice incidents (7.1 percent); 270 Loitering incidents (43.8 percent); 84 Suspicious Persons/Vehicle incidents (13.6 percent); 41 Noise/Music complaints (6.6 percent); and 35 (5.7 percent) were for Others (15 were domestic disturbances and 11 were business disturbances).

Based on this data, the research proposition isolated to American Security Services regarding the functions of the private police officers would have been correct. That is, the private police officers perform both

law enforcement and order maintenance functions, with order maintenance being the prevalent function. The results show that order maintenance amounted to 54.2 percent of the work functions (n=617), while law
enforcement amounted to only 7.3 percent (n=84), and traditional security functions amounted to 38.5 percent (n= 437). These figures support
the research proposition which predicted that the private police officers
would perform the order maintenance function in a manner illustrating
that it is the primary focus of their work.

The results of the data analysis for Majestic Protective Services are as
follows. In the four month period, the total number of incidents was 1,348.
Of these incidents, 354 were for the traditional security function. As such,
approximately 26.2 percent of their total work involved the observe and
report function, traditionally viewed as the primary role of private security. While this observe and report function is a significant percentage of
their total work, it leaves a substantial amount of their activities in areas
involving law enforcement and order maintenance.

Of this total of 354, the observe and report function was further subdivided into three specific activities. These activities were premise checks,
closing the park gates, and conducting "special attention" at the local
schools. The total breakdown for each was: premise checks, 346 (97.7 percent); park closings, 0 (0 percent); and school special attention, 8 (2.3 percent).

As to law enforcement, the total number of incidents was 329, which
results in a percentage of 24.4 percent of the total work devoted to this
function. Further breaking down this data, of the 329 total law enforcement incidents, there were 56 were Weapons related incidents (17.0 percent); 47 Battery incidents (14.3 percent); 55 Robbery/Theft incidents (16.7
percent); 78 Alarm Responses (23.7 percent); 10 Criminal Property Damage incidents (3.0 percent); and 83 (25.2 percent) for Others (51 involved
assistance to C.P.D., 19 were for "street stops" and 9 were for "building
sweeps"— more discussion and analysis on these later).

As to order maintenance, the total number of incidents was 665,
which results in 49.3 percent of the total work devoted to this function.
Further breaking down this data, there were 169 Street Disturbances (25.4
percent); 67 Public Vice incidents (10.1 percent); 196 Loitering incidents
(29.5 percent); 109 Suspicious Persons/ Vehicle incidents (16.4 percent); 7
Noise/Music complaints (1.1 percent); and 117 (17.6 percent) were for Others (of which 71 were domestic disturbances and 21 were business disturbances).

Based on this data, the research proposition isolated to Majestic Protective Services regarding the functions of the private police officers would

have been correct. That is, the private police officers perform both law enforcement and order maintenance functions, with order maintenance being the prevalent function. The results show that order maintenance amounted to 49.3 percent of the work functions (n = 665), while law enforcement amounted to only 24.4 percent (n = 329), and traditional security functions amounted to 26.2 percent (n = 354). These figures support the prediction that private police officers would perform the order maintenance function in a manner illustrating that it is the primary focus of their work.

This comparative data also illustrates a rather stark difference in the activities of each security firm. While both firms are similar in the level of order maintenance incidents, the law enforcement function was quite different. Majestic Protective Services appears from the data to be much more inclined toward aggressive criminal enforcement. This is manifested in the data which shows 329 incidents by Majestic Protective Services compared to only 84 for American Security Services. This equates to 245 more law enforcement incidents for Majestic.

Further, the arrest data also strongly favors Majestic over American. The total number of arrest incidents was substantially different. Majestic was involved in 48 arrest incidents, and recovered 5 handguns in the four month period. Comparatively, American was only involved in 9 arrest incidents, with no handguns recovered. These numbers illustrate a much greater propensity for law enforcement by Majestic.

Based on this data, it is reasonable to assert that the American tended toward the traditional security function, while Majestic appeared to take a much more aggressive approach to "crime fighting" (see ride-along section below for further development of this statement). In this sense, American acted more like a traditional security firm, whereas Majestic acted more like a tactical police unit.

Additional data supports the above assertion. The data reveals that Majestic Protective Services worked much closer with the Chicago Police Department. In the four month period, Majestic was involved in 51 assists with public police officers. Conversely, officers from American Security Services were only involved in 5 assist situations with the public police. Again, this data suggests that Majestic is more oriented toward law enforcement, which is manifested by a closer working relationship with the Chicago Police Department.

Other techniques used by Majestic are similar to those conducted by tactical police units. Specifically, Majestic recorded that it conducted 19 "street stops" during the four month period. While these numbers are not substantial compared to what would be expected of tactical police officers, the mere fact that the private police officers are making street stops presents legitimate questions relating to legal authority and constitutionality. Similarly, the reports noted that 9 "building sweeps" were conducted. A building sweep is, in essence, a procedure in which the private police officers go through the hallways of apartment buildings, and confront individuals who happen to be in the common areas. The stated purpose of this function is to prevent the property from being used for drinking, drug usage, and prostitution. Notwithstanding the legal and constitutional questions raised by this method, it is safe to assert that the building sweeps are an aggressive action on the part of these private police officers.

Another important indicator is the number of weapon incidents in which they were involved. Majestic again showed itself to be the more aggressive firm, as its officers were involved in 56 weapon incidents while American was involved in only 14. In this regard, Majestic was involved in four times as many weapon incidents as American. Since the data was derived from the same time frame, this substantial variance cannot be attributed to seasonal differences. This statistic is particularly telling when considering the possible danger involved in these incidents. One can argue that it takes a special person to respond to a "shots fired" or a "man with a gun" call. When most reasonable people would run in the opposite direction, certain officers are eager — or at least have the courage to respond to the call — to confront an individual with a weapon. In this light, the data clearly shows that Majestic was much more aggressive in this important law enforcement function.

Finally, one additional aspect needs to be addressed relative to the law enforcement orientation of Majestic. The officers employed by Majestic commonly used a radio scanner to monitor the police communications traffic in the 8th police district. The use of this scanner allows these private officers to be much more involved in the activity within the area. Obvious evidence of this involvement can be shown from the level of alarm response between the two firms. Majestic responded to 78 alarms, while American responded to only 9. This data is even more obvious considering that alarm responses are commonly assigned through police radio communications. The difference in the level of alarm response between the two firms could not have been merely happenstance. The difference, at least partly, can be reasonably attributed to the use of police scanners by Majestic.

The documentary review also will be used to assess the third research proposition that the private police officers would violate certain constitutional protections in the performance of their patrol functions. There are several different techniques used to test this constitutionality question. The methods used for such examinations will be described as appropriate.

As to American Security Services there are a number of incidents that raise constitutional concerns. There are six separate incidents in which the private police officers made decisions which were questionable, at best. For example, on one occasion, the officers confronted individuals who were gambling on the public way. The officers noted in their daily report that they "took the dice" and sent the gamblers on their way. While it is impossible to verify that the officers actually took the dice from the gamblers, there is no reason to disbelieve the report. There also is no notation of any kind that the dice were inventoried as contraband. Assuming that the report is true, the officers clearly violated the law in that their action could be deemed a theft.

In another pointed example, the private police officers confronted a teen with a knife. The officers noted on their daily report that they "advised get rid of knife. Teen threw it away." This use of discretion — assuming the report is true — also leaves a lot to be desired. While this decision is probably not illegal, the implications of this decision are rather obvious. What would happen if the knife was later used in a crime? What if a child found the knife, resulting in someone being seriously injured? Clearly, any number of problems could arise from how this matter was handled.

Additionally, there were three separate occasions in which the officers encountered individuals having sex and drinking in vehicles. On each occasion, the report merely noted that the individuals were told to leave the area. While this seems to be an appropriate discretionary decision, the report does not note how the officers conducted the stop. The report does not mention whether the vehicle was searched, whether there was any evidence that the sex act involved prostitution, and whether the driver was intoxicated and allowed to drive away. These questions—and others—raise legitimate concerns as to the decision making of the private police officers.

Other examples more directly concern constitutional questions. In four separate instances, the private police officers detained — and possibly searched — suspects without effecting an arrest or even preparing a report. In each instance, the officers merely noted the following language in their daily report: "no drugs found," "no merchandise found" (twice), and detain suspect "order no longer in [e]ffect." The logical inference drawn from this language is that the officers conducted some search. It is impossible to determine whether the suspects themselves were searched, or if only the ground was examined. In another example, the officers noted in a suspicious person incident that they [suspects] "seemed ready to smoke drugs." In each of these examples, it is reasonable to conclude that some search was conducted. The only questions are how invasive the search was, and whether it would have conformed to constitutional protections.

There were also numerous instances where the private police officers were involved in domestic disturbances *within private residences*. In at least four occasions, arrests were made during these domestic disturbances. As mentioned earlier, it is unsettling to consider that the private police officers were being used to quell domestic disturbances within a private residence. At least part of this concern involves the purpose for their contractual function. They were hired to "patrol" the Marquette Park community. Are domestic disturbances in private residences considered part of their patrol duties? This question would arguably, at least, be answered in the negative.

Beyond this contractual function, there are larger questions raised by private citizens enforcing order and effecting arrests on private property. Even if the private officers were invited into the residence, this raises public policy questions as to whether it is appropriate for private citizens to regulate human behavior within the property of another citizen. If they were not invited into the residence, it also raises constitutional questions.

Finally, the American Security Services officers were involved in a number of incidents in which citizens either refused to comply with their directives or actually used threats and physical confrontations. On at least four separate occasions, the private officers noted in their daily report that the suspects "refused to move" or "refused to re-locate." On two separate occasions, arrests were made at least partly due to the suspects' refusal to comply with the directives of the private police officers. This also raises obvious questions. Do the private police officers have the legal authority to order a citizen from a street corner? Even if they have such authority, does the fact that they are not sworn law enforcement officers impact their ability to assert either moral or legal authority?

These rhetorical questions, however, are complicated by the realities of street police work. On at least four occasions, the private police officers were threatened with bodily harm. In a couple of these instances, the private police officers noted in their incident reports the language used in these threats. The language is illustrative of the lack of legal or moral authority vested in their patrol function. For example, one report stated a suspect yelled, "f… those mother f…er's, don't move, they ain't the police." Another report noted that a suspect said he was "going to kick her [the officer's] ass." In yet another example, the private police vehicle was bombarded with rocks and bottles. In two other examples, the private officers were physically struck in the performance of their duties. It is important to emphasize that these were the incidents that were *recorded* on their reports. It is reasonable to assert that additional such incidents occurred — possibly many more given the gravity of the incidents described above.

Similar incidents take place every day while officers police streets in this country. This could occur whether the officers were private or public. Indeed, there are few rules on the street, especially for those who do not respect authority or the rule of law. Unfortunately, these individuals will always exist. The problem with such conduct, however, is that it may be exacerbated by the questionable authority attached to private police officers. While the private police officers may be deemed agents of the government (i.e., state actors), a number of important questions are raised by the amount of actual or perceived authority. These questions include selection, training, accountability, and liability. This raises one of the more important implications of this research. That is, the question of governmental sovereignty in light of the possibility that private security will become a dual provider of public safety. These issues will be more fully developed later.

As to Majestic Protective Services, the aggressive nature of their patrol function — as illustrated by the data derived from the daily reports— raises legitimate questions on the constitutionality of their actions. The relationship between aggressive police tactics and constitutional violations seems apparent. Case law overwhelmingly considers proactive or aggressive tactics as being more likely to result in a constitutional violation. This is particularly relevant in arrest situations, including search and seizures.

There are specific types of incidents which tend to raise these questions. In 10 different instances, Majestic officers made arrests in street encounters dealing with either suspicious activity or street stops. Each arrest was for two diverse crimes, either drug possession or for possession of a stolen vehicle. In each case, the reports reveal that the arrests were initiated by proactive street stops. From a purely law and order perspective, these arrests appear to be examples of good police work. By this perspective, the officers initiated an interaction resulting in the arrest of individuals committing crimes, or violating certain criminal laws. If the only goal was to capture criminals, then this was good police work — regardless if it was performed by private or public police officers. This being said, there are larger issues involved than capturing criminal offenders. That is, were the arrests constitutional?

The two critical indicators of this constitutional question are the utilization of "street stops" and "building sweeps." While it may be presumptuous to state that these functions are — on their face — unconstitutional, it is difficult to envision circumstances that would justify these actions. Simply put, the information derived from the study does not provide for any other explanation.

The 19 recorded street stops conducted by Majestic security personnel, plus 10 additional instances in which arrests were made, illustrate a rather aggressive functional approach to the job. However, when one considers that these private police officers are private citizens, with questionable police powers vested in their actions, then their "good police work" raises significant questions. Considering that these individuals, who are conducting traffic stops of vehicles or are stopping people as they walk down streets and alleys are private citizens, then this assessment must viewed in a different light.

The obvious question is: Does the status of the officer (as being a private citizen) contribute to what is deemed good police work? The analogy is similar to a private citizen imposing his or her presence in an apartment for the purpose of quelling a disturbance in the residence. It is unlikely that most citizens would believe that this is appropriate. Similarly, most people would object to private citizens stopping vehicles or pedestrians as they move about the public way. This issue certainly raises controversial questions. Even in the public sector, the assertion of street stops has raised legitimate concerns and has been the subject of numerous U.S. Supreme Court decisions.

With this in mind, consider again the presence of private police officers in domestic disturbances. Majestic officers responded to at least seven domestic disturbances, and made arrests in six. In one such incident, the officers noted that they searched for a weapon allegedly used in the disturbance. The only logical inference which can be derived from this notation is that the officers searched the residence for the weapon. Whether or not this is constitutional depends on the facts of the incident, including whether appropriate consent was provided, whether any plain view evidence would justify an extension of the perimeters of the search, etc. Notwithstanding such rhetorical questions, the function of responding to domestic disturbances and making arrests must be considered in light of other functions described below.

While the nuances of the constitutional assessments in this area are beyond the scope of this research, it is sufficient to assert that decisions relating to street stops by public police may not be applicable to similar conduct by private police officers. This is so because the private police officers would need to be deemed "state actors" to have the constitutional provisions apply. Only a court of competent jurisdiction can answer the ultimate legal question: are the private police officers state actors?

Putting aside this technical legal question, it is reasonable, given the data and facts described in this case study, to conclude that the private police officers are state actors. In this light, consider that these private police officers—as state actors—can assert certain police powers above and beyond those of private citizens. Even so, the street stop function is still extremely disconcerting for a number of reasons.

First, the private police officers do not have the training and experience afforded to police officers. This can be problematic in terms of their understanding of the law. It can also raise practical or safety considerations for both the officers and the citizens who were stopped and questioned (or searched) by the private police officers. As an individual who has participated in literally thousands of street stops, it is my contention that there is an "art" to safely and respectfully conducting such encounters. It is important to understand the core concern of this issue. Individuals who are stopped did not invite the encounter nor is it likely that they are happy to be stopped and questioned—not to mention searched or arrested. A street stop is always at least potentially adversarial, if not confrontational or even deadly.

The job of the police officer is to conduct this function in a manner that maintains a level of respect and dignity for the person being stopped, and at the same time maintains an appropriate amount of control over the encounter—to ensure the safety of all individuals. This is often a delicate balance. It is, indeed, sometimes extremely difficult to achieve. This is why I believe it is an "art" because it requires both technique and a certain sense or judgment which can only be honed from appropriate training and substantial experience. As will be described in detail in the ride-along section, the private police officers whom I worked with simply did not have a clue as the nuances of how to conduct a street stop.

Second, related to the experiential and training issues raised above, the more important question in terms of this research regards the constitutionality of such street stops. Given that this case study determined that the private officers are state actors, this does not mean that they have conformed to the dictates of the constitution. In essence, the issue is, if the private police officers are deemed state actors, then they are required to adhere to the dictates of the constitution (as defined by literally hundreds of court cases) just as the public police are expected to do. Can anyone reasonably expect private police officers to adhere to the nuances of this important, and yet technical, area of the law? My contention is that they will not do so because they are ill-prepared to conform to the laws governing such encounters.

When considering whether the private police officers have the legal or technical ability to adhere to constitutional prohibitions, it is possible that company policies and procedures can provide certain guidance. The information derived from this study, however, revealed that neither company provided anything close to substantive policies or guidelines to provide direction in this area.

I inquired with officials of Majestic, with the sole service provider, and with commission members for such documents. Based on what was tendered and represented to me, Majestic had absolutely no policies or guidelines related to this issue. It may be possible that such policies and guidelines existed. This is highly unlikely, however, as it is unreasonable to believe that the company would go to the trouble to implement such policies and procedures, and then refuse to disclose them. I can think of no reason that the sole service provider or the commission would withhold these documents if they possessed them.

As to American, they developed what was entitled "Suggested Procedures/Guidelines for Marquette Park SSA [Special Service Area]." This document provides some minimal guidance:

> American security officers will make continual vehicular patrols of the SSA concentrating their efforts equally throughout the neighborhood, giving special attention to specific areas as needed.

> If criminal activity occurs, the police should be notified via 911, then American Security should be contacted. American officers will not monitor police channels or interfere if police are already at the scene.

These guidelines are, in essence, the articulation of the "observe and report" function described in this book. If these guidelines are to be taken literally, the extent of involvement by American officers was limited to driving around the community, and calling the police when criminal activity occurred. Their own daily reports, however, demonstrate that their functions were much more involved than merely observing and reporting criminal activity. In fact, this policy also requires that "officers will document daily activity and all incidents we are involved in." The guidelines fail to mention anything relative to conducting street stops. Based on this document, it would be reasonable to suggest that the assertion of street stops was either not considered as part of the job, or the company made a conscious decision to remain silent on this matter.

In this regard, there is absolutely no evidence derived from this study which would support the notion that the private police officers were adequately trained or guided as to the legal limitations of street stops. Majestic failed to even develop any guideline for its employees as to street stops.

American provided some "guidance" as described above. Even the sole service provider and the commission failed to address this issue. The closest that any official document gets to addressing this issue is the model proposal drafted by the city. The proposal states:

> Security Firm agrees to provide security in SSA (Special Service Area) 14 comprised of mobile patrols (and foot patrols when and where required as designated by Contractor) on the streets and in the alleys of SSA 14; report any suspected or actual criminal activity to the police; where practicable, detain individuals who are believed to have committed criminal offenses until the police arrive and take charge of the investigation and/or arrest; and sign court complaints and/or appear in court as witnesses as may be required for the prosecution of criminal offenders.[9]

This language does little to provide any real guidance to the street level employees charged with the patrol duties envisioned in this program. It is highly unlikely that any officer who participated in the street patrol ever even saw this language. Assume, for the sake of argument, that this provision was made available. It is my position it provides nothing useful to an officer on the street. At best, it provides a general framework in which lawyers can negotiate intent, or argue in a litigation setting. It clearly does not guide or educate the officers who are charged with the service provision. This is particularly problematic in light of the significance of the issue, that is, adherence to protections guaranteed by the constitution.

At this stage of the study, it is sufficient to assert that the ride-alongs provided evidence that the private police officers routinely violated the constitution in the performance of their functions. This was particularly valid for instances such as street stops and other proactive functions which require the assertion of police powers. However, for the flow and organization of this study, the description of such will be confined to the ride-along section. Nonetheless, there are additional factors which will be considered in light of this constitutionality question.

The last element of the documentary analysis was a litigation check for lawsuits filed against either security firm. As to American Security, there were no federal lawsuits filed against this firm. In state court, there were three separate lawsuits. Two of these seem to be completely unrelated to the Marquette Park patrols. For example, case 97 L 013413 filed on October 27, 1997, appeared to be an employment matter between the firm and a former employee. Also, case number 97 L 009833 filed on August 22, 1996, is unrelated to the involvement of the security firm at the study site. The case dealt with a personal injury in which a bicycle on a sidewalk apparently injured someone.

The third case has a direct bearing on the research study. Case 97 L 050450 was filed on April 24, 1997, in which the firm appealed an adverse decision from the Illinois Department of Employment Security. The case essentially stems from an employee of American Security who was arrested with his handgun by a Chicago police officer. The American officer was off duty at the time of his arrest. While a security officer has authority to carry a handgun, this authority is expressly limited to the tour of duty, and traveling to and from work. As such, the possession of the weapon — at the time the private police officer was arrested — violated the law.

What is notable is that the Chicago police officer apparently did not afford the American officer any regard because he was involved in "police work." In a responsive pleading filed by the firm, they argued that the decision to award the former employee unemployment benefits was improper because "his [the employee] actions were harmful to us, as he jeopardized our relationship with the Chicago Police Department, as well as our Marquette Patrol armed account." Taken in this light, this arrest illustrates that the relationship between the private and public entities leaves room for improvement. It also illustrates that the arrest could create a schism between the private and public police. Based on what I observed, the relationship between the two groups was tolerant, and sometimes actually adversarial.

As for Majestic Protective Services, there were no federal lawsuits filed against this firm. In state court, there was one lawsuit filed against the firm. This lawsuit also involved an appeal from an Illinois Department of Employment Security case. The case 99 L 050795 filed on August 3, 1999, was an administrative review of an adverse decision in an unemployment claim. The employee in this case, however, was not assigned to the Marquette Park patrols. Hence, this lawsuit is not relevant to this research.

RIDE-ALONG NARRATIVE RESULTS

This aspect of the study will present a unique perspective of private police officers as they performed their patrol function on public streets, as it will demonstrate what these officers did and how they did it. This information can also test the third research proposition: whether the private police officers conformed to the dictates of the constitution.

The ride-alongs were done over a two month period while Majestic Protective Services had the contract for private patrols within the Marquette Park community. For this reason, the participant observation aspect of the study focused only on this firm. The total amount of time spent "on the street" as a participant in these ride-alongs was approximately 48 hours, which consisted of six eight hours tours. In these forty-eight hours, I was able to directly observe numerous incidents and speak at length with the respondents.

There were three vehicles used by Majestic for the patrols. Each vehicle was a Chevrolet affixed with a "police package" consisting of side spotlights, and a radio scanner attached to the dashboard. Two vehicles were completely unmarked with no obvious police identifiers to signify that it was a patrol vehicle. The other vehicle had a blue "Majestic Security — Marquette Park Patrol" insignia on the front doors. This vehicle had a phone number of the firm printed on the back quarter panel, and had police "emergency lights" on the roof. The marked vehicle was white with blue pin stripes. It looked fairly similar to Chicago Police Department marked vehicles, with some obvious exceptions, such as the insignia. Overall though, the vehicles and the officers presented themselves in a manner that looked and felt like the public police.

The dress of the officers was fairly typical and consistent. Each officer wore a large black bullet proof vest with a Marquette Park Security badge affixed to the vest. Each officer wore a handgun (usually a semi-automatic) on his belt. Some officers wore two guns, one a .357-caliber handgun on a pants belt, along with a semi-automatic in a shoulder holster. Each officer also wore handcuffs, extra ammunition in "magazine" clips, a radio affixed to the vest, and often a small flashlight attached to the pants belt. Each officer wore "civilian" dress, usually consisting of jeans, a button down collared shirt, and a baseball cap. In short, each officer was dressed almost identically to a tactical police officer.

In terms of background and personal characteristics, the officers were both diverse and similar. They were diverse in the sense that they were black, white and Hispanic. They were of varying ages, but typically in their late 20s to early 40s. Their backgrounds were fairly similar in that all wanted to be "the police," a couple actually worked in suburban police departments, and one worked in the county jail. There was also an individual who worked for the firm who was a Chicago police officer, but I did not work with this individual. In any case, none of these officers had legal authority to conduct themselves as "the police," except for the Chicago police officer, whom I did not ride with.

Each officer I worked with seemed to really like the job, and appeared to care about doing good "police work." I personally liked each officer. I felt that each wanted to provide a service to the community. It was not just a job to them. It was the "good guys" against the "bad guys" mentality. It was cops versus robbers. I believe they had good intentions, and were good people doing a rough job. As some evidence of such, these officers were paid ten dollars per hour. They were not going to get rich on this job. In fact, they were exposed to the same dangers as public police for much less money with little or no benefits. Nonetheless, I got the impression from each officer that they liked what they were doing, and that each felt that his work contributed to the betterment of the community.

The initial ride-along was an ice-breaking encounter. Much of the evening was spent talking about our respective backgrounds, the nature of the patrols, and about policing in general. I am sure that this initial tour was communicated throughout the firm. Most individuals whom I later rode with were at least partly aware of my presence. My background as a former police officer and a practicing attorney (who had dealt with security and police labor and disciplinary matters) seemed to be disarming and appealing to the officers. It was clear they did not look at me as a threat. They seemed to view me as one of them. In each case, I explained to the officers that I was "doing a study on private policing." I then described in very general terms that the study focused on how the patrols operated. This seemed sufficient for each officer. They did not question me about my motivations, or attempt to discern the details of the study.

The ride-alongs, like most of police patrol work, usually consisted of riding around and talking about personal issues and making observations about people and happenings on the street. I will present certain highlights of the tours, and make certain inferences of what I consider relevant observations of the data. I will — as best that I can — try to present the data in narrative form from the perspective of the private police officer, and from the perspective of an objective observer. While I realize that my biases cannot be fully removed from this study, in some ways my experiences as a police officer and as an attorney can help flush out certain issues which are not otherwise readily apparent. In any event, I found the experience to be enlightening.

The typical tour commenced with coffee at a local gas and food center. We would take our coffee into the patrol vehicle and drive around the community. The community was a mixture of some well kept residences and others that were abandoned or badly deteriorated. The east side (around Western Avenue) of the community had more abandoned and deteriorated buildings, and had a larger percentage of apartments. The west side (around Kedzie Avenue) had more single family brick homes, consistent with the typical Chicago bungalow home.

While we drove around the community, we talked and observed. While doing so, I tried to get to know the personality and backgrounds of each officer. We also talked about how and why they did certain things relative to the patrols. For example, one officer had a habit of going the wrong way down one way streets. He mentioned that "you'd be surprised as to how often you drive up on things by going the wrong way down the street — because people on the street are looking the other way." This statement in some ways illustrates the approach taken by the Majestic officers. They all seemed to want to catch criminals. They were not just driving around seeking to "observe and report." They wanted to capture the "bad guys." They did not want to merely call the police, they wanted to *be the police*. An example of this approach is illustrated by the following story.

Early in the initial tour, I was introduced to "Danny," who was a block leader in a neighborhood association. Danny was the first black person to move into the neighborhood, thirteen years ago. He was seventeen years old at the time. Now Danny is married with two children. He was a very engaging person who obviously cared about the neighborhood. He was active in politics and in community development. Danny was very complimentary of Majestic — which is possibly the reason I was introduced to him. Danny told an interesting story about a drug house which plagued the neighborhood. He described this "dope and alcohol infested" house two doors down from his own home. As he did so, I noticed that the home was boarded up, with a large message spray painted on the boards: "POSTED — NO TRESPASSING — CALL 773-...-....." The number was to Majestic Protective Services, Inc. It was to the phone carried in the vehicle.

Danny went on to describe the previous tenants of the building as "project people," who "probably lived in the projects all their lives," who had no concern for others or for the community. He spoke of the "constant disturbances," including all kinds of drug dealing in the house. Danny said that the police were called, sometimes two or three times a day, without much help. The "break" came, as he described it, when Majestic entered into an "agency agreement" with the property owner — who lived in California. This agreement essentially gave Majestic the authority to enter the building pursuant to the consent and permission of the owner. The agreement also gave Majestic the "right" to sign the owner's name on any criminal complaints stemming from any arrests made on the property. After this agency agreement was executed, which was actually drafted by a principle of the firm, officers from Majestic would literally walk into the building and confiscate drugs and make arrests. Sometimes this would be done with police officers, sometimes independent of them. The end result, according to Danny, was the individuals could no longer "stand the heat," and they moved away. In this way, the community ridded itself of a constant source of nuisance and criminal activity.

Subsequent to this conversation with Danny, the officer proudly noted that he engaged in other "agency agreements" with other property owners. He also emphasized that Majestic was "probably the only company using this type of document." Unfortunately, I never obtained a copy of the agency agreement. I asked a number of times for it. Each time an excuse was given. At some point, I felt that they apparently did not want to give it to me. I do not know why. It was probably is due to the fact that "they are the only company using it." Maybe they viewed it as a proprietary secret. Whatever the reason, I decided to not push too hard for it at the risk of damaging my relationship with the company.

From a legal standpoint, however, the basis for the agreement is interesting. The logic is as follows. The owner of the property, the principal, engages a security firm to act as the agent to maintain a safe and secure premise. From this perspective, the owner gives consent and permission to the agent to act on behalf of the principal. This would include a limited power of attorney to execute certain documents (including criminal complaints), and to take certain actions necessary for the safety and security of the property — not necessarily the tenants. It would seem appropriate to write this provision into the lease, thereby giving the tenants some notice that this "right of entry" exists. I do not know if this was done, as the officer had no knowledge of such. I also do not know if such a lease provision — if it existed — would be deemed too intrusive. In any event, the concept of an agency agreement is an interesting — albeit a rather draconian — technique to clean up a neighborhood.

During the remainder of the initial tour, we stopped to talk to approximately 20 to 25 people on the street. Most of the encounters were due to public drinking, loud music, and loitering on the street corners or in front of stores. The technique of the officers was to confront the individual and tell them to "move along." In each case they did move along, some quicker than others. As will be described below, this was not always the case.

Probably the most intrusive stop of the tour was with a vehicle parked in an alley. As we drove by the alley, a vehicle was parked with its doors wide open. Music blared from the car. As we approached, we noticed one of the occupants urinating next to a garage. The officer told two individuals to exit the vehicle and stated, "Put your hands where I can see them." By this time, the other individual had finished urinating. The officers ordered all three to put their hands on the car. They complied without a word. At this time, the officer called for another Majestic vehicle working in the area.

In the meantime, we waited. As we stood there, the youths said nothing. The officers said little. A couple of tense minutes later, the back up vehicle arrived with two officers inside. This vehicle was the marked car used by Majestic. Once they arrived, both officers immediately began to search the detainees. The search was rather intrusive, whereas their pockets were emptied and examined, and other parts of their body were checked for guns or contraband. The vehicle was also extensively searched, including the glove compartment, the trunk, and under the seats. No evidence of any wrongdoing, other than urinating and open alcohol, was found. After the search, one of the officers chastised the individuals—all male blacks in their late teens—to leave the area. He also asked the individual who was urinating if he "would like it if someone did this in front of his mother or on his property." He stated that he would not like it. The officer then told them to "get rid of the beer" and leave. The suspects then *thanked* the officer and left the scene.

This "street" stop raises questions both in terms of its constitutionality and of security services to the community. In constitutional terms, it is likely that the officers exceeded their authority in this situation. Based on the facts, the officers may have been able to conduct a brief pat down for weapons only to protect themselves from a potential attack (known as a *Terry* stop). However, the intrusiveness of the search both in terms of the person and the vehicle was probably constitutionally unreasonable. Given that the stop was conducted by private police officers, with questionable police powers, this further complicates the constitutional analysis.

In terms of security to the community, however, the larger purpose of the stop seemed reasonable. From the perspective of the particular property owner, or from the community as a whole, the stop probably was warranted. The youths may have been breaking into a garage, they may have been dealing drugs, or they may have been committing any number of illegal acts. Since the officers did not know what they were up to, they stopped and talked to them. In this manner, the officers were clearly performing an order maintenance function. This situation could also have resulted in the assertion of law enforcement, supposing contraband was found. In this way, the private police officers were performing both functions simultaneously. While it is impossible to know if the incident had any effect on the teenagers, it did represent the type of work that the larger community would likely applaud. From a constitutional perspective, however, the officers probably violated the law in their quest to maintain order.

Another example of the difficulties in balancing order and law was illustrated in an incident that involved the same officer. We drove past a group of four people in their teens or early twenties. As we drove by, a female black looked at the car and stated "fuck you!" The officer immediately stopped the vehicle and got out. He confronted the group and asked, "What did you say?" Almost immediately, a male — seemingly her boyfriend — stated that he was "sorry," she was "just kidding." At the same time, a middle aged woman came across the street and also began to defuse the situation. After a few words back and forth, the situation broke off in a fairly amicable manner. We drove off and continued to patrol. The officer never discussed the matter at all. I hesitated to raise the issue since he seemed to want to leave it alone. So I left it alone.

The "incident" illustrates the delicate balance required in policing. On one hand, as authority figures, the officers must garner some level of respect from the community. When respect is not given, however, the officer must react in some fashion. Otherwise little regard will be shown from certain citizens—typically those who are young and tough. This is easier for sworn police officers because most people will not directly challenge them. Of course, some people do challenge — and harm — police officers. However, most police officers can at least partly "hide behind the badge." With private police officers, they do not have a "real badge" to hide behind. They only have whatever moral (or legal) authority that they can personally exert. To say that this is a challenge facing private police officers is an understatement of immense proportions.

The mindset of the private police officers was illustrated by two other individuals whom I rode with. During the course of the tour, each officer remarked — several times— on how quiet it was on the streets. The fact that it was quiet meant that no criminal activity was going on. Hence, without crime, they could not make arrests. Their clear assertion was that they wanted action. This mindset is common for young, aggressive police officers. Based on my many years in dealing with police officers, I know the desire to make a "good pinch" is both common and understandable. It is understandable because most people who join the police force have a certain personality type which is manifested by the desire to find and capture "bad guys." While there are certainly less aggressive, maybe even passive, young police officers, it has been my experience that almost all young officers desire to impact crime — and make arrests. This attitude — if it can be called that — is also possibly a function of the training all police officers go through. The experience of the police academy, with its orientation toward physical conditioning, classroom instruction, and weapons training, all tend to develop a certain esprit de corps, which is consistent with the traditional quasi-military mission of the police.

This same attitude appeared to resonate in the words of one particular officer. While speaking generally about the firm (Majestic) and about the Marquette Park patrols, he stated that "this is the closest thing to being a cop, without being a cop." The significance of this statement is both top-ical and somewhat chilling. This individual, while seemingly well intended in his desire to impact crime, has been vested with the job of being "the police," without the training and formal recognition of governmental authority. Stated another way, he is "the police," without the training and without the authority of government.

What made this statement rather chilling is in the way he said it. He made the statement in a completely casual manner, without any hint of the irony or the implications. His mindset seemed to be that he can be the police, without "being the police." I do not know if the believed that this job was some shortcut for his career aspirations. It may simply have been a means of doing police work prior to being officially deemed "the police." Whatever the motivation behind the statement, the significant of his state-ment was that he, in fact, was doing the work of the police. In fact, as will be explained later, he was probably doing more than the typical police officer—for less money, and with less training and authority. Notwith-standing this assertion, the officer mentioned later — in an unrelated con-versation — that he intended to take the test for the Cook County Sheriff's Department. For now, however, he patrolled the streets of Chicago for Majestic Protective Services.

This same officer later described an incident which plainly illustrates the work of this security force. He explained that about one month pre-vious to our conversation, he was involved in a shooting incident while conducting a patrol. He described the incident as follows. He and his part-ner were on routine patrol when they observed a large group of young adults partying in a yard. The officer drove the vehicle into the alley near the party. They exited the vehicle and began asking (or telling) the crowd to disperse from the alley. While doing so, an individual approximately 18–20 years old pulled out a gun and fired four shots at the officers. Upon doing so, the crowd began to run or fall to the ground. The officer briefly took cover and then began to chase the shooter and another person, who ran through the yard and into a building. He pursued the shooter into a third floor hallway, where the shooter attempted (unsuccessfully) to enter an apartment. The officer pointed his 9mm semi-automatic weapon at the shooter, who fell to the floor — begging him not to shoot. The officer stated that he did not shoot. He stated, almost incredibly from my point of view, that the individual was not even arrested! His reasoning was that he did not arrest this person because he "could not find the gun." Apparently, or at least according to the officer, the shooter had dropped the weapon while running.

From the perspective of a former police officer, the fact that the individual was not arrested is simply amazing — if the story is true. If, in fact, an individual fired four shots at these officers, I can almost guarantee that if this same scenario occurred with Chicago police officers, the individual would — at a minimum — have been arrested, and possibly taken a "few lumps" while being arrested. It is important to consider the "law of the street" in making this assertion. The law on the street sometimes involves the police effecting "justice," regardless of the form it happens to take. In this scenario, justice would have resulted in a felony charge of, at least, aggravated battery, or quite possibly attempted murder. Beyond these charges, the "shooter" would have been fortunate not to have been subject to some other informal sanction. This statement is not meant as an indictment against the police. It is certainly possible that street justice would not have occurred, indeed, this would have been appropriate.

At least from my perspective, the Majestic officer definitely did not react as would the typical police officer. He did not arrest the shooter, he did not arrest the shooter's partner, and he did not seem bothered by the fact that the individual walked away from the incident. As a former police officer, I find this most interesting — even amazing. The question which comes to mind is whether this officer, with his minimal training and street experience, actually used a higher level of professionalism and discretion than the average "peace officer." The answer is debatable. Looking at the incident as objectively as possible, it appears that the officer was both weak (from a law enforcement perspective) and strong (from an ethical or professional perspective). Whatever the "right" answer, one wonders what lesson this incident illustrates.

These same officers were conducting themselves as "the police" in several other situations which I directly observed. During one tour, they conducted a search of an individual they had observed urinating in an alley. Apparently, the officers had previously obtained a "rock" of cocaine from his person and arrested him for possession of a controlled substance. This time, the individual was confronted, searched, and allowed to walk away. No contraband was found. This is not because the officers did not try. They conducted a thorough search of the suspect. They emptied his pockets, they searched his pants and his socks, they checked the area around the suspect — in the event that he dropped or threw contraband to the ground. This search raised obvious constitutional concerns, as the officers probably did not have legal authority to conduct such an extensive search of the individual.

In another incident, the officer responded to a domestic disturbance. In this incident, the officers did not go into the building. Instead, they parked in the alley and waited for Chicago police officers to arrive. While waiting in the alley, someone yelling from the apartment could be heard. When the police arrived, a male about 45 years old exited the back door. Since the police came to the front door, the man was initially encountered by the Majestic officers. The officers briefly spoke to the individual until the police came into the back yard. At that time, the Chicago Police officers searched the man, and some bags he was carrying. Upon completion, the police officer asked the Majestic officers if they "wanted him." The Majestic officers stated no. Later, one of the private police officers mentioned that the fact that the question was posed is a sign of respect toward the private officers. The point was that the police officer was deferring to the discretion of the private police officers as to what they may want to accomplish with this incident.

Another example of such thinking was illustrated in an incident with two individuals who were loitering on the street corner. The officers pulled up, parked directly across the street from these individuals, and stayed there without any communication with these individuals for approximately 20 minutes. This represented a standoff between the participants. Who was going to leave first, the officers or the teens? This is another form of the "respect game" that is played out on the streets. During this time, it began to rain. The youths stood in the rain, the officers sat in the car. Each did what they are supposed to do. The gamesmanship on the street "required" these rules. The youths stood on the corner — tough and oblivious to the rain and to the officers. The officers — by their continued presence — indirectly communicated that they ruled the street. The message was, we can sit in the car — warm and dry — and show you that this is our corner, not yours. In the end, the youths opened their umbrellas — to the great amusement of the officers. The youths, no doubt, heard the laughter and walked away — defeated. The officers won, they outlasted the young toughs. They won the corner. This is the game of the street.

During another tour, one of these officers worked with another older officer. On two occasions, the older officer verbally removed youths from front porches of abandoned buildings. In both instances, the younger officer seemed bothered by the fact that the older officer focused his attention on such matters. The older officer, however, demonstrated the knowledge of the "broken windows" theory. Broken windows is a term made popular by author George Kelling to describe clues of the physical deterioration in a community. He seemed to understand that much of "crime fighting" is not simply arresting criminals. Instead, by knowing the trouble spots — like abandoned buildings — the officer exhibited an understanding of order maintenance techniques. Focusing on these trouble spots, theoretically, provides a deterrent to crime, and serves the community that contracted with the firm. This same scenario occurred numerous times during the ride-alongs. Consequently, an order maintenance approach can and was used by the private police officers.

In three other examples, the service of the security firm was manifested in a very real way. On these occasions, the Majestic officers responded to "in-progress" calls. In-progress calls are just as the term signifies—the crime is in progress, it is happening now. These calls are given priority in policing. It is typical that officers will respond to the location even though they are not assigned the call. In one example, the call was a "burglary in progress." The officers responded to the scene. They were on the scene about ten minutes before any Chicago police officer arrived. At this location, the complainant was an elderly female property owner who lived alone. She was about 70 years old, and was visibly shaken. She was extremely grateful for their response. The officers secured the area and took time to speak with her. They explained how to call them, how to get involved in the block club, how to secure her home, etc. It was apparent that the value of their response and advice was worth many times more than this lady paid in taxes for the patrol service.

In another in-progress incident, the Majestic officers arrived at the scene, exited their vehicle, walked the area, and drove off before any Chicago police unit arrived. In total, the Majestic officers were there at least 10–15 minutes prior to the police. In fact, as the Majestic officers pulled away from the scene, the police officers arrived and asked if the call was "anything." The Majestic officers responded "nothing there." The vehicles pulled away in opposite directions.

In yet another incident, the Majestic officers responded to a call of "shots fired." Also responding were an 8th District tactical unit, and a railroad police vehicle. We were the first on the scene. We toured the area for several minutes before any of the other vehicles arrived. The call appeared to be unfounded. The 8th District beat car responded about ten minutes later. Their response was less than appropriate, especially given the nature of the call. Maybe the other patrol vehicles were busy. Maybe they were not.

These examples clearly illustrated that the security patrols have value — at least in terms of responsiveness. There were numerous other instances in which I witnessed the same level of responsiveness. It was clear, in the time frame that I participated in the ride-alongs, the security patrols provided more responsive service to the community than the 8th District police officers. This statement is not meant as a slight against the police. It is simply a factual statement based on my experience in this research. Some may argue that this assertion represents a skewed version of reality. This may be true. It was, nonetheless, what I observed.

Another example of the implications of the work performed by Majestic involved a confrontation with a man drinking on a street corner — in full view of passing cars and children playing. The individual was drinking from a quart bottle of beer in a brown paper bag. Upon observing such, the private police officer exited the vehicle and approached the man. He requested identification from the man. In response, the man immediately stated that "I live around the corner." The officer responded by saying "if you do, then why don't you drink there?" The man replied with some unintelligible answer. The officer ignored his response and insisted that he produce an "ID." The man pulled out his wallet — showed his identification — and again insisted, "I live around the corner." The officer verified his address and told him to "empty the bottle." The man complied, pouring out about two-thirds of the bottle into an empty flower box, which he used as his lounge chair. As he was emptying the bottle, a man who represented himself as the "caretaker" of the building walked by. He stated, "Thanks, they are always throwing the bottles here." With that, the bottle was given to the caretaker, and the man walked away while the caretaker continued cleaning up around the property.

This incident, in my opinion, illustrates the conflict between the social good of security and the constitutional constraints inherent in private patrols. From a security perspective, the act of ridding illegal and inappropriate drinking from public streets serves a larger public good. As described in the incivilities literature, the presence of disorderly behavior, such as public drinking, has a deteriorating effect upon the community — particularly the youth in the community. As is often the case, the apprehension of the drinker was "witnessed" by several preteen youths. One can only wonder what they were thinking. Through their eyes, can they even see the societal and symbolic implications of this action? Even assuming that the action failed to communicate a positive message, it seems fair to say that the larger community benefits from the removal of such disorderly behavior.

From a constitutional perspective, however, this seemingly innocuous incident presents some troublesome implications. First, apart from the immediate social benefit of removing a public drinker from a street corner, the fact is this function was accomplished by a private citizen. This private citizen has the appearance of authority, but lacks actual police powers. Regardless of all the appearances of authority — the gun, radio, squad car, and such — the fact is that one private citizen imposed his will on another. One citizen forced another citizen to be deprived of his liberty and property without due process of law — for the purpose of promoting the public good of a safe and orderly community.

Upon closer inspection, the ramifications of this seemingly innocuous incident will be apparent. The ramifications go to the heart of policing in contemporary America, and to our long cherished constitutional protections. For example, the requirement that the man produce an identification as commanded by another private citizen, while both are on a public way, represents a level of authority that the courts have not even vested in the public police. The fact is the police could not have commanded the drinker to produce an ID. In reality, of course, the police often ask people on the street to produce an identification card and an explanation for their actions or presence on the street. Citizens usually comply and cooperate. The law provides, however, that citizens do not have to comply and cannot be arrested for their failure to do so. The reality is people usually comply with such requests by the police — or they are arrested for a crime unrelated to the failure to produce an identification card. Aside from these legal technicalities, to further complicate this scenario, the fact is that the person demanding the ID was a private citizen who did not possess police powers.

Street stops for loitering have similar constitutional implications. In many instances, the private police officers admonished youths away from the street corners. In one particular incident, the private police officers observed numerous youths loitering in a narrow gangway next to a small store. One officer told the youths to get out of the gangway. They responded that they "live in the building." The officer asserted that "you do not lease the gangway." He again insisted that they move on. At this point, all of the youths walked away except one individual. This person just stood there eating potato chips from a bag. Additional words were exchanged between the officer and this person. Finally, the Majestic officer asked, "Are you going to dare me?" as he angrily began to open his door. He proceeded to exit the vehicle and moved quickly in the direction of the rebellious youth. The youth finally relented and quickly retreated into the gangway — in the opposite direction of the approaching officer. The standoff was over; the "good guys" win again.

This incident — again — illustrates the inherent interpersonal and extra-legal dilemmas facing private police officers. The street smart youths know that the Majestic officers are not the "real police." They do not have the same respect, or at least, regard for their presence and their authority. Indeed, it is sometimes difficult to impose compliance. Because of such, many of the youths—especially those tied to gangs—challenge and dare the private police officers.

This poses the potential for dangerous confrontations, and also poses the assertion of questionable legal authority. These issues—of course—

are tied to each other. The lack of legal authority (or the perceived lack of such) coupled with the desire to accomplish the job creates a dilemma. The dilemma is that the private police officer often is faced with the decision to avoid confrontations at the expense of failing to do his or her job. For those who care about doing a good job — like the Majestic officers — this is a difficult dilemma. Unfortunately, this is one dilemma which is unavoidable. It is part of the nature of the job and of the nature of their authority (or lack thereof). This issue will be further developed in the last chapter of this book.

Later in the same tour, we responded to a disturbance call of a "fight with a knife." This incident presented two issues relevant to this study. First, the police tactical unit who responded to the call specifically asked for the "Marquette Park patrol" to assist them. This request—coupled with the subsequent conversations—illustrates the level of cooperation between the private and public entities. In legal terms, this cooperation would be deemed a "nexus," thereby showing a connection to possibly impose constitutional prohibitions on the actions of the private police. In the event that an arrest was effected from the cooperative and coordinated efforts of the two entities, then constitutional prohibitions are likely to apply even though the private entity effected the arrest.

Upon responding to the incident, we observed two plainclothes tactical police officers in front of a four story apartment building. Two males and two females were also in front of the same building. It was clear that these individuals participated in the disturbance. As soon as we pulled up, one of the tactical police officers asked if we had the keys to the apartment. The private police officer looked into the glove compartment and removed a set of keys. As it was, this apartment complex was one of several in which an Agency Agreement was utilized. This time, however, the keys for this building were in another Majestic vehicle. This prevented the entry into the apartment, and possibility the ability to make an arrest.

Immediately thereafter, the private police officers met with another tactical unit in an alley around the corner from the disturbance. Here, the private officer provided information to the tactical unit relative to drug dealing. Two significant implications can be shown from this meeting.

In one regard, the meeting exhibited a level of respect for the knowledge and expertise that the private officer possessed. It is important to note that tactical police officers are expected to make arrests— much more so than patrol officers. Further, tactical officers who make "good" arrests, meaning arrests with guns, significant amount of narcotics, or both, are given high levels of informal, and sometimes even formal, recognition. As such, any good tactical officer is always looking for information from "the street." This is clearly what these officers were motivated to talk about with the Majestic officer. But did they view him as a credible source of information, or were they just testing the waters?

The second issue illustrated by this meeting is the desire to produce results versus the obstacles attached to such. In essence, the issue, as articulated by the private police officer, is that the youths selling drugs can be identified, but it is difficult to arrest them — and locate the drugs. The Majestic officer stressed that the youths could be arrested for a minor offense, such as disorderly conduct. This type of arrest, however, does not get the drugs off the street, nor does it deter the offenders from selling drugs. According to the Majestic officer, the best solution is to arrest the offender for drug possession, and at the same time confiscate the drugs. The ability to make such an arrest, however, often requires many hours of surveillance and coordination between police units.

The dilemma for the private officers is that Majestic is not equipped for such an operation. The alternative, therefore, is to pass the information to the tactical units. What, if anything, the tactical units do with the information is beyond the control of the private officers. This was obviously a source of frustration for this particular private police officer. He wanted more control. He also wanted more evidence that his work (and that of Majestic overall) had a positive effect in the community. He wanted to produce for and please his clients— the community, the sole service provider, the commission, the police department, and even city officials. Therefore, this problem presented a difficult dilemma. Making an arrest for disorderly conduct "would not do any good." Giving the information to the tactical unit may result in no action because they often "do not want to bother." The result, for this officer, is troubling and a source of significant distress.

During another ride-along, I had the occasion to observe an informant stopping our Majestic vehicle for the purpose of providing information on an imminent drug transaction. The informant stated that two youths— known to the Majestic officer — were about to enter into a $10,000 drug purchase from a "Mexican." This transaction was to take place at 1:00 a.m., at a local store. The officer obtained the information, and again, called for an 8th District tactical unit. He talked to the tactical sergeant, who took the information, supposedly to be passed on to his officers. While it is unclear whether this information led to an arrest, it is obvious that, once again, the Majestic officers and the district police officers cooperated in developing information designed for law enforcement purposes. In this instance, they clearly were "state actors," at least from a legal standpoint.

The cooperative efforts between these groups were described by other

Majestic officers, independent of these scenarios explained above. The relationship was explained by another Majestic officer, who stated that they (Majestic) have a good rapport with the 8th District police. He stated that "it was clear that the [private] patrols get a lot of respect from the community." He based his opinion on the amount of interaction with the community, from both property owners and youths on the street. He emphasized that the patrols have done "a lot," and that they "are good for the community." He believes that street crime, and the related presence of gangs, have been reduced due to the patrols. It is difficult to assess— objectively—whether the patrols had any effect on crime. The alleged reduction of gang members on the street, however, is almost impossible to objectively assess. His statement illustrates that perception, not fact, is often the key factor when assessing crime — and the fear of crime. This is consistent with the literature on crime and the effects of crime.

After describing the benefits of the private patrols, these officers then asserted that certain companies who previously provided the patrols were problematic. For purposes of this study, these companies shall remain anonymous. The officers asserted that one company was "abusive," in that its officers were known to exert physical abuse against gang members. Both officers strongly maintained that another company was corrupt, with its employees literally being "criminals." They stated that it was common knowledge that this particular firm was too close to the neighborhood gang members, possibly to the extent of "protecting their drug operations." They maintained that many of these officers took money in exchange for protecting the street drug operations. Unfortunately, I could not independently verify this information. Since this particular firm was not a subject of this study, I believed the information — even if true — was too far removed to explore at this time.

During the course of this same tour, these officers were involved in a number of street stops and searches of suspected drug dealers. On two occasions, the same individuals were stopped and searched. The first encounter was relatively slight — with only a brief "frisk" of the suspect's jacket. The second time, however, the search was intrusive. On this occasion, four people were observed in an alley. The officers had all four suspects place their hands on the hood of the patrol car. Each individual was searched. The search revealed that one suspect had a lighter in the shape, size, and weight of a .22-caliber semi-automatic handgun. The "gun" looked and felt authentic. During this same search, the officers recovered a marijuana cigarette from the pants pocket of another individual. At this point, the officers called for their supervisor.

Upon arrival to the scene, the supervisor instructed the officers to "tear their car apart." One officer stated, "I already searched it." The supervisor replied, "Search it again." The officer did not do so. Instead, he stayed with the suspects, who were still positioned with their hands on the patrol car. At this time, the supervisor took it upon himself to search the vehicle. He removed seats, searched under the dashboard, and basically "turned the car upside down." He did not find any additional evidence.

After another ten minutes, the suspects were released, each being warned that they must stay off the street. When the suspects left the scene, the supervisor stated that he took every CD out of its case, and threw them about the vehicle. The individual who owned the vehicle was obviously upset when he discovered this. The marijuana cigarette remained in the patrol vehicle's ashtray for the remainder of the tour. I do not know what the officers did with the contraband.

It seems rather obvious that the extent and intrusiveness of the search was unreasonable — and even malicious in terms of throwing the CDs around the interior of the car. The officers could have only legally extended the search under these facts based on a lawful arrest. They did not arrest the individuals. Instead, they checked everywhere they could to find contraband. Since they did not find enough to arrest, they effected "street justice" instead. It is my belief that this incident — on its face — manifested a constitutional violation. This incident precipitated a lengthy discussion about this particular supervisor. Without any probing, one of the officers began to make a series of charges against this supervisor. He stated that he was "double dipping" or "ghosting" the payroll. He asserted that the supervisor was making "a whole a lot of money from this contract" by billing for contract patrol time when no one was present. The seriousness of these allegations was stressed several times. The officer even stated that the supervisor could be indicted since the contract was a government account.

The seriousness of the allegations was underscored by the fact that the supervisor had been terminated by Majestic a couple of months prior to this conversation. The officer maintained that the decision to terminate the supervisor was because the owners found out about the "double dipping." Both officers were offended by the idea that while they made $10.00 per hour, the supervisor made "big money" in this illicit manner. For some reason unknown to the officers, the supervisor "did not stay fired." He was allowed to return to his employment with Majestic. According to these officers, he was reinstated to his position a couple of days after being terminated.

This issue presented a number of problems for this case study. It was simply too controversial to broach with the owners of Majestic. Probing into it was sure to complicate, if not destroy, my ability to participate in the study. I could not think of any way to verify the information, short of making this supervisor the subject of inquiries with other officers. This was too risky. If I mentioned the issue to the wrong person, the supervisor could have easily destroyed my ability to participate in the study. Since this issue did not directly relate to my research questions, I decided to leave it alone.

This being said, the implications of this accusation are fully appreciated. For purposes of this book, however, this accusation must be regarded as just one individual's word against another individual. There has been no independent verification of this accusation. At this point, the accused remains anonymous. The accusation is included in this case study because it was part of the data. While I cannot verify the accuracy of the data, the statement was deemed too important to ignore. For this reason, and to add context of the implications of privatized patrol services, it seems appropriate that this issue must be raised. To do otherwise would be intellectually dishonest, or at least represent a failure to objectively present the data in an unvarnished manner.

The officers further contended that this same supervisor had conducted himself in a manner which they found offensive. They described an incident which occurred two months previously in which they along with the supervisor went to an apartment. The supervisor banged on the door of the apartment, yelling "police!" Since the supervisor was not the "police," the officer asked him what was he doing declaring a police presence. From this time on, the officers stated that they are careful around the supervisor. He added that many 8th District police officers viewed the supervisor as essentially "impersonating a police officer." This assertion is particularly interesting in light of the American Security Services officer who was arrested by Chicago Police for an illegal possession of a weapon.

One final example is illustrative of this issue — with pointed implications of private policing — and involves a drug "arrest" made by this supervisor. According to the officer, the supervisor arrested and handcuffed a drug suspect. Apparently the individual was caught with marijuana and cocaine. The stop was supposedly based on a call monitored on the police radio. When the assigned police unit arrived, the police officer refused to "arrest" the suspect. The reason, according to the Majestic officer, was that the apprehension and confiscation of the drugs was not observed by the police officer. This fact created a concern in the mind of the police officer.

The obvious concern was the police officer did not know that the drugs were, in fact, recovered from the "arrestee." He was concerned that the supervisor could have planted the drugs on the individual. Again, this was simply an allegation. There are no independent facts to support his contention. However, this accusation goes to the heart of the private-public policing relationship. If the public police do not trust their "subordinate" private comrades, then what does that say about the ability of these groups to control crime? What does it say about the viability of private patrols, or the relationship between the two groups? What does it mean to public safety?

In summary, the ride-along data revealed that on several occasions the private police officers violated the constitutional rights of certain citizens. The data, therefore, supports the prediction that such constitutional violations would occur. The implications of such constitutional violations, and the issues raised in this discussion, will be addressed in the next chapter.

INTERVIEW AND MEETING RESULTS

The final research technique was interviews with key decision makers in the private patrols, including observations from two commission meetings and one police beat meeting. I will briefly describe the meetings then relate the substance of the interviews.

The initial meeting was an opportunity to introduce myself and the case study project to the commissioners, the sole service provider, and the security firm. I briefly described the study by simply stating that I wanted to study the private patrols. From there, the respondents seemed to be pleased that someone would want to study their program. I think this naturally appealed to the desire in people to do something worthy of study.

In any event, the initial meeting involved the selection of the security firm. The firm selected was Majestic Protective Services. As stated previously, the selection process was largely geared toward saving money. The firm with the lowest bid was awarded the contract. Once the firm was selected, I engaged one of the principals of the firm relative to the study. He was very happy to be part of the study.

The next commission meeting I attended was halfway through the annual contract. The meeting was very informative. This was a key meeting in that it would be a good indicator of the work of the security firm. The representative of the sole service provider stated that the firm "was doing what they are supposed to be doing, they're doing their job. I have heard nothing but good." Upon making this statement, a couple of commission members nodded in agreement.

A representative of the security firm then gave his report to the commission and the public. He stated that loitering was the biggest problem facing the community. Of course, this assertion directly relates to the order maintenance function discussed throughout this study.

In response to this assertion by the security firm, the police representative explained that the department has a loitering response. The response was to be addressed through tactical missions. The police representative also emphasized that "we are working closely with the Marquette Park patrols." He related that they share information on crime activity. He pointed to an example in which the police conducted a drug raid *in which the authority to enter the building was derived from an Agency Agreement.* This was the first independent confirmation by the police of the use of this Agency Agreement. As amazing as it is, this police lieutenant did not seem to question the legality of the document. Not only did he announce this in a public meeting, but he did so without any hint that the use of this document raises serious legal or constitutional questions. Apparently, the issue did not trigger any concerns from the commission, as none of the members raised any questions, nor did they seem uncomfortable with the legality of the Agency Agreement.

Following this assertion, the security firm representative seemed happy to emphasize that information received by Majestic officers goes to the 8th District police. He added that "we [Majestic] are not in the gang and drug business." While this statement played to the audience, the data derived from this study points in the opposite direction. There is ample evidence that Majestic was aggressive in drug and gang enforcement. While it is clear that Majestic did not have the resources or personnel for this "business," it did not stop them from trying. In fact, the ride-alongs illustrated a rather vigorous effort, albeit a losing proposition, given their limitations.

I later attended a police beat meeting, in which representatives of the security firm are expected to attend—and in fact, do attend. The police beat meeting was uneventful and rather innocuous. I came away with the overriding impression that it was a chore for the police, and irrelevant for the Majestic officers. The meeting was led by a police sergeant, who exhibited poor organization and little professionalism. The sergeant was dressed in shorts, gym shoes and a tee shirt. He sat in his chair throughout the meeting. His chair was turned away from the audience, so as to be angled toward the police officers seated at the speaker's table. His posture alone communicated to the crowd that he did not really want to be there.

The responses to the questions posed to the sergeant were answered in a very general manner. The sergeant did not answer any question with specific facts. His answers essentially revolved around a series of excuses, pushing as much of the accountability back to the community. "You must call the police, you have to give us good descriptions of the offenders, you must stay alert to community conditions and troublemakers"; these and other canned answers were readily provided by the sergeant. While these answers are all true and undisputable, the issue I found most interesting is that the audience did not challenge the police for more definitive answers. The participants in the audience seemed satisfied with the fact that "the police cannot do it alone." They seemed to accept that the community is part of the solution — and the problem.

Interestingly, no one questioned what role the private patrols had in this equation. The police never mentioned them. Neither did any of the audience members. I was most surprised that the private patrols did not seem to play any part in the discussion of crime and crime conditions. The fact that the private firm was not even included in the discussion speaks volumes.

The first interview was with a commission member. According to this person, the major duties and responsibilities of the commission are the preparation of the security budget, the selection of the sole service provider, getting feedback from the community relative to security or crime, and working with the sole service provider on various operational issues. They do not directly deal with the police, but let the two groups work together without interference from the commission.

The relationship between the commission and the community is informal. There are no formal procedures set up to obtain information or complaints. The commission member emphasized that communication with the community is based on an "informal understanding based on a cohesive framework between all groups" — community, security firm, sole service provider, and the commission. In this way, the communication is not "bureaucratic." However, when probed on how a citizen could complain about poor service or abusive treatment from the security provider, the commissioner could not give a direct answer. The answer was that the key reporting is from the people — "that's it." There are no procedures set up to track a complaint, no policies on accountability in how a complaint is handled, and no forms or other procedures to capture data on complaints. Contrast these reporting procedures, or the lack thereof, against those established by the Chicago Police Department. The distinctions are dramatic. Possibly in response to the obvious lack of accountability, the commission member added that more formalized channels for such may be instituted when the program is re-certified (the program is certified every three years).

The commission member stated that the proper functions of the security firm are to observe questionable behaviors and activity, and interact with the Chicago police on such information. The commissioner also added that the security personnel may "detain" suspects for the police. Upon saying this, however, the commissioner quickly added that the security personnel have "no authority to arrest." Based on the data derived from both the documentary analysis and the ride-alongs, it is reasonable to assert that the security firms—in fact—do much more than "observe and report." They also do more than detain suspects. It is clear that the security firms are functioning in a much more aggressive fashion than described by the commissioner. I have no reason to believe that the commissioner knows this fact. I believe that the commissioner was being honest when making the statement. To my knowledge, at least part of the reason that the actual functions of the security firms are not known is based on the substantial lack of any real reporting mechanism. Without such a mechanism, the security firm operates in a void, whereby it is difficult to determine what is being done and how they are doing it.

According to the commissioner, the most tangible benefits from the private patrol program is the promotion of community stability, reduction in crime and fear of crime, and a "major reduction" in the amount of graffiti in the community. Incivilities literature calls this the order maintenance function, which has been shown to be the most prevalent function of the security providers. Here again, at least from the perception of the commissioner, the functional research proposition had been validated.

The most tangible problem, according to the commissioner, still facing the community is the level of loitering on the street corners. The commissioner stated that the presence of loiterers fuels the perception within the community that there is a "gang problem." The commissioner noted that for this reason, loitering has been "under the microscope," and that the solution is for security to "tell people to get off the corner because of community concerns." The commissioner emphasized that this approach has been the "philosophy" of the board, and it has been communicated to the security providers. Given this philosophy, it is interesting to consider the interpersonal aspects of the relationship between the private police and the community residents. As described in the ride-along section, there are a number of nuances which impact this relationship, not the least of which is the level of legal and moral authority attributed to the private police officers. Based on the statement by the commissioner, it seems clear that these nuances were not considered.

Finally, I asked the commissioner what factors would be considered in determining the success or failure of the program. The response was thoughtful but somewhat contradictory. The commissioner focused on two factors—communication and accountability.

Relative to communication, the commissioner stated that the security firm must know what is going on in the community, including identifying the "hot spots." However, as noted above, there are no real communication channels designed to facilitate the transfer of information between the community, the sole service provider, and the commission. Instead, the program essentially relies on informal communication, such as the "good faith" and desire of those involved to "speak to each other on a regular basis." While these methods are important, the informal nature of the communication — in my mind — is not sufficient to effectively articulate important and fluid information.

Relative to accountability, the commissioner stated that the "board holds the security firm accountable for what goes on in the community." Again, this statement sounds good, but there is no mechanism in place to account for the actions or inactions of the security providers. As stated previously, there are no policies or procedures to provide for accountability. The stated desire for accountability was further negated by a statement made by the commissioner. When discussing the greatest obstacles to an effective security program, the commissioner noted that security procedures "are not necessary." If security procedural guidelines are not necessary, then how can accountability be assessed? It seems reasonable to assert that you cannot have accountability without procedures, or procedures without accountability.

Whatever the right answer, it is apparent that the commissioner desired to provide an important service that contributes to the betterment of the community. It is also clear that the commissioner believed that the security patrols have provided for the betterment of the community. While this case study has shown some evidence of this perception, there are a number of larger issues which should be considered, such as accountability for legal and constitutional constraints, and the legal and moral authority derived from the private security providers.

The next interview I conducted was with an administrator of the sole service provider, the Lithuanian Human Services Council, Inc. The administration of the security patrols is one of the functional responsibilities of this community based corporation. Other services that they perform include immigration procedures, translation and counseling services, family and domestic violence prevention programs, and a number of programs focusing on elderly citizens. The administration of the security patrols represents from 10 percent to 20 percent of the work product of the service provider.

The administration of the security program focused on two areas—contract administration and the operations of the actual patrols. In terms of contract administration, the service provider is charged with the responsibility to advertise and hire the security firm, prepare the contract proposals, and organize the information for the selection of the security provider by the commission. As to the operational support for the patrols, the service provider compiles data on crimes, arrests and the activity level of the firm. It is important to note that this information is provided directly from the security firm. This data is not compared or contrasted with crime statistics from the Chicago Police Department. The service provider merely organizes and compiles the data for presentation at the commission meetings.

The service provider also is charged with monitoring the activities of the security provider, monitoring community conditions, and working with block clubs for special requests and other similar matters. As emphasized above, these services are not tied to any specific policies and procedures. Instead, they are done in an informal manner, without any written guidelines to accomplish the actual service.

The administrator viewed the overriding purpose of the security patrols as providing a "feeling of security or safety" within the community. According to the administrator, the patrols have been "very beneficial to the community." In this light, the most tangible benefit of the patrols was the reduction of crime, an enhanced feeling of security and safety, and less graffiti. Notice that these factors were echoed by the commission member. Unfortunately, just as with the commission member, this opinion was based on a subjective belief. There was no evidence that this assessment was based on any specific, objective criteria. Here again, these concerns, as echoed by the crime and incivilities literature, related to order maintenance. Consequently, at least from the perception of the administrator, the functional research proposition has been validated.

When asked to describe the most problematic aspect of the patrols, the administrator responded that there "were none." In this regard, the administrator emphasized that there have been "no complaints" from the community relative to the patrols. The only negative point made by the administrator related to the continued presence of loitering around the community, but this person was quick to add that "there probably would be more if security was not there." In this light, the administrator noted that "some people would like to pay even more" for additional security patrols. This was at least partly related to the desire to further reduce loitering.

Both the administrator and the commissioner spoke almost exclusively in positive terms regarding the patrols. I believe, as I did regarding the commissioner, that the administrator held this assessment in an honest manner. I do not believe that there was any attempt to hide or ignore potential problems. I believe that the administrator viewed the patrol program in a manner devoid of any concern for issues such as constitutional rights, appropriate accountability and legal authority. Instead, the concern was for safety and security. These issues may provide the motivation for continued and sustained use of private patrols. Whatever the causal factors, this study has shown — in a compelling manner — that the patrol function raises serious concerns related to these larger issues, which were ignored or overlooked within this private patrol program.

Finally, the last interview was conducted with an administrator of the security firm. This interview proved to be the least informative, possibly because, as the respondent with the most to lose if his firm made a bad impression, the administrator was the most cautious about the information that he provided. It was my impression that the administrator knew more than he said. The information derived from the interview is as follows.

The firm of Majestic Protective Services, Inc., was incorporated in the State of Illinois on February 5, 1997. The typical accounts of the firm are construction sites, rental car lots, parking garages, and some shopping mall security. According to the administrator, the purpose of the private program was for "patrolling and visibility — to provide for a safer neighborhood." It is fair to say that these are "observe and report" functions. The words of the administrator directly reflect this particular function. As stated above, however, the data derived from this study show otherwise.

When probed about the community response to these patrols, the administrator stated that the "community likes Majestic, our company is friendly — not arrogant." The administrator was asked if there have been any complaints from the community related to the patrols. The response was, "not to my knowledge." The administrator added that "the city" did not provide any guidelines relative to operational procedures. It is noteworthy that the administrator was cognizant that such guidelines are necessary.

The blame for the lack of guidelines, however, did not rest with Majestic but was directed at *the city*. Without belaboring this point, this assertion by the security firm administrator speaks volumes as to the nature of privatization. In essence, the lack of accountability for private patrols was a *systemic* problem — it was not the fault of the particular security firm. Instead, the problem rested with the failure of government to adequately administer the program — at least from the perception of the security firm administrator.

Case Study Conclusions

This study has shown that each of the research propositions was found to be valid. First, the documentary data and related facts evidenced that the private police officers would be deemed state actors. The data revealed that law enforcement and order maintenance functions accounted for 68.1 percent of their total work product. This data, coupled with the factual and situational attributes described earlier, clearly illustrates that the private police officers are state (or public) actors. This conclusion relates directly to the predicted instances of constitutional violations. In this regard, the constitution would only apply if the private police officers are state actors. Since it has been determined that they are, then the constitutionality assessment will be made with this conclusion in mind. If the research proposition relating to state actors was not validated, then legally and logically, it would be impossible to violate the constitution, since it would not apply to private citizens. Consequently, the state actor assessment will trigger the subsequent assessment relative to constitutional violations.

Second, the documentary data also showed that the private police officers perform order maintenance functions as their most common and pervasive function. The two firms collectively devoted 51.5 percent of their work to order maintenance. This data was further broken down to the activities of the respective firms, with each firm evidencing a preponderance of their time on order maintenance. This conclusion was further validated by the interviews of key decision makers. In each case, the focus of their concern was on loitering and graffiti, the order maintenance mandate of the private patrols.

This study further illustrated that the order maintenance function, made popular in community policing parlance, is applicable to private policing. This is consistent with the theory posited in this study. That is, order maintenance is consistent with the typical functioning of private security. Security firms have tended to focus on deterrence, rather than enforcement. The reasoning is that since order maintenance is believed to act as a deterrent, or as a means to prevent more serious criminal activity, this proactive approach is consistent with the role typically played by private security. Consequently, this research demonstrates that the order maintenance function is naturally suited for private policing and was its predominant function.

Third, both the documentary data and the ride-along narrative observations have shown that private police officers violated certain constitutional prohibitions as a direct consequence of their involvement in law enforcement and order maintenance functions. This conclusion was based on two independent data sets. First, the documentary analysis revealed that neither security firm provided any real guidance relative to policies and procedures. Without such guidance, and considering their relative level of training and experience, it is reasonable to infer that the private police officers would violate the constitution. Indeed, without such guidance, the private police officers would be placed in fluid, dynamic and dangerous situations and be expected to perform their job within the confines of the constitution. Speaking from personal experience, this is difficult even when educated and trained far in excess of the minimum standards required for security personnel. From my perspective, it is simply impossible to assume that private police officers will conduct themselves in accordance with the constitution, absent defined guidance, policies, and training.

Going beyond the issue of policies and directives, the documentary analysis showed that in a number of instances, private police officers clearly violated the constitutional rights of certain citizens. Specifically, the data revealed that the use of street stops and building sweeps were conducted by the two firms. It defies explanation as to how these activities could have been constitutionally valid. Indeed, the evidence suggests that the security firm conducted these activities without regard for constitutional concerns.

Additionally, the data shows that the private police officers were involved in a number of arrests, and assisted Chicago police officers in the performance of their duties. This data suggests that the private police officers—particularly Majestic—aggressively sought out criminal activities, including weapon violations and violent criminal incidents. Of course, it is difficult to definitively determine—based on just the documentary evidence—that any of these incidents actually resulted in constitutional violations. However, it is fair to say that there is a greater propensity to commit constitutional violations when conducting such proactive activities. The case law provided in this book validates this assertion.

While the documentary data may not be definitive relative to constitutional violations, the ride-along observations have established that such violations, in fact, took place in my direct proximity. Several instances of vehicle stops and searches, particularly the search in which the CDs were thrown about the car, were clearly unreasonable and excessive under 4th Amendment standards. There were a number of other street encounters where the private police officers exceeded their authority. There were a number of incidents when the private police officers conducted rather intrusive searches without effecting an arrest. Their actual police powers, however, remain questionable in relation to these functions. While the case law analysis illustrated that private police officers have essentially the same arrest power as public police, there are concerns raised when private police officers do not effect an arrest. This presents a situation in which private police officers are performing a function without a clear determination that they have the legal authority to do so. Consequently, I believe that the aforementioned conclusion is consistent with the data and information derived from this case study.

The results of this case study were quite telling and insightful. However, this was not just an experiment. It was real life. It was a community banding together in an attempt to provide a safer environment. It was relatively uneducated, ill trained and ill prepared individuals acting as "the police" because they wanted to help the community, because they needed to feed their families, because they needed a job, and because of a thousand other reasons we will never know. What we do know is the data on how private police officers perform patrols on public streets is available for public consumption. What we do with this information is another question. How widespread will these patrols be in the years to come? I predict they will be commonplace. The next chapter discusses the implications of this case study, focusing on the information derived and the lessons learned.

VIII

Where Do We Go from Here?

The title of this chapter poses a question which can be viewed from at least two different perspectives. The question seems appropriate because so little research has been done by others that would support the data and information from this case study. Nonetheless, we must start somewhere. Hopefully, this book will be viewed as a start, possibly even a significant commencement. Aside from these assertions, the two perspectives are as follows.

First, the operative word in the question is *we*. In the context of this case study, the *we* entails a host of different, often conflicting, interests and entities. A short list of the entities would include the police, the security industry, government administrators at all levels, civil rights attorneys, civil libertarians, prosecutors, corporate attorneys, business leaders, community activists and property owners, to name a few. In this sense, the questions raised here must be addressed at all levels of American society. This is because the issues of security and constitutional rights touch everyone. From the janitor to the C.E.O., from the line level security officer to the president of the company, from the police beat officer to the mayor, from the halfway house to the White House, each person has an interest in a secure environment and in constitutional safeguards.

Second, the difficult balance between security and the constitution is finding a security regiment which will reduce crime and diminish the effects of terrorism, on one hand; while doing so in a way that maintains the integrity of critical constitutional protections. This book demonstrates that this will not be an easy task. To borrow a term often used by Olympic judges, "the level of difficulty" in obtaining this delicate balance will likely be related to the amount of destruction caused by terrorism and crime. If sustained and large scale terrorist attacks do not occur, or if terrorists are rooted out and prosecuted before they can strike, then the clamor for more security, with greater limitations on freedom of movement and constitution protections, will not be substantial. However, if there are any additional 9/11 type destructive attacks, or we are exposed to the use of nuclear, chemical or biological attacks, then the clamor to "do something" may cause our leaders and our citizens to institute "remedies" that are as bad or worse than what the terrorists could inflict on us. By now, the reader is quite aware what this admonition means. Of course, these remedies entail the use of "police powers" to the detriment of critical constitutional protections.

As with any challenge, of course, there is hope and a message. The hope is that American society pulls together as it did in the days and months after the 9/11 attacks. The hope is that the citizens who live in this society will adhere to the principles which made this country great. The hope is that the diverse groups of people who consider themselves as "hyphenated" Americans will view this country as their home and thereby pledge their allegiance to the constitution. My hope is that we as a free and brave people can fight the good fight in the challenges that surely lie ahead.

Additionally, my hope is that this book provides both an insightful view of the issues facing contemporary America, as well as a road map as to how best to maneuver around the forthcoming challenges. In this sense, it is a message. Admittedly, the literature review and the case study illustrates there are no definitive "answers" to the challenges ahead. At best, this book can make the issues more succinct and comprehensible. The following implications may be useful in developing a road map for the appropriate and proper use of private policing.

Since the focus of this book is to shed light on the phenomenon of private patrols, these implications are confined to this specific environment and to those issues which generally affect the security industry — such as training, standards, wages and accountability. Of course, there are many issues related to private security which are not addressed. Those issues specifically dealing with private property are largely beyond the scope of this work. Certainly, there are a number of dynamic and fluid issues facing the private security industry in light of recent terrorist attacks. It is important that these factors are addressed since the threat of terrorism is largely centered on public locations or symbolic governmental institutions. In this way, the implications discussed below limit their perspective to the issues related to private patrols in public environments. These can be broken down into two broad categories: operational or societal.

Operational Implications

The issues related to operational factors include accountability, training, experience, and wages. Each of these issues will be addressed below.

This research raised relevant questions regarding the level of accountability attached to the patrols, particularly as it relates to improper or illegal conduct. Accountability plays an important role in limiting such abusive or illegal conduct. This case study has shown that the functions of private police can adversely impact constitutional protections. Indeed, the research has shown several instances of constitutional violations. Accountability would result in the implementation of certain policies and procedures specifically designed to limit such violations.

There are two sides of the accountability issue related to these patrols. The first is the failure to adequately define the nature or functions of the patrols. The second is the failure to provide any real policies or procedures to handle complaints of misconduct on the part of the patrol officers. I assert both failures are tied together.

The most glaring weakness is the failure to define exactly what functions the patrol officers were to perform. As explained in the findings, neither of the security firms, the commission, the sole service provider, or even the city provided any real cogent direction as to *what* functions were to be performed and *how* were these functions to be accomplished. Indeed, the contract and bid documents merely provided broad, non-descriptive language, such as *security patrols*. This is such a broad term that it has no real meaning attached to it. The best definition for this term was provided in the model proposal drafted by city attorneys. This language was "explained" by listing various functions, which included:

1. Reporting suspicious or criminal activity
2. Detaining individuals believed to have committed criminal offenses
3. Signing complaints and testifying as witnesses at criminal trials

While listing these functions has some explanatory basis, in my opinion such an "explanation" has no value from an operational perspective. As asserted earlier, there is no reason to believe that any patrol officer was made aware of the language in the model bid proposal. Indeed, even if this language was presented to street level officers, it would provide no real direction. At best, the benefit of this language is limited to the liability exposure of the city. If a lawsuit was filed due to the actions or conduct of a patrol officer, the city likely would use the model bid proposal as a basis to contend that the city did not sanction such conduct nor was it even aware of such. Consequently, it is my opinion that the City of Chicago desired broad, non-descriptive language because it provides for a potentially effective legal defense.

This language allows the city to contend that they did not intend for the patrols to conduct certain activities. For example, is it appropriate for the patrol officers to conduct street stops? While the bid documents allows the officers to "detain" suspects or individuals who commit crimes, it does not articulate under what circumstances the detention could take place. Nor does it limit detentions to any specific types or categories of "crimes." This raises several questions. Does the city view loitering as "criminal activity"? How about drinking alcohol on a street corner? What about loud music or loud arguments in a private apartment? There is absolutely no direction given for these questions. Certainly, city attorneys and political leaders should be aware of these questions.

None of this program's legal documents addressed such questions. The reason — in my opinion — is that this allows the city to assert "plausible deniability," that the city never intended the private patrol officers to conduct themselves as police officers. In this way, the city has a much more effective legal defense. They can properly — and honestly — contend that the city never intended that the functions of the private patrol officers would include law enforcement or even order maintenance. As an attorney, I cannot say that this approach by the city was legally incorrect. In fact, from a purely legal perspective, I would agree with the approach taken by the city. However, from an operational perspective, this broad language acts as "definitional or situational" silence. The failure to adequately define the functions and circumstances of the patrols leaves silent a critical aspect of the contract. That is, exactly what are the patrol officers expected to do?

Instead of answering this basic question, the city includes broadly defined indemnification language which seeks to place any and all liability on the shoulders of the sole service provider (or the security firm). It is important to note that the city does not directly contract with the security firm. The city contracts with the sole service provider. In this contract, the city shifts the blame for any liability to the sole service provider. The sole service provider then contracts with the security firm. In this contract, the sole service provider shifts the liability to the security firm. Therefore, in both contract documents, the city comes out the winner.

While this contract language does not guarantee definitive protection from legal exposure, the city and the sole service provider have built a rather effective barrier from liability. Probably the best legal arguments to penetrate this contractual barrier would be "public policy" or "agency" theories. While these are highly technical legal and factual questions, suffice to say that the city will probably be liable — at some level — for the actions or conduct of the patrol officers, if it can be shown that the misconduct was foreseeable or if the city was deemed a co-employer.

The other aspect of accountability relates to the failure to provide any meaningful complaint mechanism to track, administer or remedy misconduct on the part of the private patrol officers. Based on the information provided in the research, the only mechanism set up to deal with such complaints would be an informal communication channel from the sole service provider to the commission and the security firm. At best, if a complaint was made by a citizen, the sole service provider should communicate the complaint to both the commission and the security firm. The commission — theoretically — would have the ability or the obligation to raise this complaint with the administrators of the security firm. However, there is no mechanism to record any such complaints, there was no data to account for any previous complaints, and there were no procedures designed to investigate or verify the veracity of any such complaints. In short, if there were complaints raised, there is no way to verify the existence of such nor were there any procedures in place to remedy them. Consequently, there is little or no accountability built into the patrol program.

The lack of any policies or procedures related to accountability must be viewed with some degree of pragmatic optimism or skeptical criticism. From a positive standpoint, the patrol program is a rather novel and unusual policy initiative. There is not much data or information available for an administrator to use as a model to implement or mirror. While some authors have voiced concerns about accountability, there is little or no information or data on how other programs deal with this important issue. Consequently, administrators who are worried about accountability must "invent" their own policies and procedures. While it is possible to use police department policies and procedures as models, it is not practical to require such formalized methods in this type of program, which is vastly limited in scope and resources as compared to most municipal police departments.

Further, administrating the patrol program is done on a part-time, almost *ad hoc*, basis. The administrators from the commission and the sole service provider are not making any money running the program. Indeed, the commission members are politically appointed volunteers from the community. The sole service provider spends approximately 10 to 20 percent of its time devoted to the program. Only the security firm administrators stand to incur a financial gain from the patrol program. It is reasonable to assert that developing policies and procedures would not be a high priority for the security firm administrators. One could argue that they have a vested interest to downplay or even conceal questionable conduct on the part of their employees. As such, there is no incentive, or at least no practical reason, to take the time and the effort to develop an effective and demonstrable accountability program.

From a more critical standpoint, there are a host of reasons why accountability would be downplayed, ignored or even actively concealed. As stated above, the city is not looking to invite litigation for the misconduct of the private patrol officers. Further, the city's loosely defined patrol "functions" illustrate that the city sought to legally isolate itself from any misconduct done by any private police officer in the performance of their job. Additionally, there were little or no resources afforded by the city to the commission or the sole service provider to develop accountability methodologies. Given these factors, it would be extraordinarily presumptuous to believe that accountability policies and procedures would be enacted by these part-time administrators. In fact, this is just what occurred — policies or procedures were not developed. The security firm administrators have little incentive to develop such an accountability program which could expose itself to liability.

It seems reasonable to conclude that the lack of accountability policies and procedures was either a reasonable oversight due to lack of information, resources, or incentives; or the program was intentionally designed to limit accountability. In either case, most people would say this is unacceptable. This is particularly so if such private patrol programs become more commonplace or popular — which is what I believe will occur. As such, this directly reflects the concerns of authors who worry about the ability of the public to hold private firms accountable to the larger interests of society (see Bilik, 1992: 342; Johnston, 1992: 25; Shenk, 1995: 19; and Hebdon, 1995: 9–10). Consequently, this issue raises far reaching concerns as described by Zielinski, who stated:

> In a democracy, public police forces, with all their abuses, have at
> least a theoretical potential for accountability through citizen
> review boards and other community pressures. Private security
> firms, however, are inherently a law into themselves, only account-
> able to the corporate bottom line [1990: 10].

Another issue raised by this study is the lack of training and experience of the private patrol officers. The data and information derived from the research illustrates that the private officers are performing similar functions as the public police, with substantially less training and experience, which is so different it is hard to compare. Specifically, pursuant to state regulations, private police officers are only required to have 40 hours of training (20 hours if unarmed), while most public police officers receive from 400 to 800 hours of instruction plus additional on-the-job training during a probationary period and in-service training thereafter (DuCanto, 1999: 15). Some states require much less training than does Illinois. Both Tennessee and Washington require only four hours of training (Long, et al., *Chicago Tribune*, Oct., 14, 2001). This variance in training has substantial implications, including greatly enhancing the possibility that constitutional violations could occur for no other reason than lack of knowledge.

The disparate training and experience can be a consequence of the constitutional violations noted in this study. These issues represent particular concerns for a variety of reasons. As noted in the Privatization and Public Safety chapter, one of the criticisms of private policing relates to reduced training and accountability standards. Some authors attribute the relative economic benefit of privatization to these lower standards (see for example Shenk, 1995: 16). The argument is that the lower wages offered by private employers is related to the decreased skill and training of private employees as compared to their public counterparts. At least at the lowest levels of the public safety industry—especially those conducting the patrols—it is quite clear that this assertion is true.

Any privatization advocate would be hard pressed to assert that most low level private security personnel are more skilled or better trained than even rookie police officers. However, this does not mean that private personnel do not have a significant role to perform in the public safety industry. It is my assertion that the role of private security is critical—and likely to grow. Because of such, it is important that the standards and training increase to the relative significance of its growing role.

There has been a growing chorus of authors who advocate increased standards for private security personnel (see Azano, 2001: 174; Theim, 2002: W5). In the aftermath of terroristic violence, these advocates are likely to sound a more compelling and convincing refrain. This research should add to this refrain. The case study helped to make clear the need for increased training for private security personnel. This is particularly relevant for private police officers who perform a function very similar to that of public police officers. When one considers the substantial variance in training for these groups, the need for additional training for private officers who perform a patrol function becomes even more critical.

One solution is to provide for additional levels of training—in relation to the function or type of work performed by particular private police officers. Consider the substantial difference from a security guard who stands at a post in an empty office building at 3:00 a.m. Consider the security guard who tours a construction site on the weekends. Both of these individuals are not likely to need much specific training or skills. This is not to demean the value of these jobs—as they are often critical to the protection of substantial assets. However, the function of these officers is quite likely limited to "observe and report." As such, the skill and training levels for these jobs do not compare to those needed to perform within a public environment—particularly if the job involves dealing with criminal activity on a regular basis. The point is those private police officers who patrol public streets, parks, and alleys must be better trained and skilled than those who patrol empty offices or construction sites. This is just common sense. However, as it has been said many times, common sense is not that common, as most state licensing standards are not prepared to make such a distinction.

This disparity in skill and training levels should be remedied according to job requirements. Just as family doctors do not perform brain surgery, so should security professionals be trained and skilled for their particular environment. Similarly, as the typical real estate attorney would not be allowed to litigate cases in federal district courts, so should security professionals be required to demonstrate certain levels of competency. Why should it be any different for security officers? The honest answer is there is no difference.

To my mind, the solution is to provide gradations of skills and training in direct relationship to the requirements of the job. Just as most states require different classifications of driver's licenses to conform to the skill level and types of vehicles driven, so should the security professional be required to demonstrate certain skills, experiences or tests for competency, based on the work he or she is to perform. To use the analogy of driver's licenses, a class "A" security officer would have minimal training or skills. This level of skill or training would only allow the security officer to work at jobs or facilities with minimal risks or responsibilities, such as empty warehouses or construction sites.

As the risk and responsibility level increases, so should the requisite training and skill levels. For example, a security officer who performs patrols on public streets should have much of the same training and skills as do their public police counterparts. Further, security personnel who guard nuclear facilities should have specialized training and skills similar to military personnel who secure valuable or sensitive facilities. These security officers—and others in similar environments—would be considered the "elite" of the security profession, just as gang and drug tactical police officers and specialized military units, such as the Navy SEALs, are deemed elite units in their respective organizations.

Consequently, I envision a continuum of requisite training and skill levels from the minimum class "A" designation (20 hours of training) to a class "D" or "E" designation requiring in the range of 300 to 400 hours of training. Some cutting-edge security firms have similar graded classifications. For example, Wackenhut (now Group 4 Falckas) has its "custom protection officer" level, which provides better pay and training for certain clients, such as the federal government (Perez, 2002). With these variable levels of training, the needs of the specific client or the specific environment could be more appropriately applied — for the optimal level of security services.

The implementation these initiatives are long overdue, and are becoming increasingly necessary. Such initiatives, however, require a paradigm shift in the way we as a society view security. The adage of the night watchmen as an old, tired and feeble "guard" must be changed. The adage of the teenager who can work at the hamburger stand or as a "security guard" must be changed. The adage of the dysfunctional or problematic worker who cannot otherwise hold a job — but who can perform a "security function" — must be changed. These changes must reflect the dictates of a world where gangmembers, drug dealers, petty thieves, rapists and terrorists are much too commonplace.

This is not to say the "sky is falling." It is to say that the world of security has changed because the world is evolving. As Kaplan asserts, the environment will be *the* security issue of the 21st century. The current environment promises to include crime and terroristic violence. If this society does not comprehend or appreciate these factors, then it will pay — dearly — in terms of lives, assets and the quality of life for all Americans and those in civilized society. The days and years ahead will likely be very violent — possibly unprecedented. Are we prepared for the changes needed to address them?

As this study infers, one way to address the level of training and skills within the security industry is to increase wages. At least, arguably, the enhancement of training and skills would simultaneously increase the quality of service, including the capabilities of those in the labor pool. In the event that these standards are increased, it becomes more likely that accountability and performance standards would also increase. This desire for enhanced standards and accountability has been a controversial issue in the security industry for many years (see for example DuCanto, 1999). Indeed, this criticism has taken on new significance in light of the recent terrorist incidents.

Many have begun to address the wage scales of private security personnel with critical and compelling arguments. How much longer are we as a society going to accept pay scales for security providers on the same level as those who serve hamburgers? The argument goes, "We will get what we pay for" (Azano, 2001: 173). As such, we should not be shocked to learn or observe that the security providers we pay minimum wages are not motivated or attentive. We also should not be surprised to know that many security personnel become part of the problem by committing crimes when they are supposed to be protecting against such (see Avano, 2001: 174). Additionally, it is not unusual to learn that many security officers have themselves been convicted of crimes (see Long, *Chicago Tribune*, Oct. 14, 2001). The *Tribune* reported that 4,200 license applicants during a two year period were rejected by the state governing agency — mostly for criminal histories.

If increases in standards and wages occur, the relative cost effective benefits for private police officers may correspondingly decrease. In the event that wages actually increase, then the attractiveness of privatized policing — at least from a purely economic perspective — will decrease, thereby diminishing the cost effective benefit of privatization. However, this economic assertion should not change the level of demand. The demand for security is likely to grow. It was already increasing even before the advent of terroristic violence. For example, a recent *Wall Street Journal* report noted that the volume, revenues and profit margins of security firms have increased since 9/11. According to the report, the days of 3 percent margins seem to be giving way to 5 percent or 6 percent and even 8 percent profits (Perez, 2002). Beyond the margins, the billable rates are showing signs of increasing. Clients are now more willing to pay increased rates, which allows the security firms to pay their top notch personnel wages in the $20 per hour range. Indeed, Perez notes that this increase stands against the vast majority of firms paying wages in the $7 per hour range (2002). This is significant, especially considering the wages of public police. I personally know of municipalities paying their police officers in the $15 per hour range.

While the opponents of privatization contend that the wages attached to private policing may be illusory, the demand for security may exceed the supply. This is especially true if the standards, training and skill levels increase to reflect the current security environment. While wage, training and skill increases may dampen the desire to privatize, this study suggests that higher standards are necessary to facilitate more professional, skilled, and capable private police officers. This study suggests that increased skill and training levels may increase the quality and type of security service delivered to the citizen/client. It is my hope this research facilitates these long needed improvements.

Societal Implications

The wage and accountability standards also extend to a more societal (or political) based argument against privatized delivery of police services. The essence of this argument is that private firms will be concerned only about limited financial interests, while public agencies have the larger interests of the public in mind (Bilik, 1992: 342). Johnston argues that public police agencies are better able to maximize social values, thereby promoting social controls. This is because, at least partially, police services could be allocated by need, instead of cost-effective concerns exhibited by private firms (1992: 25). These concerns are largely framed on discretionary decision making related to the delivery of such services. Both Spitzer and Scull (1977: 20) and Johnston (1992: 25) assert that too much discretion by private firms is problematic. Their concerns are echoed by Shenk (1995: 18), who stated, "Decisions that should be the province of elected officials fall into the hands of hired guns." When dealing with private policing, the use of the term "hired guns" has both literal and symbolic meaning.

The use of privatized police services entails many far reaching implications. Many authors emphasize there are substantial and troubling aspects of privatized policing due to the nature of the services provided (see Wessel, 1995; Shenk, 1995; Linowes, 1988; Johnston, 1992; Cunningham, et al., 1991; and Hebdon, 1995). Opponents of privatized policing argue for democratic ideals, and assert that law enforcement is too important to be placed into the hands of private firms (see Wessel, 1995; Shenk, 1995; Manchester, 1989; Linowes, 1988; Johnston, 1992; Cunningham, et al., 1991; and Hebdon, 1995). For example, Herbert Williams, when he was president of the Police Foundation Research Group, stated that "corporations are developing huge private, gun-carrying armies which raise questions about the very nature of the republic" (Tolchin, 1985: 27). In this regard, privatized policing arrangements involve issues potentially much more important than "cost effective" and pragmatic political arguments. Maghan (1998), writing on the privatization of prisons, emphasizes that prisoner "clients" have little or no political influence, and thereby are unable to affect the financial arrangements in the market (1998). These comments provide a telling editorial on the state of private security, and of the implications on such within society.

The essence of the arguments against privatized police services are illustrated by the following statements. Shenk argued that "Americans believe, legitimately, that businesses can't be trusted to care for their health and safety" (1995: 22). This concern addresses the notion that corporations would place too much emphasis on economic and financial matters.

Further, Manchester asserts that "public safety ... bear[s] too directly on the common welfare to have service levels determined on the basis of demand responses" (1989: 30). Significantly, according to Moe:

> The fundamental difference between the sectors is based on public law and not upon economic or behavioral theory ... thus, the primary importance should be given to determining if the service involves powers reserved for the sovereignty, economics should be a secondary consideration [Hebdon, 1995: 9].

As inferred by the above quotations, much of the opposition against privatization of policing is based on substantive public policy arguments. The criticism centers on the democratic ideals of this country. Both Bilik (1992: 342) and Shenk (1995: 17) argue strongly against privatization of policing due to the belief that such services can fundamentally alter the democratic system. Similarly, Stanley E. Morris, when director of the United States Marshal's Service, stated that "if you turn over public safety to private industry, you're condemning our system of government" (Hebdon, 1995: 9). Interestingly, this assertion coincides with the belief of an early advocate of public policing, none other than Sir Robert Peel, who stated: "You cannot have good policing when responsibility is divided, the only way to consolidate responsibility is through government" (Benson, 1990: 74).

Additionally, Kaplan contends that the utilization of privatized public safety services can attribute to the breakdown of governmental sovereignty, thereby leading to the "balkanization" of society (1994: 74). In this way, the development of modern private policing raises the possibility of the sovereignty shifting from the state toward private entities (Shearing and Stenning, 1983: 504; and Johnston, 1992: 69). Zielinski (1999: 5) pointedly described the possibility of a dual system of policing by asserting that the use of private police to supplement (or even replace) public police has created a "separate and unequal system" in which "the rich protect their privileges and guard their wealth from perceived barbarians at the gate ... in which heavily armed private guards are accountable not to the public, but to the well-manicured hand that feeds them." This viewpoint caused security expert Richard Kobertz to comment that "we seem to be reverting to the days of the highwayman, when everybody got into the castle at night and pulled up the drawbridge" (Farnham, 1992: 43). As the dual nature of policing continues into the future, the implications may become more problematic.

Notwithstanding such criticism, as illustrated by this research, the movement toward privatization seems to be marching on. This is not without justification. As explained above, the need for adequately trained, skilled and capable security professionals will not go away. The statistics and trends point to an increasing need for security professionals. One of the key aspects of this research is to assert that the need for security is growing — both in numbers and in scope. The increase in scope includes more — possibly many more — private patrol programs which operate within the public domain. If this is true, then the concerns raised by the authors quoted above must be addressed. The key concerns or criticisms center on democratic ideals, such as governmental sovereignty and the possibility of establishing a dual system of policing. While this work cannot disavow these concerns, it can address them in a forthright manner.

In order to deal with these issues in an intellectually honest manner, we must agree that security will be driven by the needs and demands of society. If society demands more security, then two alternatives are possible — that it is provided by government or by private firms. As illustrated by the statistics presented earlier, if we as a society required the same level of police to crime ratios as we had in the 1960s, then we would need to hire five million new police officers (Walinsky, 1993: 40). This is not going to happen. It is financially impossible to sustain this level of policing, funded exclusively by taxpayer monies. Instead, what has occurred is that the private sector has dramatically increased its proportion of security personnel, to its current amount of approximately two million people employed within the security industry. While this does not equate to a one-to-one ratio from the 1960s levels, the increased ratios demonstrated by security industry data are significant by any reasonable assessment.

The numerical proportions and scope of the private security industry has created much ironic concern and criticism. Those same authors who criticize privatization do not advocate increasing public policing to the ratio levels of the 1960s— or at any other time. These authors realize that the public funding needed to accomplish these ratios is not available. Based on the growth of the private security market, however, it seems apparent that the funding is available from private sources. Therefore, market forces of supply and demand are shaping the public safety industry in contemporary America. Consequently, those authors who pointedly criticize the security industry fail to admit that someone is hiring the guards, someone is willing to pay for security. Even the low-to mid-income residents of Marquette Park were willing to pay for additional protection.

This raises a question begging to be answered. Is it wrong that people are willing to pay for security? Should this be viewed as a problematic departure from democratic norms? The answer is not as simple as the criticisms offered by many authors. It is my assertion that the issues are not simply public versus private provider. As illustrated in the Privatization and Public Safety chapter, the distinction is not that clean. There are many complex conceptual, economic and legal issues. To my mind, the answer is the optimal level of security and safety which this society can afford — tempered by significant conflicting issues such as liberty and constitutional protections. Indeed, whether the person who saves your life is employed by the Chicago Police Department or Majestic Protective Services is not a significant concern to most people. As demonstrated by this research and by the privatization sites described herein, most people focus on security and safety — not esoteric issues such as constitutional prohibitions or even the sovereignty of government. This is not meant to minimize the importance of the constitution. Of course, one of this book's key components was based on constitutional concerns raised by private police patrols. The study has shown that significant constitutional violations occurred, and as such, must be addressed.

This being said, those authors who struggle with the impact of private security upon governmental sovereignty, or who worry about the balkanization of society, have every right to be concerned. These are complex and substantial concerns. However, there are competing concerns dealing with the protection of lives, assets, and the viability of our way of life. Of course, the question is not simply — or necessarily — one service provider versus the other. The functions of public and private policing are becoming closer and closer, or are even indistinguishable. Hence, the question is, where is the right balance?

To answer this question, there are substantive changes that can be implemented to protect the competing interests represented by security versus liberty (or constitutional protections). In this sense, the solution may rest on additional regulation and standards within the security industry, creating various classifications of security personnel, providing increased training and skill development, and providing more and better governmental involvement in the public safety industry. This may be facilitated by increased use of "special police" officers largely supplied by private firms. These special police officers would have the additional benefit (or power) derived from the fact that they are sworn peace officers, thereby receiving the acknowledgement or "blessing" of government. This will, at least partly, resolve the questionable legal and moral authority articulated in the case study. Consequently, we need to view both private and public policing as part of the same industry — the public safety industry — which is devoted to providing a safe and secure environment for all citizens and residents in a manner consistent with our constitutional ideals. While this is a tall order, it can and must be accomplished.

The growing movement toward cooperative or combined public and private policing is adequately illustrated from various legislative initiatives. While there have been many initiatives introduced in state and local governmental bodies, arguably the most significant legislation has occurred in the national and international levels. The significance of this legislation stems not just from the governing bodies. It also relates to the substance of the initiatives. In this regard, certain examples of such legislation are summarized below.

House Resolution 2996 was introduced by Rep. McCollum in the 104th Congress, 2nd session. The bill entitled the Law Enforcement and Industrial Security Cooperation Act of 1996, was designed to encourage cooperation between these groups to facilitate the control of crime (H.R. 2996). The bill provided for the appointment a bi-partisan committee to study "appropriate cooperative roles ... to offer comprehensive proposals for statutory and procedural initiatives." The stated specific purposes of the legislation were fourfold:

> To identify critical issues in crime control which may be better addressed through improved cooperation between public law enforcement agencies and private sector security professionals.
>
> To examine existing models of public-private cooperation, and improve such models or develop new models for cooperation in crime control and law enforcement.
>
> To encourage public agencies and private businesses and institutions to make use of effective models for cooperation in crime control and law enforcement.
>
> To analyze Federal, State, and local statutes which either enhance or inhibit cooperation between public law enforcement and private security, and recommend changes to such laws that enhance cooperation [H.R. 2996].

While this legislation did not become law, it mirrored many of the recommendations of a report presented to the 9th United Nations Congress on the prevention of crime and the treatment of offenders. The report, entitled *Urban Insecurity: Conditions, Causes and Cures*, made the following assertions:

> Increasing violence and crime will not be reversed by traditional juvenile justice and criminal justice approaches.
>
> Prevention should take priority over punishment.
>
> New directions at the international, national, and local level for justice, safety and security are essential.

Development of metro area public-private partnerships and coalitions [is needed] to facilitate democratic participation in the creation of security strategies and goals [Weisburg, 1995: 1–4].

These recommendations from two substantial legislative bodies, Congress and the United Nations, are consistent with the trend toward privatization of public safety services. Significantly, these recommendations mirror many of the issues and elements raised in the privatization literature. The desire to develop cooperative efforts between public and private entities for more effective crime control is at the core of both initiatives. Indeed, both initiatives emphasize the need for more and better cooperation between private and public police. These initiatives, however, fail to address both operational issues such as training and accountability, and the larger societal issues such as constitutional and public policy concerns. This research has shown that these matters cannot be ignored.

Recent legislation reveals that these matters are becoming increasingly subject to public debate. For example, a Michigan state legislator introduced House Bill 4694 designed to establish training standards for private security guards, private detectives, and alarm service providers within the state. The bill would create a security provider advisory commission, staffed by representatives from both the public and private sector, charged with the establishment of minimum training standards. The bill was introduced, at least partly, in response to three recent deaths of shoplifting suspects in the hands of security guards earlier that year.

Even more sweeping legislation has been introduced on the national level — in direct response to the terrorist incidents of 9/11. On October 8, 2001, President George W. Bush introduced an Executive Order establishing the Office of Homeland Security. While this act is directed specifically toward terrorism, there are a number of provisions which directly relate to cooperative public and private responses. Particularly in section 3 (e), the act provides for a number of initiatives designed to enhance our ability to protect against terrorist attacks. In this framework, the act provides for cooperative efforts between "federal, state, and local agencies, and private entities, as appropriate" to protect various facilities, systems, infrastructures, and the like from terrorism. This act — as with the other legislative initiatives— supports the notion of public and private cooperative efforts against crime and terrorism. Consequently, these legislative and executive initiatives indirectly support some level of privatization in such important "governmental" functions.

These initiatives do not imply that private policing is necessarily the solution for crime and terrorism. This study has demonstrated, however, that there are real benefits derived from the private patrols, including the responsiveness of policing services to the community. Indeed, the level of service provision often appeared to be superior to those provided by the police department. Additionally, statements from numerous participants indicate that the patrols have resulted in a reduction of crime and fear of crime, a reduction in the incidence of graffiti damage, and some impact on loitering. These are certainly commendable manifestations of the private patrols. As such, the responsiveness of the service provision, and the reduction of crime and these related "incivilities" has been a strong incentive in the movement toward privatization. Each of these relate to the desire to reduce crime (or the fear of crime) and to enhance the orderliness of the physical environment.

However, this study has shown that the "privatization solution" also has substantial shortcomings. One obvious shortcoming was the incidence of constitutional violations. Few people would defend such a critical deficiency. Even proponents of privatization admit it is no panacea (Morgan, 1992: 264; Donahue, 1989: 218; Benson, 1990: 193; and Johnston, 1992: 219). Based on this study, one can make the case that the shortcomings are already evident. In fact, this assertion will likely become increasingly relevant in the future, if or when private patrols become increasingly common.

Consequently, this research, at its core, illustrates the longstanding interplay between constitutional rights and individual security. As described in the advent of public policing, much of the criticism of early municipal policing stemmed from the concern for the "ominous intrusion upon civil liability" (see Miller, 1977: 4). Indeed, in contemporary America, critics of privatized policing make the same statements. On the other hand, many in contemporary society are advocating greater controls, and demonstrate less concern for an all-too-powerful government. For example, Larry Ellison, the president of the software company Oracle, speaking about the need for better and more centralized data bases, stated, "It's our *lives* that are at risk, not our liberties" (Rosen, 2002: 50, emphasis in original). These viewpoints demonstrate — again — that there is great diversity on this issue of security versus liberty.

These well founded concerns have resulted in literally thousands of legal decisions, particularly within the past generation or so, relating to the use of police powers by the public police. While these decisions often reflect the ideological or philosophical makeup of the courts, it is fair to state that the issue of "police powers" has been a substantial focus of many significant legal decisions (see Murphy and Pritchett, 1986). In the years ahead, there promises to be much case law developed relative to the use of "police powers" by private police officers. The cases listed in this research, nonetheless, provide an insight into the legal reasoning and the trends developing in this area of the law.

The underlying issues related to the use of police powers demonstrate the delicate balance between constitutional rights and personal security. On one hand, the desire for personal security in many ways facilitates the ever increasing use of police powers. The belief, in essence, is the more pronounced the use of police powers, the less likely it will be that crimes will occur. With this logic, even if crimes do occur, the offenders will more likely be apprehended. Conversely, those who advocate constitutional rights often view the use of police powers with caution, or even with disdain. This viewpoint would place greater priority on the free exercise of rights than the personal desire to be safe from crime.

It is certainly true that such conflicting viewpoints vary over time. In times of great public concern, such as during war — or under the threat of terrorism — it is not unusual for security concerns to outweigh constitutional "niceties." Conversely, in good economic and peaceful times, the desire for constitutional protections takes precedent over "obtrusive" security methods. It is also arguably true that most — if not all — people would possess both viewpoints at some time in their lives. Indeed, when faced with extreme danger, even the greatest advocates for constitutional rights would likely desire personal security. From the opposite perspective, individuals particularly concerned with security are likely to respond poorly to abusive conduct imposed on them by those in authority.

This interaction illustrates an inherent conflict between the basic contentions of power versus presence. Broadly speaking, as the power of the state decreases, the ability to affect crime and disorder also decreases. Conversely, the effect of crime and disorder will have some corresponding response or desire for the presence of more security — or at least the perception of more security. Based on the literature of crime and the fear of crime, there appears to be a relationship between these two variables. In this sense, the use of order maintenance functions are designed to foster a more orderly environment, thereby making it less conducive to conditions which seem to invite crime or criminal activities. As such, there is a certain logic tied with the desire to reduce crime through the use of order maintenance functions.

Order maintenance functions, however, tend to impact the ability of people to conduct themselves in a unrestricted manner. A classic example of such is loitering. When loiterers are removed from a street corner, this order maintenance function satisfies a security concern to some, but frustrates others interested in freedom of assembly. Indeed, the conflict is clear. To some people, it is the exercise of their right to freely assemble. To others, it represents a barrier to the free flow of pedestrian traffic. Worse yet, it may represent a threat to the personal safety of those who interact with the individuals congregating on the public way.

The use of private police has an increased significance should the terrorist threat become sustained within this society. This is so for a number of reasons. First, from an economic and operational perspective, many authors have made the assertion that the public police are already overworked — and underfunded. Most people would agree with this assertion. This is partly the result of the nature of police work, and of the expanding scope of the work derived from the requirements of community policing. Even without the impact of terrorism, many authors and officials—from both the public and private sectors—are advocating that some supplemental service by private police could free up the public police to focus on more serious crimes. In the event of a sustained terrorist campaign, the workload and the stresses placed on the public police will prove to be substantial. If this occurs, then the need for supplementary services from private police will likely outweigh any of the current impediments, such as opposition from police unions and police officials. As asserted in this research, the likely focus of such supplemental services will be on order maintenance functions.

Second, order maintenance will become increasingly important in a sustained terrorist campaign. In such a circumstance, the environmental focus of order maintenance will be critically important. Consider that the presence of litter, including boxes and garbage, is no longer just an eyesore, it can also be deadly. The placement of bombs in boxes lying on a sidewalk in a downtown business or shopping district could be terribly devastating, both in human and financial terms. Further, the significance of unattended vehicles left on the same street corner may be even more terrible. As such, the need for an orderly and well surveillanced environment will be absolutely critical. Order maintenance techniques are an excellent means to maintain order and surveillance. It is my opinion that the public police will not be able to handle this critical function without substantial assistance from private police personnel.

There is a connection between power and presence. The less power derived from the state, the more it becomes necessary that some corresponding presence should exist. The presence of authority figures— such as private police patrols— may provide a perception of safety, even though the level of police powers associated with their presence is ambiguous. Their presence, nonetheless, may do much to keep people safe. This connection between power and presence, therefore, intersects with the conflict between rights and security. It may be that the presence of private police patrols leads to constitutional violations. To some people, this may not be as important as the perception of safety. To others, the utilization of security techniques through police powers would not justify constitutional violations. Indeed, it is a complicated mixture of priorities. The "proper" approach may depend upon the value system of the individual or of the society. Do constitutional rights trump individual security? Does individual security — the freedom to be alive and free from crime — trump the right to live in a free society?

These are difficult questions to answer. The answer may lie somewhere in the middle of the two extremes — a balance of rights and security. The real question, however, is how do we as a society achieve the balance? We must acknowledge that security requires some degree of inconvenience. It also creates limitations on our freedoms. This is of particular significance in a terroristic environment. It may be that the utilization of private police creates additional inconveniences and limitations on our freedoms. Private police may also help to save lives and property. These are difficult choices to resolve.

This research was cognizant of the search for balance. Many seemingly well-intended individuals were involved in the private patrol program. The private police officers put their lives at stake in conducting these patrols. I believe that they cared about doing good "police work." I also believe the individuals who administered the program wanted to make their community a better place to live. These are important considerations to keep in mind in any criticism of the program.

Any such criticism should be focused on the structural components of the program. In my opinion, this is where the concentration of effort and initiatives should lie. This research has illustrated that many abuses and questionable actions can occur in an unstructured environment. The dangers and abuses inherent in policing must be controlled in the fullest extent possible. The arrangement described in this research site failed to provide such controls. It failed to provide any real accountability to both the public and its "clients."

Hopefully this book will serve as a guide to address the issues and implications inherent within private police patrols. The case study revealed many shortcomings which must be addressed. There are many questions, however, which were left unsettled. Such questions include the following. Are there any factors which account for the functional differences between the two firms? One firm tended to focus on law enforcement, while the other tended toward traditional "observe and report" functions. Does the approach by the governing commission or the administrator impact the functions on which the private patrols ultimately focus their attention? Does the level of interaction between the private and public police entities have any impact on the functional approach taken in the program? What differences would standards relating to selection, training and accountability have on the incidence of constitutional violations, or on the economic viability of the program?

These questions, and others, can and should be the focus of further research. Indeed, this study emphasized one central theme. That is, private policing *will* continue to grow both in its relationship with public policing, and its significance to the public safety of citizens within this society. This continued growth will result in additional private patrol programs throughout this country. As such, policymakers need to pay attention to the implications of such programs. Indeed, this area is ripe for further debate and research. Any such research should be communicated to site administrators, governmental officials, security industry representatives, and any other persons interested in private patrol programs. It is my hope and belief that this research can serve as an example to those interested in the important constitutional and public policy issues raised in this study.

Appendix A:
Map of Marquette Park
Special Service Area No. 14

MARQUETTE PARK SPECIAL SERVICE AREA NO.14

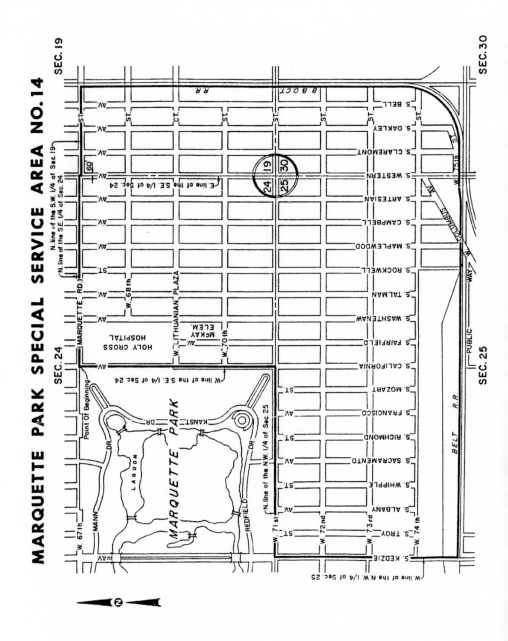

Appendix B:
Comparison of
Security Firm Bids

	A	B	C	D
Hourly rate	$31.70/hour (2-man)	$32.00/hour (2-man)	$34.00/hour (2-man)	$31.00/hour (2-man)
Extra Patrol	same rate	same rate	same rate	same rate
Hourly rate for Holidays	$31.70/hour (2-man)	$48.00/hour (2-man)	$51.00/hour (2-man)	$46.50/hour $62.00/hr. X-mas & Thanksgiving Day
Vehicle Cost	$390.00/mo.	$840.00/mo.	$470.00/mo.	$1083.00/mo.
Additional Vehicle	$390.00/mo. prorated for actual use	$840.00/mo. prorated for actual use	$470.00/mo. prorated for actual use at Contractor's request NO CHARGE if put on at vendor's discretion	$1083.00/mo. NOT prorated for actual use
Operational Overhead Costs	$320.00/mo.	$475.00/mo.	$346.00/mo.	$3.00/hour ($1,392/mo.)
Court costs	Same as regular rate	Same as regular rate	Same as regular rate	Will be billed for accordingly
5 years Experience:	Yes	Yes	Yes	Yes
Incorporation Date	2/5/97	1/9/97	10/3/94	10/9/86
Initial License Received	Prior Company—1991 3/17/97	Prior Company—1970 2/15/97	Parent Company—1984 8/21/92	1/2/87
References checked	Yes	Yes	Yes	Yes
Marked Vehicles Available	Yes	Yes	Yes	Yes
Mars Lights	Yes	Yes	Yes	Yes
Radio Communications with Dispatch Center	Telephone/Two-way Radios	Radio Telephone	Two way radio	Car Phone
Insured	Yes	Yes	Yes	Yes
Uniformed Guards	Yes	Yes	Yes	Yes
Firearm Registration	Yes	Yes	Yes	Yes
Litigation	No	No	No	No
Other Considerations:	*City of Chicago Certified DBE/WBE Directory *Illinois Female Business Enterprise Certification *Can add extra car and guards on short notice *Phone answered after hours *Local Company-based on Southwest side *Computer in vehicle for reporting	*Available at no extra cost: -Mountain bikes with security devices(guards Extra) -Video Cameras mounted in vehicles *Could be reached after hours *Licensed by Village of Alsip *Can add extra car and guards on short notice	*Owner is registered firearms instructor *Can add extra car and guards on short notice *Phone answered after hours *Will place 2000 flyers in stores & 1000 business cards to SSA#14 with dispatch number in Jan. & June '99 *Has 6 employees from SSA area	*Can give extra vehicle with 1 week notice *Phone answered after hours *Amended contract regarding indemnification

Company A
(based on 102 hrs. Per week)

2 man Patrol: 52 wks. × 102 hrs. = 5304 hrs. × $31.70 = **$168,136.80**

Holidays: [New Year's Day (14 hrs.), Memorial Day (14 hrs.), Independence Day (16 hrs.), Labor Day (14 hrs.), Thanksgiving Day (14 hrs.), Christmas Eve (14 hrs.), Christmas Day (16 hrs.), & New Year's Eve (14 hrs.) Total Holiday hours: 116]

NO OVERTIME PAY FOR HOLIDAY HOURS

Vehicle Cost: $390.00 × 12 months = **$4,680.00**

Operational Overhead Costs: $320.00 × 12 months = **$3,840.00**

Total Cost for year: $176,656.80   NO OVERTIME COSTS

Company B
(based on 102 hrs. Per week)

2 man Patrol: 52 wks. × 102 hrs. = 5304 hrs. – 116 Holiday hrs. = 5188 hrs. × $32.00/hr. = **$166,016.00**

Holidays: [New Year's Day (14 hrs.), Memorial Day (14 hrs.), Independence Day (16 hrs.), Labor Day (14 hrs.), Thanksgiving Day (14 hrs.), Christmas Eve (14 hrs.), Christmas Day (16 hrs.), & New Year's Eve (14 hrs.) Total Holiday hours: 116]

116 hrs. × $48.00 = **$5,568.00**

Vehicle Cost: $840 × 12 months = **$10,080.00**

Operational Overhead Costs: $475.00 × 12 months = **$5,700.00**

Total Cost for year: $187,364.00   NO OVERTIME COSTS

Company C
(based on 102 hrs. Per week)

2 man Patrol: 52 wks. × 102 hrs. = 5304 hrs. – 102 Holiday hrs. = 5202 hrs. × $34.00 = **$176,868.00**

Holidays: [Martin Luther King Day (14 hrs.), Memorial Day (14 hrs.), Independence Day (16 hrs.), Labor Day (14 hrs.), Thanksgiving Day (14 hrs.), Christmas Day (16 hrs.), & New Year's Eve (14 hrs.) Total Holiday hours: 102]

102 hrs. × $51.00 = **$5,202.00**

Vehicle Cost: $470.00 × 12 months = **$5,640.00**

Operational Overhead Costs: $346.00 × 12 months = **$4,152.00**

Total Cost for year: $191,862.00 NO OVERTIME COSTS

Company D
(based on 102 hrs. Per week)

2 man Patrol: 52 wks. × 102 hrs. = 5304 hrs. – 116 Holiday hrs. = 5188 hrs. × $31.00/hr. = **$160,828.00**

Holidays: [New Year's Day (14 hrs.), Memorial Day (14 hrs.), Independence Day (16 hrs.), Labor Day (14 hrs.), Thanksgiving Day (14 hrs.), Christmas Eve (14 hrs.), Christmas Day (16 hrs.), & New Year's Eve (14 hrs.) Total Holiday hours: 116]

86 hrs. × $46.50 = **$3,999.00**

30 hrs. × $62.00 = **$1,860.00**

Vehicle Cost: $1083.00 × 12 months = **$12,996.00**

Operational Overhead Costs: 102 hrs. × 52 wks. = 5304 hrs. × $3.00 = **$15,912.00**

Total Cost for year: $195,595.00 + unknown overtime costs

Notes

1. "Observe and Report" is the traditional technique used by security personnel. The technique, in essence, is to observe suspicious or criminal conduct, and immediately report such to the public police.

2. "Order Maintenance" techniques focus on the environment whereby disorderly conduct and conditions are addressed for the purpose of deterring more serious criminal activity. Disorderly conduct and conditions includes such things as public drinking and drug usage, loitering, graffiti, and other similar such matters.

3. Marquette Park is located on the southwest side of Chicago, roughly between 67th and 74th streets, from Bell to Kedzie.

4. As described in the historical section, the actual functioning of private citizens entailed certain functions, including "observe and report" and the arrest of those persons suspected of violating criminal laws. Over time, however, private security personnel tended to limit their focus to protect specific property. The typical way this was accomplished would be to "observe and report" suspected criminal activity to the public police. The public police would then be charged with the enforcement or the arrest. As such, the "observe and report" function has been known as the traditional role of private security–but it is not historically accurate, as private citizens have enforced law and order prior to the advent of public policing.

5. Data taken from *U.S. Bureau of Justice Statistics*, Census of State and Local Law Enforcement Agencies, 1996; as compared to *U.S. Bureau of Justice Statistics*, Census of State and Local Law Enforcement Agencies, 1993.

6. For example, from 1989 to 1996, Gallup Poll data illustrates that annually from 71 percent to 89 percent of the respondents believe crime is increasing, as shown in *Public Opinion*, 1998.

7. Taken from the 4th Amendment of the United States Constitution, from the section known as the Bill of Rights.

8. Taken from the model proposal prepared by attorneys for the City of Chicago relative to private patrols from January 1, 1999, to December 31, 1999.

9. Excerpted from the Model Proposal drafted by city attorneys.

191

Bibliography

Azano, Harry J. (2001). Will the New Threat Result in Real Change? *Security Management*, December.

Bailin, Paul (2000). Gazing into Security's Future. *Security Management*, November.

Barron, Kelly (1997). Your Money or Your Life. *Forbes*, November 17.

Bastian, Lisa (1995). Criminal Victimization 1993. *National Institute of Justice*. Office of Justice Programs, U.S. Department of Justice, May.

Benn, Stanley L., and Gerald F. Gaus, ed. (1983). *Public and Private in Social Life*. St. Martin's Press, New York.

Benson, Bruce L. (1990). *The Enterprise of Law: Justice Without State*. Pacific Research Institute for Public Policy, San Francisco, California.

Benson, Bruce L. (1996). Are There Trade Offs Between Costs and Quality in the Privatization of Criminal Justice? *Journal of Security Administration* 19 (2): Pp.19–50.

Benson, Bruce L. (1997). Privatization in Criminal Justice. *National Institute of Justice*. Office of Justice Programs, U.S. Department of Justice.

Bilik, Al (1992). Privatization: Defacing the Community. *Labor Law Journal*, Pp. 338–343.

Black's Law Dictionary. Fifth Edition.

Blyskal, Jeff (1996). Thugbusters. *New York* 28, No. 11, March 16.

Bole, Kristen (1998). Meet the Force: Ex-Cop Takes His Security Firm into Public Housing. *San Francisco Business Times* 12 (30), March 6.

Boyce, Joseph N. (1996). Making a Stand: High-Crime Developments turn to "Ninjas" for Calm. *The Chicago Tribune*, October 19.

Burdeau v. McDowell (1921), 256 US 465 (U.S. Sup. Ct.).

Carlson, Tucker (1995). Safety Inc.: Private Cops Are There When You Need Them. *Policy Review* 73, Summer.

Chanken, Marcia, and Jan Chaiken (1987). Public Policing — Privately Provided. *National Institute of Justice*. Office of Justice Programs, U.S. Department of Justice, June.

Clemow, Brian (1992). Privatization and the Public Good. *Labor Law Journal*, Pp. 344–349.

Clotfelter, Charles T. (1977). Public Services, Private Substitutes and the Demand for Protection Against Crime. *The American Economic Review* 67 (5): Pp. 876–876.

Clutterbuck, Richard (1975). The Police and Urban Terrorism. *The Police Journal.*

Cohen, Lawrence E., and Marcus Felson (1979). Social Change and Crime Rate Trends. *American Sociological Review* 44: 588–607.

Commonwealth v. Leone (1982), 435 NE 2d 1036 (1st Dist).

Connors, Edward, William Cunningham, and Peter Ohlausen (2000). Operation Cooperation: Guidelines for Partnerships between Law Enforcement and Private Security Organizations. *Bureau of Justice Assistance.* Office of Justice Programs, U.S. Department of Justice.

Corman, Hope, and Theodore Joyce (1990). Urban Crime Control: Violent Crimes in New York City. *Social Science Quarterly* 71 (3): Pp. 567–583.

Covington, Jeanette, and Ralph B. Taylor (1991). Fear of Crime in Urban Residential Neighborhoods: Implications of Between and Within Neighborhood Sources for Current Models. *The Sociological Quarterly* 32 (2): Pp. 231–249.

Cox, Steven M. (1990). Policing into the 21st Century. *Police Studies* 13 (4), Pp. 168–177.

Crenshaw, Martha ed. (1983). *Terrorism, Legitimacy and Power: The Consequence of Political Violence.* Middleton, Connecticut: Wesleyan University Press.

Cruickshank, Ken (1994). Frenchman's Creek Provides the Ultimate in Security. *Manager's Report* 8, November.

Cunningham, William C., John J. Strauchs and Cliffiord W. Van Meter (1991). Private Security: Patterns and Trends. *National Institute of Justice.* Office of Justice Programs, U.S. Department of Justice, August.

Cunningham, William C., and Todd H. Taylor (1994). The Growing Role of Private Security. *National Institute of Justice.* Office of Justice Programs, U.S. Department of Justice, October.

Dalton, Dennis R. (1993). Contract Labor: The True Story. *Security Management,* January.

Davis, James R. (1982). *Street Gangs: Youth, Biker and Prison Groups.* Dubuque: Kendall-Hunt.

Dexter, Anthony Lewis (1970). *Elite and Specialized Interviewing.* Evanston, Illinois: Northwestern University Press.

Diesing, Paul (1971). *Patterns of Discovery in the Social Sciences.* New York: Aldine Atherton.

Dilulio, John J. (1995). Ten Facts About Crime. *National Institute of Justice.* Office of Justice Programs, U.S. Department of Justice, January 16.

Dodds v. Board (1867), 43 Ill 95 (Il. Sup. Ct.).

Donahue, John D. (1989). *The Privatization Decision.* New York: Basic Books.

DuCanto, Joseph N. (1999). Establishment of Police and Private Security Liaison. Manuscript presented at 45th Annual Seminar of the American Society for Industrial Security, Las Vegas, Nevada, September 27–30.

Einhorn, Robin L. (1991). *Property Rules: Political Economy in Chicago, 1833–1872.* Chicago: University of Chicago Press.

Ezeldin, Ahmed Galal (1987). *Terrorism and Political Violence.* Chicago: University of Illinois at Chicago Press.

Farnham, Alan (1992). U.S. Suburbs Are Under Siege. *Fortune,* December 28.

Feliton, John R., and David B. Owen (1994). Guarding Against Liability. *Security Management,* September.

Fenno, Richard F. (1978). *Home Style: House Members in Their Districts.* Philadelphia: Scott, Foresman.

Figlio, Robert M., ed. (1986). *Metropolitan Crime Patterns.* New York: Criminal Justice.

Finley, Lawrence K., ed. (1989). *Public Sector Privatization: Alternative Approaches to Service Delivery.* London: Quorum.

Fisher, Bonnie, and Jack L. Nasar (1995). Fear Spots in Relation to Microlevel Physical Cues: Exploring the Overlooked. *Journal of Research in Crime & Delinquency* 32 (2): Pp. 214–239.

The Gallup Poll (1998). *Public Opinion 1997.* Wilmington, Delaware: Scholarly Resources.

Geyelin, Milo (1993). Hired Guards Assume More Police Duties as Privatization of Public Safety Spreads. *The Wall Street Journal,* June 1.

Gibbs, Jack P., and Maynart L. Erickson (1976). Crime Rates of American Cities in an Ecological Context. *American Journal of Sociology* 82: 605–620.

Glaser, Daniel, ed. (1970). *Crime in the City.* New York: Harper & Row.

Goldberg, Ceil (1994). New Roles for Private Patrols. *Security Management,* December.

Goldstein, Herman (1993). The New Policing: Confronting Complexity. *National Institute of Justice.* Office of Justice Programs, U.S. Department of Justice, August.

Gordon, Corey, and William Brill (1996). The Expanding Role of Crime Prevention Through Environmental Design in Premises Liability. *National Institute of Justice,* April.

Graham, Thomas, and Ted Gurr, eds. (1971). *History of Violence in America.* Princeton, New Jersey: Princeton University Press.

Greisman, H.C. (1979). Terrorism and the Closure of Society: A Social Impact Projection. *Technological Forecasting and Social Change,* Vol. 14.

Hadden, Jeffrey F., ed. (1967). *Metropolis in Crisis: Social and Political Perspectives.* Philadelphia: F.E. Peacock.

Hebdon, R. (1995). Contracting Out in New York State: The Story the Lauder Report Chose Not to Tell. *Labor Studies Journal* 20 (1): Pp. 3–24.

House of Representatives for the United States Congress, H.R. 2996, 104th Congress, *Law Enforcement and Industrial Security Cooperation Act of 1996,* introduced by Rep. McCollum on February 29.

House of Representatives for the United States Congress, H.R. 1764, 106th Congress, and Senate 842, introduced by Rep. Ted Strickland and Sen. Russell Feingold.

Hsieh, Ching-Chi, and M.D. Pugh (1993). Poverty, Income Inequality and Violent Crime: A Meta-Analysis of Recent Aggregate Data Studies. *Criminal Justice Review* 18 (2): Pp. 182–189.

IOMA. *Security Director's Report,* May.

Jackson, Pamela Irving (1984). Opportunity and Crime: A Function of City Size. *Sociology & Social Research* 68 (2): Pp. 173–193.

Jacobs, David (1982). Inequality and Economic Crime. *Sociology and Social Research* 66: 12–28.

Jacobs, David (1978). Inequality and the Legal Order: An Ecological Test of the Conflict View. *Social Problems* 25: 515–525.

Johnston, Les (1992). *The Rebirth of Private Policing.* London: Routledge.

Jorgensen, Danny L. (1989). *Participant Observation:* A Methodology for Human Studies. Newbury Park, California: Sage.

Kaplan, Robert (1994). The Coming Anarchy. *The Atlantic Monthly,* February.

Karow v. Student Inns, Inc. (1976), 43 Ill App 3d 878, 357 NE 2d 628 (4th Dist).

Kelling, George (1995). Reduce Serious Crime by Restoring Order. *The American Enterprise,* May/June.

King, Gary, Robert O. Keohane, and Sidney Verba (1994). *Designing Social Inquiry: Scientific Inference in Qualitative Research.* New York: Princeton University Press.

Klein, Edward (2002). We're Not Destroying Rights, We're Protecting Rights. *Parade Magazine,* May 19.

Kolderie, Ted (1986). The Two Different Concepts of Privatization. *Public Administrative Review* 10 (2): Pp. 285–290.

Kolpacki, Thomas A. (1994). Neighborhood Watch: Public/Private Liaison. *Security Management,* November.

Lewis, Dan A., and Michael G. Maxfield (1980). Fear in the Neighborhoods: An Investigation of the Impact of Crime. *Journal of Research in Crime & Delinquency,* July, Pp. 160–189.

Lindquist v. Friedman's, Inc. (1937), 366 Ill 232, 8 NE 2d 625 (Il. Sup. Ct.).

Linowes, David F. (1988). Report of the President's Commission on Privatization. *Privatization: Toward More Effective Government.* Washington: U.S. Government Printing Office.

Liska, Allen E., Joseph J. Lawrence, and Andrew Sanchirico (1982). Fear of Crime as a Social Fact. *Social Forces* 60 (3): Pp. 760–770.

Litsikas, Mary (1994). Security System Installations Up in 1994. *Security Distributing & Marketing,* September.

Long, Ray, Douglas Holt, and Flynn McRoberts (2001). Security Laws Face Scrutiny. *The Chicago Tribune,* October 14.

McKenzie, Evan (1994). *Privatopia: Homeowner Associations and the Rise of Residential Private Government.* New Haven: Yale University Press.

McLennan, Barbara N., ed. (1970). *Crime in Urban Society.* London: Cambridge University Press.

McNulty, Paul J. (1995). Natural Born Killers: Preventing the Coming Explosion of Teenage Crime. *Policy Review* 71: Pp. 84–87.

Maghan, Jess (1998). Cell Out: Renting Out the Responsibility for the Criminally Confined. Pp. 49–67 in *Negotiating Responsibility in the Criminal Justice System,* Jack Kamerman, ed. Carbondale, Illinois: Southern Illinois University Press.

Mancusi v. DeForte (1968), 392 U.S. 364 (U.S. Sup. Ct.).

Mayhew, Bruce H., and Roger L. Levinger (1976). Size and the Density of Interaction in Human Aggregates. *American Journal of Sociology* 82: 86–110.

Meadows, Robert J. (1991). Premises Liability and Negligent Security: Issues and Implications. *Journal of Contemporary Criminal Justice* 7 (3): Pp. 112–125.

Miller, Wilbur R. (1977). *Cops and Bobbies: Police Authority in New York and London, 1830–1870*. Chicago: University of Chicago Press.

Miranda, Rowan A. (1993). Better City Government at Half the Price. In *Chicago's Future in a Time of Change*, Richard Simpson, ed. Stipes.

Mokwa, Joseph, and Terrence W. Stoehner (1995). Private Security Arches Over St. Louis. *Security Management*, September.

Moore, David C. (1995). *Government Contracting: How to Bid, Administer and Get Paid*. Washington: John Wiley.

Moore, Mark H., and Robert C. Trojanowicz (1988). Perspectives on Policing: Corporate Strategies for Policing. *National Institute of Justice*. Office of Justice Programs, U.S. Department of Justice, No. 6, November.

Morgan, David R. (1992). The Pitfalls of Privatization: Contracting Without Competition. *American Review of Public Administration* 22 (4): Pp. 251–268.

Murphy, Walter F., and C. Herman Pritchett, eds. (1986). *Courts, Judges and Politics: An Introduction to the Judicial Process*. New York: McGraw-Hill.

Nalla, Mahesh, and Graeme R. Newman (1991). Public Versus Private Control: A Reassessment. *Journal of Criminal Justice* 19: Pp. 414–436.

Nemeth, Charles P. (1989) *Private Security and the Law*. Cincinnati: Anderson.

Olick, M. (1994). Private Response: The No Response Solution. *Security News*, December.

Palango, Paul (1998). On the Mean Streets: As the Police Cut Back, Private Cops are Moving In. *MacLeans*, 111 (2), January 12.

Patterson, Julien (1995). Forging Creative Alliances. *Security Management*, January.

People v. Lawson (1976), 37 Ill App 3d 767, 345 NE 2d 41 (1st Dist.).

People v. Stormer (1987), 518 N.Y.S. 2d 351 (Co. Ct.).

Perez, Evan (2002). Demand for Security Still Promises Profit. *The Wall Street Journal*, April 9.

Reiss, Albert J. (1998). Private Employment of Public Police. *National Institute of Justice*. Office of Justice Programs, U.S. Department of Justice, December.

Reppetto, Thomas (1974). *Residential Crime*. Cambridge: Ballinger.

Reynolds, Morgan O. (1994). Using the Private Sector to Deter Crime. *National Center for Policy Analysis*, March.

Robinson, Frank W. (1996). From Blight to Bliss. *Security Management*, February.

Robinson, Matthew (1997). Why the Good News on Crime. *Investor's Business Daily*, April 30.

Rosen, Jeffrey (2002). Silicon Valley's Spy Game. *The New York Times Magazine*, April 14.

Roth, Jeffrey A. (1994). Understanding and Preventing Violence. *National Institute of Justice*, Office of Justice Programs, U.S. Department of Justice, February.

Rubenstein, Jonathan (1973). *City Police*. New York: Farrar, Straus & Giroux.

Sampson, Robert J. (1983). Structural Density and Criminal Victimization. *Criminology* 21 (3): Pp. 178–211.

Savas, E.S. (2000). *Privatization and Public-Private Partnerships*. Chatham House.

Schine, Eric, Richard S. Dunham, and Christopher Farrell (1994). America's New Watchword: If it Moves, Privatize It. *Business Week*, December 12.

Seamon, Thomas M. (1995). Private Forces for Public Good. *Security Management*, September.

Shearing, Clifford D., and Philip C. Stenning (1983). Private Security: Implications for Control. *Social Problems* 30 (5): Pp. 493–506.

Shenk, Joshua Wolf (1995). The Perils of Privatization. *The Washington Monthly*, May.

Smith, Lynn Newhart, and Gary D. Hill (1991). Victimization and Fear of Crime. *Criminal Justice and Behavior* 18 (2): Pp. 217–240.

Spencer, Suzy (1997). Private Security. onpatrol.com/cs.privsec.html. Phoenix Mosaic Group.

Spitzer, Steven, and Andrew T. Scull (1977). Privatization and Capitalist Development: The Case of the Private Police. *Social Problems* 25 (1): Pp. 18–28.

Statistical Abstract of the United States (1997). *The National Data Book*. U.S. Census Bureau, U.S. Department of Commerce, Economics and Statistics Administration.

Statistical Abstract of the United States (2000). *The National Data Book*. U.S. Census Bureau, U.S. Department of Commerce, Economics and Statistics Administration.

Tafoya, William L. (1990). Future of Policing. *F.B.I. Law Enforcement Bulletin*, January.

Theim, Rebecca (2001). A Secure Future. *Chicago Tribune*, October 24.

Tolchin, Martin (1985). Private Guards Get New Role in Public Law Enforcement. *The New York Times*, November 29.

Travis, Jeremy (1997). New Approaches to Juvenile Violence. *National Institute of Justice*. Office of Justice Programs, U.S. Department of Justice, February 10.

Trojanowicz, Robert C., and David L. Carter (1990). The Changing Face of America. *FBI Law Enforcement Bulletin*. January.

United States v. Francoeur (1977), 547 F. 2d 891.

Walinsky, Adam (1993). The Crisis of Public Order. *The Atlantic Monthly*, July.

Walsh, William F., Edwin J. Donovan, and James F. McNicholas (1992). The Starrett Protective Service: Private Policing in an Urban Community. Pp. 157–177 in *Privatizing the United States Justice System*, Gary W. Bowman, et al. (eds.). Jefferson, North Carolina: McFarland.

Wardlaw, Grant (1982). *Political Terrorism: Theory, Tactics and Counter-Measures*. Cambridge: Cambridge University Press.

Warner, Sam Bass, Jr. (1968). *The Private City*. Philadelphia: University of Pennsylvania Press.

Waugh, William L. (1982). *International Terrorism*. Salisbury, North Carolina: Documentary Publications.

Weisberg, Barry (1995). Megacity Security and Social Development. *United Nations Crime Prevention & Criminal Justice Programme*.

Wessel, Robert H. (1995). Privatization in the United States. *Business Economics*, October.

West, Marty L. (1993). Get a Piece of the Privatization Pie. *Security Management*, March.

Wolf, John B. (1981). *Fear of Fear: Survey of Terrorist Operations and Controls in Open Societies*. New York: Plenum.

Young, R. (1977). Revolutionary Terrorism, Crime and Morality. *Social Theory and Practice*, Vol. 4.

Zalud, Bill (1990). Law, Order and Security. *Security*, June.

Zielinski, Mike (1999). Armed and Dangerous: Private Police on the March. *Covert Action Quarterly*. Caq.com/caq/caq54p.police.html.

Index